This book may be returned to any Wiltshire
library. To renew this book phone your library
or visit the website: www.wiltshire.gov.uk

Wiltshire
COUNTY COUNCIL

LM6.108.5

MY LIFE
IN THE SHADOWS

SAM ALEXANDER

ATHENA PRESS
LONDON

ISBN: 978 1 84748 261 7

First published 2008 by
ATHENA PRESS
Queen's House, 2 Holly Road
Twickenham TW1 4EG
United Kingdom

This book is dedicated to my family;
I couldn't have done it without them.

And the Lord said unto the servant, Go out into the highways and hedges, and compel them to come in, that my house may be filled.

Luke 14: 23

FOREWORD

I do not intend to use this book to give away any secrets. Indeed, I believe that most of the practices I describe have already been written about. I also do not intend to give a glorified account of life in these organisations, as some books do, but to give my own perspective on life in some very unusual military and other covert organisations. When I left the Army, I was one of the very few people in the whole of the armed forces with wide and varied experience in the different organisations described later. I spent fifteen years in covert organisations, including six years in Special Forces, and have now been out of the intelligence business for over nine years. I believe that any operations I describe or was involved in are long dead and buried. Indeed, my organisation in Northern Ireland has been disbanded and replaced by a new Special Forces Regiment with a worldwide remit; I wish them the very best of luck. Perhaps one of my reasons for writing this is that everyone so far writing about this subject has portrayed things from a personal standpoint for their own benefit. My aim is to say how things really happened and how the guys on the ground actually felt. In this book, anyone that I believe is still living I have referred to by a different name. Those who are dead are referred to by their real names except for members of the security forces who still have families.

1

MY EARLY LIFE

I was born in Malta, the son of an army family, and nearly died soon after because I contracted bronchial pneumonia. If it hadn't been for Sir Alexander Fleming's discovery of penicillin, I wouldn't be here today. Apparently, I was hours away from going to see my maker. We stayed in Malta until I was six months old when we were then posted back to England, to live in a prefab in Dover. Dover was going to play a major part in my growing-up process (or not).

When I was two, we moved to Edinburgh for a few years. Edinburgh was a great place for a young kid. At the back of our house was a big wood that for us was a real scary place to go into. All the stories were that the bogeyman lived in the woods and you were considered dead brave even to go in there. I had visions of this faceless thing propelling itself around on a bit of wood with wheels at each corner. The reason for this is because we were always making 'bogeys', which were a set of wheels either end of some sort of platform to sit on and we would race down the hill at the side of our house, hence the 'bogeyman'. I suppose that these days you would liken it to a very large skateboard. At that time, my dad used to have a double-barrelled twelve bore shotgun and he and my brother used to go in the woods on Sundays and nearly always come back with a hare or rabbit for the pot. I used to hang out the back window watching them go and thought it was unfair because, at four years old, I couldn't go with them. Probably a good job, because the way I was always disappearing and running around it would probably have been *me* in the pot. We also used to do our bit for the environment with tree conservation. Because money was tight and coal was expensive we used to make the most of natural resources. I used to go off to the woods at night with my mum and a bowsaw and 'liberate' the occasional tree, which we would then drag back to the house and saw it up for logs for the fire. Modern open gas fires with the log effect are fine but you can't beat the real thing, especially when you have just 'liberated' it! For an Army brat, life proved to be quite difficult. Although I made friends easily I never really kept them and that, unfortunately, still applies to this day. I find that when I move on the past stays behind me and it's only the future that counts. What's done is done. When my father was posted, I quickly lost touch with a lot of childhood friends.

We went from Edinburgh to Singapore in the early 1960s before the country became modern. I was six. I remember living firstly amongst the Singapore Chinese community, which to a very young round eye was a real experience. The people were great but to a young kid the culture shock was unbelievable. At that time, there weren't many things for a child to worry about in a foreign country but there are certain things that stick in my mind – such as the time I nearly got run down. I was chasing my mate and ran out between two parked cars and went smack into the side of a taxi. We didn't know about the Green Cross Code in those days! A few seconds earlier and I would have been under it. It was a tremendous shock, but I was very apologetic to the taxi driver because I'd knocked his hubcap off.

I also remember going out with another mate on our bikes when I took the corner of a road and he took the shortcut. I could see this truck coming up the road and I could see him bombing it across this piece of waste ground. I could see what was going to happen, but neither the truck driver nor he could because there was a bloody big hedge in the way. I was screaming at him to stop but he must have imagined that I was just shouting at him and pedalled faster. He came out of the waste ground and the truck caught him broadside. I will never forget the look of horror on the truck driver's face because he had just mown down a soldier's son. The truck carried him across the road and he ended up in the monsoon drain. If it hadn't been for that drain and the depth that it was he would have been killed. I don't know what was going through my mind at that moment but the only thing I could think of was to get his mum. I pedalled like a madman back to his house and told his mum that Barry had been run over. She went into overdrive and after that I don't really remember what went on because I think I was in a bit of delayed shock. It's amazing how resilient kids are though, because after he had been taken to hospital and I found out he was going to be OK, I forgot about it, and then he came out and we teamed up again.

With us being the sons of ordinary soldiers there was great rivalry between the officers' kids and us. We used to be on one side of the valley and they used to live on the other. I don't know when it started but we ended up having battles. There was no given signal but we would man our side and they would try to get our position. Both sides dug holes to get at the clay and we would make clay balls and pelt each other with them. They nearly got us once but we were never defeated!

There was also one time – Halloween I think it was – when a couple of us decided to play a prank on a mate's dad. This bloke used to have some plants on his veranda and he used to spend quite a lot of time looking after them… so we thought we'd have a laugh. Being only seven, we thought he'd also have a laugh – but we were wrong. We got some bangers, put them in his plant pots, rang the bell and lit the fuses then legged it across the road and hid down the bank. As he came to the door they blew up and sent little clouds of soil into the air. Now we thought that would be the end of it but no, he wasn't impressed. He must have guessed where we were and started across the road. I think we realised that we'd made a bit of a boo-boo and ran down the valley thinking he'd give up – but he didn't. He chased us down the valley, up the other side, round the officers' quarters, back round the camp to the medical centre until we found somewhere and hid. We were in a panic that he'd find us and beat ten bells out of us. He eventually gave up but we stayed where we were for ages, in case he was hiding around the corner. At last we took the chance and came out. We slunk off home expecting trouble when we arrived at our respective houses but it was OK. If he knew who it was nothing was ever said, thank God.

One of the largest streets in Singapore was called Orchard Road and had two places of importance. One was the Cold Storage, an air-conditioned store where Mum used to take me for a milkshake. At that age to get out of the heat was bloody marvellous. The other was the market a little way down the road, where, we could buy just about everything. The two things that come immediately to mind were the kangaroo meat we used to buy for the cat and the mixes for curries we used to buy for my dad. Mum would tell the stallholder how strong she wanted it and they would put all the spices on to a banana leaf and wrap it up. At the time, Mum's instructions meant nothing to me. However, over the years I have become an avid curry eater and I wish I could find proper curry somewhere in this country. With what happened in my younger life I could now look back and think that kids these days are missing out on a lot. There were no computers and we only had one TV in the house, so there was a lot more interaction with our parents. These days I can cook most things because it used to be a case of watching my mum in the kitchen – there was nothing else to do. I think my kids would probably have a struggle to make anything in the kitchen unless it came out of a packet. Take the microwave away and they'd be stumped. Although my youngest son does actually make some really mean bacon butties. There was also conversation among the family whereby these days if you get an occasional grunt you could call it social interaction.

The whole culture in Singapore was incredible for a young kid. Obviously there were aspects of the Singapore culture that I was never allowed to see, such as Boogie Street. Sometimes we would go to restaurants in the evenings and that was probably where I got my love for food. Now I hardly eat, because I need to watch my weight, although I am not a fat bastard yet! I particularly remember a pavement restaurant called Fatty's where you would sit at the side of a smelly road and eat the tastiest satay. You could also choose a good fat duck when you arrived and it was then taken and cooked. At the end of the night, Fatty would just add up all the satay skewers and work out your charge from them.

Being an Army brat you met many characters when you were growing up, but to describe them all would need another book. The two that particularly remain in my mind from Singapore are Alec Durham, who was a short Geordie, and 'Wingy' Baines. I didn't know 'Wingy' that well but he had lost the lower part of his arm, hence the name 'Wingy'. What I do remember is that when we went to the Mess I would play snooker with him. Whenever I scored points, which he let me win, he would whack me around the head with his stump.

At this time I obviously had no idea what would happen in my life but a career in the army and covert intelligence services would have been the furthest thing from my mind. My brother was more Army minded and spent two years at Sandhurst after leaving the school. At that time two years was the norm but these days I believe that you are in and out in five minutes with a commission. He used to get really pissed off with me because I always used to tease him about taking his 'squaddie' exams. He did, however, go on to become a Lieutenant Colonel in the Royal Engineers and was once CRE (NI) (Commander Royal Engineers Northern Ireland). He was more academic than I was and to follow in his footsteps was always difficult. We both went to the same boarding school, the Duke of York's Royal Military School (the Dukies) in Dover. As the younger sibling I was expected to emulate him and even when he left I was sometimes in his shadow. I will give you an example of this.

In 1993, some twenty-three years after I left the school, my wife and I were thinking of putting our eldest son into boarding school.

We were in Germany at the time and didn't think the Army schools there were up to standard; the Dukies was one of the ones we went to have a look at. When we turned up for the interview we were met by the then deputy head, who had been a housemaster when I left.

'Ah, good morning Mr and Mrs Alexander, welcome to the Duke of York's. Aren't you the Alexander who was captain of the 1st XV?'

'No, that was the other one.'

He got off to a flying start – not! Before his comment, the school in its more up-to-date mode could have been the best thing since sliced bread. However, after that comment he'd lost it. Always do your research!

We did, however, have a look around the school and particularly at the dormitories. The actual construction hadn't changed at all, but now, there were cubicles where each boy had a captain's style bed with a cupboard for his kit and a desk to study. In our day there were just twenty beds, ten on each side with lockers in between. Despite these changes, we decided against it. Seeing the modern dormitories made me think that perhaps things had changed. When I was there the whole school was run like a barracks. For example, the heating would go on, at a certain date and go off at another date. It didn't matter if it was freezing or boiling, that was when the heating went on and off. We used to have a big clock tower on the dining hall and it was run by water. In the winter it wasn't unusual for the clock to stop because the water had frozen. The school was on top of the Dover cliffs and it used to get really cold, especially with the wind chill. We were issued three blankets for our bed but what we had to do to keep warm was to double two of them and put the single one over the top to keep the whole lot in place. That and a pullover over your pyjamas was normally enough to keep the cold out. Continental quilts, hah, never heard of them although now, mine must be one of the thickest there is. There is a saying I learned later on in life and that is 'Any fool can be uncomfortable'.

When I arrived at the school in September 1965 at eleven years of age my brother was in the sixth form; he was Deputy Head Boy and Captain of the 1st XV rugby team – as I said earlier, a very difficult act to follow. I think the hardest part was the culture of the school, which prevented me from going up and talking to my brother because I was a junior and he was a senior. At home I would be calling him by his first name, and other things besides, but at the school it was always surnames, even brother to brother. If we had to talk to each other it was always furtive because he would have had the piss taken out of him for talking to a junior even though I was his brother. Because it was a military boarding school, we actually wore Second World War style battledress and berets for lessons but after my first term we switched to civvies. Can you imagine all these little eleven-year-olds, first time away from home, walking around in full battledress and berets, marching to lunch to the accompaniment of the school band?

Most kids accepted the fact that they were there and got on with it but I can remember more than one kid who was so homesick that they would just lie on their bed and cry their eyes out all day. In the end there was nothing the school could do but get their parents to take them home. We were all homesick – it would be lying to say that being removed from the family home was a natural thing at that age – but some coped with it better than others. First night back after being at home it wasn't unusual to hear the occasional sob coming from a bed in the dormitory and I was no exception. The school did, however, give me a head start in bulling boots for later in my career (bulling boots is a Forces expression for spit and polish). It is also probably where my (lack of) dress sense stemmed from (these days unless I am very adventurous I normally have my clothes bought for me, although I will put my foot down if I don't like it). We used to have a Sunday church parade in full blues, bulled boots and, again, accompanied by the school band. A Junior Under Officer who carried a sword commanded each company. My brother was also one of those. I was expected, therefore, by the school staff to come in and be Alexander No. 2, taking over where he had left off. In the end it might have been this that caused me to head in the other direction. I think that is one of the things I have always done in my life. If someone tries to make me do something I don't want to do, then I will go exactly the other way, even for the most minor of things. Sometimes there's no real reason for it. It's just for the sheer hell of it, which really annoys my wife even now. However, as you will read later, once I set my mind on something nothing will stop me. I did get into sport and at different stages during my school career represented the school at rugby, hockey, cricket, swimming, judo and athletics – but not all at the same time or in that order. In fact, before I went to boarding school I was being coached to swim for Somerset. When I gave some of these sports up I was made to feel as though I had let the side down because that was not what my big brother would have done. As a result, I try not to impose my own prejudices on my own children. Everyone has the right to shape their own destiny without the constraints of what someone else has done before them.

The head boy when I first joined the Dukies is now a bishop in the Church of England. I will never forget his introduction in the school hall when he told us that self-respect and honour were the most important things in life. Throughout my life, I have tried to remember and live up to his words.

My time at the school was not easy. I tried my best but being me, I started to rebel and soon got in trouble. At one point, I was accused of taking drugs because of my behaviour. I have never taken drugs in my life, although I have been offered them. On one particular occasion we were in the third form common room one morning before school began and we were all having a laugh. Somebody said something that just creased me and I couldn't stop laughing. I think I sat there for ages just doubled over. At one point the Matron came in and saw me and must have gone straight to the Housemaster. I was called into his study and that's when he asked me if I had been taking drugs. Apart from the shock factor that he had actually asked me that question I don't think any of us really knew what they were all about. Certainly with the regime there, they would have been bloody difficult to get hold of any anyway. Being caught smoking was bad enough but being caught with drugs would have caused an automatic expulsion. I have three children now and would have a real problem with it if I found any of them taking that shit.

Boarding schools are great for education but to be perfectly honest an all-boys boarding school does not really prepare you for what to expect in life and that is why I said Dover, or the school in particular, was a major part of my (not) growing-up process. Once I discovered what life was all about, however, I don't think I have ever stopped trying to make up for it, even to this day. I have come to the conclusion that you only live once so enjoy it while you can.

Towards the end of my time at the school I became interested in the Royal Marines and, although totally uninterested in Army life, I decided I wanted to be a commando. As I said earlier, I even used to take the piss out of my brother, who by this time had left Sandhurst and gone into the Army. I'd read the bloods (war comics), got the warry attitude, seen the films and decided that this was what I wanted. However, when I left school I didn't have the necessary academic qualifications to become a Royal Marines Pig

(Officer) so I spent another three years at college trying to achieve these. Those years were probably the most wasted years of my life.

I really would have liked to become a vet but tough on me. I actually love animals but at this moment we have this cat that I can't abide. When I am at home he appears at the back door in the morning crying to get in after being out all night. This makes me think, because I always get up early and he is at the back door making me feel guilty. If I weren't there who would let him in? The rest of the family don't get up until much later. Once he's in, however, there is no peace because he will sit there with this look on his face and his attitude of 'feed me now'. *My* attitude is that he can bloody well wait because I've got the family to sort out and I'm not having my life ruled by a cat. He will then disappear for the rest of the day until about 5 p.m. At that time, I am normally in the kitchen sorting the kids' tea out and I get the feeling of a presence. There's the bloody cat in the kitchen doorway again with this 'feed me again' look. As I say I love animals but this really gets on my tits.

Anyway, back to school: I left school with four GCEs (as they were then) and two CSEs. These were hardly likely to get me into the realms of high finance or set me up for the future.

I went to Carlett Park, Technical College on the Wirral, and managed to persuade the tutors to let me take the subjects I wanted. I talked them into letting me take Physics A level, yet despite having done the subject at school I didn't even have the O level. This was a disaster because I now started to discover what life was really all about. The coffee bar and the Ferry pub in Eastham soon seemed to be where I spent most of my time. Having been in an Army environment and at a boy's boarding school, girls were unknown to me, apart from the occasional snog at a house dance. I had been brought up to be a gentleman and to treat all women with respect and I still do with certain caveats from past experiences. When I got to college I found that all women weren't as they had always been portrayed. There was one particular girl, who came from the Woodchurch estate in Birkenhead and who was used to dealing with boys. I wasn't used to dealing with girls. She made my life hell because once she found out I was an easy touch she used to pinch me and squeeze my arms. Because I had been brought up not to hit girls, I never retaliated and went home with arms black and blue. Eventually one of the lads said, 'Why don't you hit her back?'

I thought about it and one time, reluctantly, I gave her a little tap. Nothing serious but just enough to say, 'That's enough!'

You should have seen the shock on her face when I actually did but after that, she never did it to me again! She eventually, after another twenty years and two failed marriages, became my wife.

I have done some tough things in my life. I don't regret them and I think because of this I don't always see the need to act the hard man or to be disrespectful. Some of the content in this book contains strong language because that is the culture of the armed forces. I do not usually swear in the house or in front of women and on more than one occasion I have had quiet but effective words with people being too mouthy in the presence of my wife or other friends. I will still open doors for women (or should I say ladies) and be respectful to old people and genuinely try to avoid trouble. If, however, it ever came to it, the person on the other end would certainly know. There are some men who refuse to do things around the house because it isn't 'manly' – what a load of bollocks! My wife worked full-time as a support teacher for kids with special needs. Plus she acted as chauffeur to our own kids in the evenings for football, athletics, rugby and drama, so I helped around the house when I could. She also had to put up with a house full of men/boys and that, when I came home, was no mean feat. At the moment I work abroad but before that when I used to come home I cooked and did the ironing. So fucking what, I don't dust!

I was taught that whenever you fight, or are in a confrontation, you should look someone straight in the eyes because the eyes will always give them away. The eyes always give the measure of a person, which is one of the reasons why boxers try to stare each other out at the weigh-in. Normally a man will always have a quick look at where he is going to hit you. It is just that slight flicker that will give his intentions away and when you see that you have a better chance of defending yourself. My kids are older now but when they were young but I taught them the importance of eye contact and how to defend themselves. I regularly used to spar with my kids and found that they knew to watch for the eyes and they could block a lot of my punches. In fact my youngest son used to behave like Kato in the Inspector Clouseau series. He would hide behind doors and ironing boards and wait to jump out on me. He even used to try to crawl up on me but there was always that little rustle that I could pick up on even when watching TV. My kids are my life and I will do anything to protect them including things beyond the law. One saying that I always tell my kids, however, is that although they think that they are getting older and smarter is, 'Age and treachery will win out over youth and skill.'

It really gets on my goat these days when you have all these civil liberties groups bleating about the rights of the criminal. What about the civil rights of the poor bloody victim? I'm sure these victims didn't go up to the perpetrator and say, 'Hey mate, it's a great day, how about you do me a bit of GBH with maybe a bit of rape thrown in.' It's then a case of, 'Oh, let's help the poor criminal. There really must be a deep-seated psychological reason whereby he felt the need to beat the living shit out of that poor defenceless pensioner.' What a load of bollocks!

I also do something with my kids, which appears to have fallen by the wayside these days. I teach them to be well mannered and polite but it does not mean they are pushovers. I have seen my youngest son take on four Italian kids who were having a go at him and only stopped when he realised we were looking. My wife kept telling me to stop it but I could see he was OK. If I thought he wasn't I would have stepped in. On another occasion this obnoxious kid was ruining a game my son was playing so he just turned around and whacked the kid on the nose – good for him.

I will always make a point of talking to someone and look him directly in the eye. Partly because it makes them feel intimidated, but also because it means you dominate the situation. My father always used to say that a firm handshake was the hallmark of a real man. His favourite expression when he met a man with a weak handshake was 'Put that back in the goldfish bowl'. Thankfully my brother and I both have a grip like a gorilla!

I will never forget two occasions in Taunton where we lived for a time, when I went out for a night on the town with my brother. That's if you can *call* a night out in Taunton 'on the town'. Often when I went out on my own I was back home by 9.30 p.m. (Taunton was great to go for a drink at lunchtimes because all the secretaries used to go into the pubs for lunch – fuck knows where they went at night). The first was outside a chippy in East Reach when a few Hells Angels were bemoaning the fact that their 'hogs' had been pushed over. In the chippy at the time were a couple of very young matelots in uniform who obviously got their attention. Now these young lads only looked about sixteen or seventeen. I felt sorry for them because they had probably just joined up and this was perhaps their first leave and they were showing their uniforms off. The 'Angels' were about to punch the lights out of these two young lads when my brother and I stepped in and pointed out that I was in the Commando Brigade, he was in the Para Brigade and we were with the young matelots! We weren't really but we had decided that we were going to have these bastards! We told them that if they wanted to continue the conversation further we could step outside. They declined. I saw one of these jokers a while later when I was out with my mate Steve Lord. He recognised me and made a comment but then he just walked away.

The other time was when we were walking in a side street in Taunton and four blokes passed us and said something I didn't like so I turned round and asked them what they had said. They obviously thought that four to two were fair odds, as I did. After I had booted one in the balls and seriously offended another, I went to help my brother. After that, the one I had booted was on the floor saying, 'There was no bloody need for that.' Bollocks; get them down and keep them down.

We then walked the six miles home with our shirts covered in blood. As we walked along, this woman stepped out of a doorway near the railway station and said that she had been harassed and could we escort her down the street. Two more unlikely characters she couldn't have asked. We are both over six feet tall and well built but we had blood all over us. We escorted her safely but couldn't understand why she didn't get harassed again. This fight happened after my stag party, the night before my first marriage in 1977. When we got home Mum gave us a real telling-off and got into a panic about how we would look the next day. Fortunately there wasn't a mark on either of us the next morning. Because of the way we stuck together when we were young men, I have always believed that no matter what happens and how infrequently we see each other my brother and I are always there for each other. I may not see him for two or three years but I know that at the end of the day, if there is trouble, I would want him at my back and the same also goes for our cousin Mac, who's a bloody good lad – for a civilian!

While I was in college I got two summer jobs that weren't particularly brilliant but I just wanted to earn some money. The first was in a packing factory just outside the Birkenhead end of the old Mersey Tunnel near Camell Lairds Shipyard. The hours were long and I worked from 7 a.m. to 5.30 p.m. Mondays to Fridays with half an hour off for lunch. We also worked Saturday mornings until 1.30 p.m. For this I received the princely sum of four pounds fifty but it kept me off the streets. I have to admit the manager was honest with me because as this was the first job I had ever had I was bloody delighted.

'Thanks very much,' I said when he gave me the job.

'No problem,' he said, 'but you won't be saying that in a few weeks' time.'

I could have taken my words back after day one because I was so knackered that I used to go home, fall asleep on the settee for the evening and then go to bed. When I finally went out beer was only 15p a pint so you could actually get pissed on one pound – great!

At the time the factory was packing soap (buy one get a smaller one free) and about twenty girls had to tape the large boxes to the small. My job was to take the boxes of soap, large and small, to the girls at the tables and take the full ones away. It's amazing how often 'A box of large please,' shouted at you in a broad Scouse accent really pisses you off by the end of the day. If they'd shouted, 'Can I have a large one please,' it might have been different. The job did have its compensations as it was the time of the really mini-miniskirt and although the money was not good the sights were bloody marvellous. The other job was in a garage in Spital in the days when there was still attendant service. Once again, the miniskirt was an amazing thing.

Because of my interest in the Royal Marines (also known as the Bootnecks or Booties) I joined the Birkenhead branch of the Royal Marines Reserve (RMR) in Morpeth dock as soon as I reached seventeen and a half. This was while I was still at college and at the time of the hippies. I suppose I did stand out at college as one of the few with short hair but I didn't give a shit. Apart from enjoying what I was doing it gave me money to spend because I would turn up two nights a week and most weekends, so I normally had enough money for what I wanted because I was paid the same rate as a serving Marine for the time I was on duty.

Normally the maximum you were required to do was one evening per week and one weekend per month but I turned up for the extra night because we did some pretty intensive training. If I'd stayed at home I would have gone for a run anyway so I thought why not go and get paid for it? I spent many hours on Altcar ranges and other camps in the north-west freezing my nuts off. I also volunteered to act as a waiter in the Officers' Mess at regimental dinner nights, which might sound a bit naff but there was method in my madness. I would get an evening's pay plus the officers were always buying me drinks. This, coupled with all the wine that was available, meant that I was being paid to get pissed, which wasn't bad!

The best thing about the RMR was the social life. Apart from the functions in the unit, the other lads took me to all sorts of places. Because these guys were all civilians they came from all walks of life. Some of the places I ended up in Liverpool don't bear thinking about. There was one pretty rough place just outside the Liverpool end of the old Mersey Tunnel called the Royal Tiger. One time I went up the stairs to the toilet and there was this woman having a piss in the sink – charming! I heard that a couple of weeks later someone walked in with a handgun and blew a couple of people away. I was also taught that if you are in a fight in a town centre you have to know the correct angle to bounce someone off a plate glass window so that he doesn't go through it. An unusual piece of information but handy!

It may have been natural to them but to a young lad from boarding school and a fairly sheltered background it was an eye-opener. In those days we quite often used to meet up in a pub in Birkenhead on a Saturday morning, go across to Yates' Wine Lodge in Liverpool and when they shut we'd dive over the road to the pub for last orders. When they closed it was up to Chinatown to find a bar that was open and by the time you'd finished there it was back to the pubs again. All this drinking was probably one of the reasons why I needed the extra training.

When I was in the RMR, I enjoyed the summer shows where we gave demonstrations. We would travel over quite a large area of the Wirral giving demonstrations in unarmed combat. We were taught this to a fairly high degree and practised it regularly during training nights, especially when there was a show coming up. We'd be introduced to the crowd and then we'd run through our routine, which I was told actually looked quite good! We used to have a plant in the crowd who would act as the duty drunk and always be hurling abuse. The crowd didn't know about him and used to give him a hard time, telling him to shut up. He then used to stagger on to the field with a knife and threaten one of the lads, who would then disarm him to great cheering from the crowd – until they found out he was a plant. Then they would have a good laugh. At the end of the demonstration came the finale and that, quite often, used to be me showing how to take on six of the lads if it came down to it. The commentator would come on and announce, 'Ladies and gentlemen, I hope you have enjoyed the unarmed combat demonstration given by the RMR this after-noon. As a finale, Marine Alexander would like to demonstrate the action to take if confronted by six men in a dark alley.'

I would stand there poised for action while trying to look hard. The six men would then fan out in a semicircle in front of me. After they'd taken a few steps towards me I would spring into action – I turned and ran like fuck! Enough is enough!

After some fairly intensive training, the time came to go to Lympstone to do the RMR Commando course. I threw myself into this and although, at that time, it was the hardest thing I had ever done in my life, I thoroughly enjoyed it. At the end of the two-week course we received the coveted Green Beret and the right to wear the Royal Marines Commando flash on our shoulders. The only thing that distinguished us from members of the regular corps was that we had the letter R for reservist under the flash. Some of the blokes would leave it off so that people would think that they were in the Regular Corps. Some of the guys in the Regular Corps used to get hacked off because we only did a two-week course to get the Green Beret. What they probably didn't realise is that in the Regular Corps, as I found out a couple of years later, your training is intensive and culminates in the Commando tests. In the RMR you might be doing your training over a prolonged period until the Regular instructors in the unit thought you were fit enough to go to Lympstone. You would turn up and do some more training and drills on the square before doing the Commando tests. These tests were exactly the same as the Regular guys, no easy option, and if you failed you failed: end of story.

Once I had the beret, the world opened up and one of my priorities was to gain my parachute wings. I was still eighteen when I went to Abingdon to do the reservists' parachute course. This was a two-week course that entitled you to wear parachute wings on your arm if you were successful. Anyone who has done parachuting in civilian life will probably think of it as a bit of fun. Military parachuting was not. The first two jumps were from a cage suspended beneath an old barrage balloon that was raised to a height of 800 feet with four of you plus the PJI (parachute jumping instructor). There was no aircraft noise to take your mind off things, just total silence as you went up and saw the horizon come into view. Once at 800 feet the balloon came to a shuddering halt and crunch time came.

After the last week of being shouted at it was deathly quiet, apart from the sound of the wind moaning through the balloon's rigging lines. The PJI then lowered the bar at the entrance to the cage and said, 'See the red streamer on the tail of the balloon? Just jump and see if you can reach it – OK when you're ready off you go.'

'What, now?'

'Yep, off you go.'

There was no shouting, no threats – just a quiet voice, because at that time it was up to you to make the decision. I think one of the things that swung it for most people was the shame you would have felt if you refused and you were still in the balloon when it came down. Better to jump and cream in than refuse. People pay a fortune at funfairs for the latest white-knuckle rides but the RAF could make their own fortune. You stepped out from the balloon and dropped 200 feet in what seemed to be a fraction of a second before the chute opened. I say 'stepped out' but you actually had to jump out otherwise your chute would have caught on the floor of the cage and pitched you forward, creating big problems.

It's probably the nearest thing to bungee jumping except you don't come back up. If my parachute hadn't deployed I can honestly say that I would have waited with closed eyes until I hit the ground. You have a reserve chute but you have to be fucking quick firstly to realise you need to pull it, and secondly actually to pull it, before you cream in. When I was in the Regular Corps, I actually saw one of the lads who was quite an experienced parachutist have a malfunction when he came out of the balloon and he was coming down at a fair rate although part of his main chute had deployed. The ground crew shouted at him, 'Pull your reserve!'

After a while he did. We just stood there willing him to pull it. At the moment he pulled it his malfunction cleared and the reserve just flopped between his legs. The problem with that sort of incident is if the reserve inflates and goes up into your main chute it could get tangled and then both could malfunction, leaving you no chance. He landed harder than normal and kicked the parachute all around the Drop Zone (DZ) in sheer temper and also the relief that he'd made it. If the parachute packer had been on the DZ, I think the parachutist would have killed him.

When you did your first jump, as a joke you were told, 'OK, if your main chute doesn't open, make sure you cross your legs.'

'Why's that then, staff?' We always called them staff, never sir.

'So we can screw you out of the ground when you cream in.'

'Ha fucking ha!'

I have done the latest rides at Blackpool and they do not compare to that experience! I completed the course successfully and was duly awarded my wings. After that, balloon jumping became a regular thing because the RMR would arrange a day's ballooning at Altcar and we would turn up there and give it rock all. You could manage about four or five jumps but to be honest after that you were cream crackered, because the adrenaline rush had packed in. They would have run out of chutes by then anyway.

Jumping from the Hercules (Herc) was no joke either. The first couple of jumps were 'clean fatigue', which means without equipment, but if you can imagine over sixty people crammed into the belly of the Herc with parachutes, reserves and equipment of a total weight of somewhere in the region of 130 lbs or more, it wasn't pleasant. It got worse when the pilot decided to do some contour flying (using the Ordnance Survey contour lines to judge how high above sea level to fly) around the valleys in Wales before he went for the DZ. One of the reasons he did it was that after about an hour of flying along the valleys and then banking to get out, and throwing the aircraft all over the place, most people just wanted to get out anyway.

Normally when you jump it is from a height of 800 feet but I remember one time when the pilot screwed up with actual height above ground and height above sea level and we jumped from 600 feet. He admitted it afterwards but I wondered at the time why I hit the ground so soon after jumping. Once you've jumped you are supposed to carry out all-round observation before you release your equipment and pull down on the rigging lines to steer away if necessary.

I will never forget one time when I'd done all of this but some twat above me hadn't. He released his equipment and I got the fucking lot on my helmet. It certainly made my eyes water.

I still had intentions of joining the Regular Corps but I think the thing that swung it for me was a two-week training camp in Cyprus, where we worked alongside members of 41 Commando. To me this appeared to be the way forward. When not training, we went into Cyprus drinking with some of the old sweats that had been there before. Up until the final two days I was convinced that Cyprus consisted of a few dingy little streets with dingy little bars and even dingier bargirls. It was in one of these bars that, still being young and naïve, I got fleeced by one of these women and spent the rest of my time there broke. To add insult to injury I didn't even get my leg over! In the last two days, however, I discovered that the place actually had tourist beaches, hotels and good bars. Fortunately the Troop Pig (a solicitor in Civvy Street) bought me a meal and lent me some money so I could enjoy myself.

Towards the end of my time at college I became a bit apprehensive of leaving my cushy little world and the RMR and was persuaded to go into banking. I joined National Westminster bank as a trainee manager but soon realised that I had made a big mistake so decided to get out quickly. My normal mode of dress is very casual and I couldn't really see me spending the rest of my life as a suit. I think there was one other thing that happened in my life then that made my mind up for me.

My parents had had a pretty rocky marriage, mainly because of Dad's drinking and they had separated on more than one occasion. It was my mum who had held the family together over the years. When he was sober, my dad was a gentleman and a good dad, it was just when the beer, cider or whatever came out, he couldn't stop. He could be like Jekyll and Hyde. On this particular occasion we had both been out on the piss but after all the years of drinking he couldn't hold it as well as he used to and he would sometimes get abusive. We ended up at the top of the stairs having a go at each other. I couldn't believe what came next when he turned around to me and said, 'You know what your trouble is, don't you? You're just a bloody coward.'

I really couldn't believe that my dad had said that to me and I think deep down I had to prove to him that I wasn't. We did get over it afterwards, but it always remained in the back of my mind and still does to this day. It has made me determined that no matter what my kids choose to do they will always have my backing and will never hear anything like that from me.

I went into town and into the Army careers office. I spoke to the recruiting sergeant and asked, 'If I sign the entry papers now how long would it be before I could join the Parachute Regiment?'

At that time I couldn't really see myself doing anything other than joining an elite regiment because the ordinary infantry and corps didn't appeal to me. I wanted to do this, despite the fact that when he was sober, Dad had always told me never to join the infantry but to join something where I would learn a trade and have the opportunity for promotion. Too late – I had a point to prove and a mission in life.

'Ten days,' he said. Not a bad option.

I then went to the Royal Marines recruiting office and asked the same question.

'Six weeks,' he said, which made it a difficult choice.

After some soul-searching I went for my original choice and signed for the Royal Marines. On successful completion of the tests, I was allowed to sign the attestation forms, take the oath of allegiance and swear my loyalty to Her Majesty, heirs and successors. It may seem a load of bullshit to a lot of people these days but when I signed those forms I was prepared to die for my sovereign and so was my brother.

I finally joined the Corps on 23 April 1974 – St George's day. Before I left the RMR, they gave me a tremendous piss-up and a memorial tankard.

2

THE ROYAL MARINES

When the day came I packed my bags and boarded the train at Liverpool Lime Street to go to basic training at Lympstone. We actually went to Portsmouth first for two weeks but Lympstone was the ultimate destination. I had decided to take one step at a time and so did not have a clue what the future held. As we approached our final station I noticed this guy on the train with hair literally halfway down his back and thought that there was no way he could be going to the same place as me.

He did, however, get out and board the truck. Steve Lord and I were in the same troop and we became firm friends. I was best man at his first wedding and he at mine. He was awarded the King's Badge for best recruit at the end of training and we joined the same unit, 40 Commando. We served two tours together in Northern Ireland, one in Belfast and the other in South Armagh, before I left the Corps. He also lived not far from me so we used to socialise on leave. Years after we lost touch, I heard that he had been tragically killed in a car crash leaving a widow and three kids.

I did one thing at Lympstone that I think must have pissed off some of the instructors there – I wore my parachute wings. Part of me said that I would be daft to wear them, as I would attract a lot of unnecessary attention. As I have said before, I will some-times go completely the other way just for the sheer hell of it. I thought, I've earned them so I'm bloody well going to wear them. Unless you are in a certain branch of the Corps, parachute wings are as rare as rocking horse shit and here was I, a mere recruit, wearing them. Even though, as I said, I didn't get the King's Badge I did get the nickname of 'The General' because I could normally sort things out. After a while even the instructors were calling me that. When I joined 40 Commando, the unit was scheduled to go to Northern Ireland (NI) so a lot of our initial

31

training was geared towards that. At that time Support Company was short of bodies, so we were attached to it and were assigned to Reconnaissance Troop (Recce Troop).

Most of the training for NI was carried out at Lydd and Hythe ranges in Kent and that's where the Commando went before Belfast. After this training, we were given some leave. By this time my parents had moved back to Taunton and lived in a country cottage, which although very nice was really isolated. It had great countryside for running in, but getting into town was a nightmare as there were only two buses all week and none at night. So going out meant either a cab or getting dropped off and a six-mile walk back. Even if you left town fairly early there were no buses so it was either the expense of another cab or Shanks's pony. I also did something at that time that I regret.

Just before I left to go back to Plymouth I took my dad's car out for a drive, while he was sleeping off a lunchtime session, and crashed it. I got it back to the house but it wasn't in good shape. It was his pride and joy and here I was going off to Ireland and leaving him with a badly bent car. I was devastated and so, I think, was he but he didn't make a big drama out of it because, as I said, he could be a good dad, at times.

I then returned to Plymouth and the unit to make final preparations and to pack personal kit. I was supposed to travel with the advance party to Liverpool by the road convoy, which meant an early start, while the rest of the Commando came by train a week later. Our final piece of preparation though was a night out in Plymouth and I went over the top completely and got absolutely shitfaced. My apologies to the person in Union Street, whose front garden I threw up in! I managed to get back to the camp and put my name in the shakes (wake-up) book. The system was that when you were woken up you had to sign the book to indicate that you were awake so that if you went back to sleep it was your fault. The next morning I woke up to find that the convoy had gone and thought that I was in the shit. Fortunately my troop stripey (sergeant) took me to the guardroom and demanded to see the book. My signature had been forged. Apparently the guy couldn't wake me up, thought fuck it and signed the book himself, so I got away with that one.

We caught the train to Liverpool and the night boat to Belfast. Steve was still single and actually managed to find a girl on the boat, smooth-talking bastard! We approached Belfast harbour as dawn was breaking and could see the lights of the city. Those of us who hadn't been before were a bit apprehensive. It was drizzling with rain, which I found out later was normal and I was definitely asking myself questions as to what was I doing here. We were expecting to be shot at as soon as we got off the boat and the five rounds we had been issued hardly seemed adequate. Obviously nothing happened and we were transported to our home for the next four months: Fort Monagh in the Turf Lodge area of West Belfast. I think our arrival in the area and our attitude during the first week or so shocked the local residents, who had been getting away with murder with the previous Fusilier Battalion. It used to be good sport for the kids to pelt the Fusiliers with rocks and because they had enclosed vehicles, they couldn't react. However, because some of our lads had been in Aden and other operational theatres, the first thing we did was to strip the Land Rovers down so that we were riding around in open vehicles.

Not only did this give you better fields of view and fire but also if you had a contact (firefight) you were able to debus quicker. The kids obviously thought that they could play the same game with us and threw stones until we stopped the vehicles, debussed and chased after them. They thought this was really out of order but after a couple of incidents we didn't get any more rocks thrown at us. It also used to be fun for them to set the dogs on us and they would run after the vehicles with teeth bared, barking like fuck. We solved that problem by carrying slabs of concrete in the back. We slowed the vehicle down to let them catch up and gave them the good news on the head. That practice soon stopped as well. One dog in particular cottoned on pretty quick and after that used to come on foot patrol with us and see the other dogs off if they got too uppity. He was adopted as the mascot and I think one of the lads took him home. At least the poor little sod got well fed.

Our area was in fact Andersonstown but most of our problems came from the Turf Lodge. The Turf Lodge or the Turf was a horrible place with terraced houses and some blocks of flats. These flats were shit pits with large bins at the bottom of chutes, for the disposal of rubbish. Very often they were full and the rubbish would overflow or just be thrown on to the grassy areas. There are two things about the Turf that will always stick in my mind.

One was a little old lady who lived in one of the blocks of flats. Bear in mind that the Turf was a hard republican area and the Brits, and anyone who helped them, was fair game. We were moving around the bottom of the flats one night when she opened the door.

'Hey boys, would youse like to come in for a cup of tea?'

'We'd like to thanks, love, but we wouldn't want you to get into any trouble.'

'Don't you worry about me lads, those boyos don't scare me.'

So in we went for tea and bickies. It felt really good just to be able to have a good cup of tea even if you were standing there in flak jackets with weapons with one of the guys on guard just inside the door. I thought she was a real gutsy old bird.

The other was when I was doing a foot patrol and saw this little kid in a garden who was about three or four years old. As I was passing I tried to be friendly and said, 'Hello, how are you?'

The answer I got was, 'Fuck off, you Brit bastard.'

Charming!

Our tour passed relatively peacefully with only one or two minor incidents. The first was when we had received information that one of the top terrorists at the time, Deirdre McCracken, was known to be in a house in the Turf and that we were to mount a snatch operation. We screamed into the area and sealed it off, while others broke into the house and eventually found her hiding behind a wardrobe. By this time rent-a-crowd had arrived and started pelting us with missiles. We advanced on them and only the fact that I had my rifle at the high port (held diagonally across my chest) stopped me getting a bottle in the face. Now that really would have spoiled my good looks!

The other incident occurred on St Patrick's night in 1975. We were on immediate standby with two Land Rovers ready to react to any incident. Suddenly, about six shots were fired at the fort from the direction of the Turf. We crashed out and raced in the direction of where the shots had been fired. We arrived at a building site to find two drunks with an M1 carbine on the floor with a foot patrol standing over them. I think the only thing that saved their lives was the small crowd that had gathered.

One other incident occurred that also may have set me on course for what I ended up doing in the future. We were on mobile patrols one day, being briefed in the Ops room, and there was this guy there with long blonde hair, a droopy moustache and a scruffy duffel coat. We were told we didn't need to know what he was doing there but we were to act as floating cover for him and to bail him out if he got in the shit. We went out on patrol and every now and again saw this bloke wandering around in the Turf. Years later I realised what he had been up to. Also, in hindsight, I realised that I probably would have been a bit young and immature at that time. I was also a bit put off by the horror stories that some of the lads who had been on the course came out with.

Every week we used to spend twenty-four hours in Andersonstown Police Station as the guard force, it was a bit of a doddle really. The station was situated at the point of two road junctions and the main sangar (fortified position surrounded by rocket screens) used to dominate the triangle. The only times we were normally turned out at night would be for a 'rat trap'. This would be where a car had been hijacked and we would put a VCP (vehicle checkpoint) outside in the hope we could intercept them. Mind you, anyone with any sense wouldn't have driven a hijacked car anywhere near a police station. It was just across the road from the Milltown cemetery with the very large Republican plot. Most people will have seen the cemetery on TV from time to time and it was the scene of an incident where the Loyalist terrorist Michael Stone threw grenades and fired at people attending a funeral. We actually went round there a few times to see the plots of people we had heard about from past PIRA days. I'll say one thing for PIRA and the Republicans in general, they must spend a fortune on headstones – some of them are works of art and massive to go with it. Just across from the sangar was a sweet shop with living accommodation on the first floor. This was a point of interest in the evenings because two girls in their late teens, had a bedroom facing the sangar. Now I can't say if it was deliberate or not, but invariably when they got undressed for bed there always seemed to be a gap in the curtains, which they stood in front of. Night-time sangar duty was very popular!

After my first Northern Ireland tour, I volunteered for SBS (Special Boat Service) training and was accepted, which meant I was sent to Poole in Dorset. Once again, as with most other courses I have done in my life, it started in January and was bloody freezing. Early morning PT nearly always seemed to end up with a run along the jetty and a swim back to the shore before running back to camp. The diving phase was conducted in Horsea Lake in Portsmouth, which had previously been a torpedo testing lake. Diving was new to me and it couldn't have come at a worse time, as I had been to see *Jaws* only a couple of weeks before. When we were in the water for the first time, one of the other divers kicked up all the crap from the bottom and I watched with rising panic, as this cloud of mud came towards me, imagining what could be on the other side. I just kept perfectly still as the muck engulfed me and when I realised I wasn't going to get eaten and I couldn't see heads bobbing in the water I breathed a sigh of relief and carried on swimming. We were swimming on oxygen re-breather sets at the time and had to recharge them manually, which was a tiring process. I found this two-week phase very physically demanding and it wasn't uncommon to go to bed at about 6.30 p.m.

As well as the other aspects of the course the key part was the canoeing, because the role of an SBS Marine is to be a swimmer canoeist. This was one part of the course that I thought I would fail. When I was doing the initial fitness phase I was required to do a certain number of chin-ups to the bar. I could never do more than two so I thought my time was up. One of the tests was a thirty-mile paddle with a full canoe and I passed this, no problem. Towards the end of the course we were required to do the same fitness test and I could still only manage two pull-ups. Does this come down to lack of commitment or the fact that I just couldn't do bloody pull-ups?

The canoes used were two-man Kleppers, the same as those used during the Second World War by a group of Royal Marines to attack the Port of Bordeaux to disrupt German shipping. Their exploits were immortalised in the film *The Cockleshell Heroes*. These canoes have a rubberised bottom with a canvas top and can be broken down and carried by the two-man crew. One man would carry the outer skin and the other would carry the wooden framework. The whole thing weighed about 112 lbs and when afloat would carry about the same in stores plus the crew. The boat was very stable and by actually rafting up, coming together and holding on, you could walk along the canoes. In the water things were fine but when it came to moving across country, things got awkward. Moving across country would be done at night and that meant leaving the water and stripping down the canoe if you couldn't carry it complete. This might seem an easy task but when you have over two dozen wooden parts you must know where they have come from and how to put them back together in the dark. Coupled with the fact that you would also have all your food, water, spare clothing, ammunition, explosives and anything else that you might need to complete the operation, things got a bit heavy. I remember one time in particular that I was just trying to get my Bergen (rucksack) on when the strap broke with the weight; I had to tie it up with parachute cord. Running with this was not easy either, nor was trying to get over obstacles (of which I might add, in the English countryside, there are many). With all that weight, you would have to remove your Bergen and it invariably took two of you to pass it over the obstacle.

Putting it back on was no easy matter either and invariably meant propping the thing up, sitting down and putting my arms through the straps, rolling over on to my front and trying to stand. If you didn't get it right you would end up on your back kicking your legs and waving your arms like a dying fly. I was doing well on the course and when it came to the final exercise I was appointed one of the two Section Commanders which meant that at the time, I was one of the top two on the course. We went to isolation camp prior to the exercise, where the staff would disclose the details of the mission. Being in isolation, you weren't able to talk to anyone – meaning, in theory, the mission would not be compromised.

At the time we had an American SEAL (Sea, Air, Land or Special Forces) team Chief Petty Officer instructing on an exchange and I personally thought he was an arsehole. Before we were due to go out, when I thought we should have been resting if we were playing things for real, he had us out most of the night stripping and assembling the canoes and practising obstacle crossing. Coupled with the fact that things weren't going too well in my life at the time, I decided I'd had enough. With less than a week to go I rapped my hand in (quit). I realised later in life that obviously the intention had been to increase the fatigue factor but I still thought he was a twat. I told the Troop Pig the next day that I was going to rap. At first he couldn't believe it and then he started getting aggressive. Not a very smart thing to do, as that sort of thing only makes me clam up. He had only passed into the SBS on the previous course, and I didn't have much time for him either.

He walked out and must have had a conversation with the other instructors because he came back in and said, 'Right Alexander, it's been decided that you will complete the course but you will no longer be a Section Commander.'

You can fuck off, I thought, but said instead, 'This is a volunteer course and I'm volunteering to get off it.'

That threw him a bit and they actually sent for the Officer Commanding at Poole. He came out to the isolation camp and I told him exactly the same thing. They tried to get my reasons but I told them nothing and this is the first time it has ever come out. After quite a lengthy interview he said, 'Well Alexander, I'm really sorry that you've decided to rap, because after the runaround you've given me in this interview you would have flown through interrogation training.'

After that I returned to 40 Commando where I joined Recce Troop in time for the forthcoming tour of South Armagh. I later became reacquainted with one of the blokes who passed the course, in a later phase of my life. I often wonder what direction my life would have taken if I'd stuck with it, but hindsight is a marvellous thing!

My second uniformed tour was in South Armagh in a spot called Bessbrook Mill. Before the tour, I had volunteered for and been accepted into Recce Troop. The troop contained the Commando's specialists in a number of roles. However, for this trip its primary role was to mount covert observation posts. Observation posts come in two forms. An observation post (OP) is one that everyone can see. A covert OP is one that they cannot see so you have the advantage.

We were a five-man team who sometimes carried unorthodox weapons and were allowed a mixture of uniform. (This is borne out by a photograph of our patrol that appears in a book by Mark Urban called *Big Boys' Rules*.)

This caused some resentment amongst the rest of the Commando, particularly because we were also allowed to grow our hair long. We did carry out some patrolling duties but our main role, as stated, was OPs. We would be given a target and a certain amount of information (very little, as I came to find out later in my career). It was then our job to recce the target, to find out the best place to mount the OP, to identify the target and his associates and also to photograph them. At the time we thought we were the bee's knees but I was later to learn that we were just doing the donkey work for those who could make better use of the information we provided.

Bessbrook Mill in 1976 was a dismal place, as those who have been there will know. When we arrived, it was pouring with rain and when our Section was shown to the small room that was to be our home for the next four months I found that the roof was leaking on to my bed. So my first task was to get up on the roof and fix the bloody hole. Fortunately that did the trick for the rest of the tour.

When we first arrived we took over a static OP from Patrol Company, the Parachute Regiment overlooking Jonesborough/Flurrybridge. This OP was quite well established and had a sandbagged command post, living accommodation and some machine gun emplacements. We spent some time there and apart from the boredom factor it was OK. There were only five of us in there, but we felt secure because it was on top of the largest hill in the area and our fields of fire were therefore excellent. Sometimes three of us, on our handover period, would go into the village to do a small patrol and must have attracted some interest because we were in uniform but with long hair, non-standard weapons and desert boots. One time in the summer, not long before we pulled, out the hillside caught fire and the local volunteer fire brigade spent ages trying to bring the blaze under control. It was thought at the time that it might have been either the bottom of a bottle that had acted as a magnifying glass and caused the heather to catch light or PIRA trying to burn us out. What *really* happened is that the Section Commander had fired a schermully (parachute flare) to see if anything was out there. Unfortunately he fired it at a low trajectory and it hit the ground still burning. Oops, sorry! We were watching out for a particular guy at the time but also keeping an eye on things in general. The village was in a valley and on the opposite hill, below us, was a hotel and just a bit further up was a very large calor gas tank that supplied the hotel. We had one of our tripod-mounted machine guns fixed on this gas tank. The idea was that if we came under any form of attack we would fire a burst at this tank and ignite it with the tracer and hopefully that would take the enemy's mind off us long enough for us to have a go at them.

One day it was decided that the OP had outlived its useful-ness. Early one morning some choppers came in, we dismantled the place, loaded all the stores and flew back to Bessbrook. When you work with Special Forces soldiers, you find that the Army is a small place because later in my career in Germany, I ended up working with one of the blokes in the Parachute Regiment who had occupied the OP before us.

This particular OP was an overt OP but I was also involved extensively in covert OPs. These OPs require highly specialised troops to mount them successfully and the skills needed are only given to a select few. A covert OP could, and did on one occasion, mean being in some bushes in someone's back garden. The one I refer to was literally ten metres from someone's back door and to stay there for four days takes some doing. It takes a very special kind of skill to be able to carry out an OP effectively, achieve your mission, gain the information you require and avoid compromise. Compromise (or being found) in this part of the province sometimes proved fatal. There was one particular terrorist at the time called Francis Hughes. He would actually patrol South

Armagh with his Active Service Unit (ASU) and would take on OPs if they were compromised. He and his group at one time took out one particular OP consisting of four men. Later in my career I actually got to see the rifle he once used, an AR 14, and it was in immaculate condition. Although some blokes would not have admitted it I think a few of us had a grudging respect for his professionalism. Fortunately for us, he was one of the hunger strikers who starved to death. Although we considered ourselves fairly good at OPs already, we were sent to Hereford before the tour to be taught more effective skills by the Special Air Service (SAS).

I personally found these skills invaluable and without them, as a Section Commander, might have made potentially disastrous mistakes. It may seem a very simple task to get yourself into a position to observe someone but when your life is at stake you have to make sure you get it right first time – simple things like packing your Bergen correctly so that the things you need first and more often are at the top for ease of access.

The tour passed off without any real incident and I believe we were the first unit to walk away from there in years without a fatality. Perhaps the only injury we had was to a REMF (rear echelon motherfucker) in Crossmaglen. The base was mortared twice and he was actually hit twice but his were the only injuries that the Commando as a whole sustained. There was another incident when a friend of mine, Ken (who later went on to a successful career in the SAS), was in an OP and saw two men walking towards the it. They were wearing combat jackets, carrying weapons and appeared to be moving tactically. In cases like that it is not always practical to issue the yellow card warning. Ken was a trained sniper and he genuinely believed that they represented a threat to the integrity of the OP and he opened fire, killing one and wounding the other. Unfortunately it turned out that they had been duck hunting and were innocent. I would also say that they were Protestants. It was tragic but all I can say is that in that part of Ulster and at that time, they should have known better than to walk around in camouflage gear with weapons. Of course, for a time after that there were the usual morbid cracks of:

'What goes quack, quack, bang?'

'Ken in an OP!'

As most people know South Armagh, or bandit country, was a very dangerous place to work in with the threat of culvert bombs and snipers; the safest way to travel was by chopper. At that time Bessbrook, normally a small insignificant place, was the busiest heliport in the world with aircraft taking off and landing every few minutes.

I was nearly the Commando's only fatality. I almost got shot once when I went to visit my brother. He was second in command of 9 Independent Parachute Squadron Royal Engineers and was based in Castle Dillon near Armagh. I needed a new pair of DMS boots, which I would have had to pay for in the Marines. He had promised to get me a free pair, as well as a couple of rolls of HBM (Harry black maskers, or black masking tape). HBM was like gold dust. It was used to keep everything together but you could never get hold of it. They used to have it in the stores but the storeman's attitude was, 'Stores are for storing. If they were for issuing they would be called issues.' Consequently you could never get any. So I drove over to see him in a covert car with my mate Steve Lord. We arrived at the gate in our civilianised car and without thinking I got out of the car dressed in civvies carrying my rifle, which I had shortened by removing the flash hider from the front of the barrel and shortening the butt. As I approached the gate I began to realise something was wrong when the paratrooper inside the gate sangar cocked his rifle and told me fairly impolitely to stand still and drop my weapon before he put a hole in me. Mind you, with the instinctive rivalry between the Royal Marines and the Paras he'd probably already sniffed out who I was and was trying to put the shits up me: it worked. I tried to explain who I was but unfortunately (or perhaps not) I don't look anything like my brother. Our builds are similar but he has black hair and is very swarthy while I am fair verging on redheaded with freckles and a light beard. Fortunately, the sentry called my brother from the operations room and he identified me and we were let into the base. I suppose I should be grateful that my brother didn't employ his rather warped sense of humour and disown me! Anyway, I got my free boots and had a few pints of beer with my brother in the Officers' Mess, from a silver goblet. It was always nice to see him when he was roughing it on active service!

My time in Bessbrook helped me to decide that my life in the Royal Marines was at an end. I really couldn't see the rest of my life, at that time, revolving around the Mediterranean, Northern Ireland and occasionally Norway. In the forces you get an annual report on your performance and mine had been good with recommendations for promotion that never came. That, amongst other things, caused many a shouting match between the Troop Pig and me in the Ops room. These invariably ended up with him shouting, 'Clear the Ops room!' Then we would really go at it. I eventually decided that I had had enough and I bought myself out. It was shortly after I had decided on this course of action that my place on a promotion course came through. I told them to shove it. During the Falklands war, I saw that my former troop commander was commanding the Mountain and Arctic Warfare Cadre and led a very successful attack on Top Malo house. The only casualty occurred when someone was shot up the arse.

We arrived back in England in December 1976 and in January 1977 I married for the first time but I believe it was for the wrong reasons. It did not last long and fortunately there were no children.

It happened when I was twenty-three years old and a few of my friends had married or were getting married, including Steve Lord, and I was feeling a bit left out. I had known this girl for only three weeks before we got engaged and afterwards we got married. I think we both realised fairly quickly we had made a mistake. The marriage lasted three years but the divorce was amicable and we stayed friends for a while before I moved out of the area.

One of the principal roles of the Royal Marines is to be an amphibious assault force. Although many people pay big money for ocean cruises around the world, in the Royal Marines we seemed to get them for nothing although they were aboard the less-than-luxurious grey funnel line. Unless you were actually a ship's marine and were part of a ship's company, these cruises were usually aboard a Landing Ship Logistic (LSL) such as the ill-fated *Sir Galahad*. I spent a couple of trips aboard that ship and although it didn't have as much space as some of the bigger ships, it was more comfortable. One time I was aboard an LSL and I was in the well deck before the vehicles arrived. I saw someone lift one of the hatches to look in the storage spaces underneath. I wasn't too chuffed when I saw the whole space was packed with fucking explosives. I would have thought that the stuff would have been aboard another ship to minimise casualties if it was hit. Perhaps it was acceptable in peacetime exercises but perhaps it was different in time of war. I certainly hoped so but never found out.

Another favourite was *HMS Bulwark* or the 'Rusty B', as it was affectionately known. This had been an aircraft carrier before it had been converted to a LPH (landing platform helicopter) designed to transport Royal Marines and then land them by helicopter. The thing was big and fairly uncomfortable and when using them we had to conform to Navy rules, which, although understandable, got on your nerves.

For example, there were and probably still are, things called 'rounds' in the Navy. Twice a day, the duty officer came around and inspected the living accommodation. This meant that everything had to be squared away and everything cleaned. Sometimes, especially when it was captain's rounds, it involved the use of white gloves to check surfaces for dust. Being an embarked force meant that you were treated as someone who shouldn't be there. Perhaps the worst time was when there was flying that didn't include you. All the outside hatches were shut and you were not allowed on deck. With up to 600 extra people confined below decks, this could get very claustrophobic. It's amazing the number of stupid games that grown men think of to amuse themselves. One of the favourites was a game similar to Ludo but called 'Uckers'. It was played on the same board but the rules were different just to make it more interesting. Can you just imagine a bunch of hairy-arsed Commandos sitting around playing Ludo? One of the good things, at that time, on board Royal Navy ships was the food. As well as the normal meals, perhaps because of the boredom factor, there used to be supper in the evening known as 'nine o'clockers'. This used to consist of big sandwiches and went down well with the two cans of beer you were allowed per day.

One time on board the Rusty B we were returning home after a series of exercises in the Med. Some of the ship's crew ran a radio station and they decided that they were going to raise money for charity. The idea was that a mess deck would get some money together and go and pledge it to the charity of their choice for whichever record they wanted.

That record would then be played non-stop until someone came and 'bought' another record to play, and so on. If you consider we were on this ship for some weeks some of the records got played a few times. I think someone, we never did find out who, was really taking the piss but the charity must have made some big bucks out of that cruise. If I ever hear that fucking record by Rod Stewart, 'Sailing', I just scream!

The good thing about Bulwark compared to an LSL was the fuck-off big flight deck. You weren't able to do very much when the ship was steaming but when there was no flying you could actually get up on deck for a run. In port, when you weren't on duty and there was no training, you would normally go out on the piss around lunchtime. That would give me time for some training in the mornings and I used to get up there and just spend ages pounding around the flight deck. We had a stop-off in Gibraltar one time and I was training heavily for the Top of the Rock Race. Unfortunately for some reason we couldn't do it so although I wouldn't say it was training wasted, I could have done without it. All you could really manage on the LSLs was static PT and maybe a game of deck hockey now and again.

In Gibraltar at that time most of the bars had a large glass jug in a wickerwork basket on the bar top and this held what was known as 'Pussers Rum'. Being 'Pussers' was also a nickname for someone who was Corps pissed (Marines mad). This stuff had, as local legend had it, been rescued from a fleet of ships that had sunk off the coast. It was really nice to drink but it was absolutely lethal. I have actually seen Three Badge Marines who had done a lot of time in the Corps get completely fucked up on this stuff. In the Royal Marines at that time you would get a stripe, or badge, for every five years of service. So Three Badgers had done at least fifteen years' service – they were not sprogs. It might amaze some people to know that aboard British warships at that time you actually had civilians. They were the NAAFI staff, who ran the shop which was an essential part of ship's life.

Perhaps, however, the most important blokes on the ship were the Chinese laundry staff. It cost you next to nothing to hand your stuff in during the morning and to get it back in the afternoon washed, ironed and even starched if necessary. They also used to run up a nifty line in multi-coloured shorts if you found yourself in a hot climate without any.

Despite its faults, the Rusty B was a damned sight more comfortable than some American ships. In the embarked force mess decks, although you were stacked three high there was a partition between you and the guy in the next stack of three sleeping next to you. I went on board the USS *Guam*, a similar ship to HMS *Bulwark*, and we were shown to a mess deck called 'the snake pit'. This consisted of a large 'room' that housed 200 marines. The bunks were also stacked three high but there was no partition between you and the next guy so you were looking at each other going to sleep. There was also absolutely no privacy. The Yanks were so paranoid about queers that there were no toilet cubicles, so you could not even have a dump in privacy. There was just a row of pans and that was it. If anyone has seen the film *Full Metal Jacket* and you can picture the scene where the guy shot the drill instructor in the 'heads' (toilets), then you'll know what I mean. You could have a good chat to your neighbour while taking your daily dump. No wonder so many Americans are fucked up! At that time, American ships were dry with no alcohol for the enlisted guys. Consequently the guys looked for other ways to distract themselves from the boredom, and drugs were a big thing on board some of these ships.

We were told by some of the guys that it was normal to lose a few guys during a long trip because of drugs. If you stand at the stern (the blunt end) of a ship and watch the wake it can become quite hypnotic and after a while it is said that there is quite a desire to jump in. This was one of the favourite ways for the junked-up guys to go. They would just launch themselves off the stern of the ship into the water and if this was at night it might be the next day before they were reported missing.

It was also quite comical at meal times when you went to the galley (cookhouse, to non-Royal Marines), because as I have already mentioned, the food on board British ships was good, but we thought the food on board the *Guam* had to be out of this world. It must have been, because at the head of the queue was a Snowdrop (US Naval Police) with a colt .45 making sure that there was no trouble. It was during one of these Mediterranean 'cruises' that I eventually went back to Malta, the land of my birth, for the first time in twenty-two years. Obviously I hadn't got a clue as to what it looked like before but I had promised my mum that I would visit the barracks where we were stationed and the hospital where I was born. What I didn't promise was that I wouldn't visit a particular street called Straight Street or 'The Gut'. This was a street that went downhill and had seedy bars on either side with whores and bar girls everywhere. I spent several happy nights there, but after my experience in Cyprus my money stayed with me.

There was one particular exercise we carried out in Sardinia with the US Marines who had a SEAL team attached to them. Prior to going on the exercise we spent a day on board the *USS Guam*. As with most different Forces when they get together there are bits of kit that each other has that you wouldn't mind having. Quite a few of the lads swapped bits of their kit and I ended up with a pair of leather boots that came halfway up the calf. I thought they were the business and wore them on exercise without breaking them in. I was in fucking agony! I suppose the fact that they were half a size too small didn't help either. I was determined to last out without going back to British boots DMS and took them off at every opportunity to give my feet a rest. By the end of the exercise I could walk more or less normally.

We also swapped our twenty-four hour ration packs (rat packs) for the American 'C' rats. To look at one of the British packs you wouldn't believe that the contents would last for twenty-four hours, but the contents were very nutritious and had a high calorific value. At first sight theirs seemed better than ours did but after a couple of days most of us would rather have had our own rat packs. No wonder they were so keen on ours. I was talking to an ex-Foreign Legionnaire years later and he said that they used to get miniature bottles of whisky or brandy in their rat packs. They would save them up until they weren't working and then get shitfaced.

As the exercise went on, we became more involved with the SEAL team and got to know them quite well. They were actually surprised at some of the things we described that happened in Northern Ireland, because they had never been involved in urban guerrilla warfare. I was also surprised to find that at that time you could volunteer for and join the USN SEALs directly from Civvy Street without having to do any service first. In our forces if you wanted to join the equivalent – SBS or SAS – you had to join either the Royal Marines or Army, depending which one you wanted to go for, and then go through an arduous selection.

At the end of the exercise we had a big BBQ on the beach and invited them along. They were all for it as we had the beer and the Americans didn't. I had had no contact with SEAL teams before this but I can honestly say they were some of the biggest (literally) bastards I have ever seen in my life. Their contribution was to bring the biggest steaks I had ever seen. After a few beers and a chat it turned out that even though it was a BBQ, none of their blokes would be allowed any beer. I could see a quick buck to be made here, so two of us bought a case of beer and decided we were going to sell it to the Septics (Septic Tanks – Yanks) at twice the price. This was the law of supply and demand. We had it and they wanted it. We grabbed the case but decided if we walked into their camp with a case of beer to sell we would probably get the shit kicked out of us and go back minus the beer. On the way there we stashed the beer then walked in and enquired if anyone wanted to buy a case of beer. If we had ten cases we could have sold the lot but one was all we could get. We agreed a price with one of the Yanks and got our money first before we took two of them to the cache where the beer was handed over. I presume they went off and got shitfaced and we went back a little bit better off. Honour was satisfied all round.

There are two other memorable incidents during my time in the Corps which will always stay with me. The first was the firemen's strike when we were deployed to Sandwell, in West Bromwich, near Birmingham. At the time there appeared to be a lot of tension and when it transpired that we would replace the local fire service, we were a bit apprehensive. We had heard that they would be mounting pickets. The public was on their side and perhaps there would be some animosity towards us, but in the end it was a really great time. We were put up in a Territorial Army (TA) drill hall in Sandwell, and the public couldn't have been nicer. We were given free access to the public baths and at Christmas people would sometimes come up to you in the street and give you things like a bottle of whisky. The guy in charge of the drill hall must have needed a long period of rest after we had gone. For the first few weeks I don't think he saw daylight as the bar always appeared to be open so that when you came off duty it was up to the bar for a few beers before you got your head down. At one point he was walking around like a zombie and was as white as a sheet. They must have made some money off us though.

There was a pub we always used where there were some really nice-looking barmaids who were very friendly. I howled with laughter one night when we were having a drink and something was said about accents. I just happened to say, in my normal forthright but diplomatic way, 'Get lost, you're all the same, you Brummies.'

They all had a Black Country accent but were most offended when I called them Brummies. One of them drew herself up to her full 5'2" and said, in a posh Brummie accent, 'We're not Brummies, we're from West Brom.'

During this time, because people were going on leave, we were short of HGV3 drivers to drive the Green Goddesses (MOD fire engines). They got some Royal Corps of Transport testers up and some of us were given a crash course in HGV driving. I failed the first test, because I was too aggressive towards other road users, but passed the second one. I think that as soon as I got into the truck I adopted the average trucker's mentality; 'Get out of the fucking way because a good big'un will always beat a good little'un.'

The instructor who took me for my training and test was a Staff Sergeant in the Army but in the Marines we called them Colour Sergeant or 'Colours' for short. The only thing was the guy was a fucking big black guy and I'm in the driving seat calling him 'Colours'.

After a while I had to explain myself. 'Look Colours, I'm not being disrespectful but "Colours" is what we call your rank in the

Marines.' 'Don't you worry about it son, I was wondering when you were going to say something.'

We got on great after that. I have never been racially prejudiced but what I will say is that I cannot stand arrogance and that doesn't matter whom it comes from. Unfortunately, the most arrogant people that I have come across have tended to be black people because it seems they have a point to prove. I have known and worked with some very nice black people, and I'm not just saying that to be PC but arrogant honkies really give me the shits as well.

The trouble with society in these days is that most people treat the law like a piece of shit. When I was young you respected (and I still do) police officers no matter what colour they were. Despite that, I will do things beyond the law to protect my kids so maybe I am being slightly hypocritical. But they were the law and you respected them even when they clouted you around the ear.

In those days, that was all it took because these days there are too many cases of some little toerag who has committed a lot of offences turning around and saying, 'You can't do fuck all to me 'cos I'll get my brief on to you.'

Bollocks, the little twats need a good kicking. Just let the next social worker that has been done over by these little tossers turn around and say, 'He was just misunderstood.'

Anyway, back to the driving, the whole process took just two days. After that I was a Green Goddess driver. It really used to piss us off at first because all we had to start with was a fucking bell outside the cab that one of the team had to rattle if we were on a shout and it didn't really attract attention. Things changed when we got the 'blues and twos'. We used to have police outriders with us, who acted as guides because they knew the area and we didn't. We could have lost valuable minutes if we'd had to go by street maps with the risk of getting lost.

The second memorable time was when the troop went to Switzerland to do some mountain climbing. We stayed at a small campsite in Lauterbrunnen using civvy gear because we weren't supposed to look like soldiers. The only thing that let it down was the 'civilianised' four-ton truck that we used for transport. The campsite was good and because the weather in the mountains was bad, we spent a lot of time there. We did not have a cook and did not receive rations so we were given what they called CILOR – cash in lieu of rations. This meant that you bought your food, presented the receipts and got your money back, up to a certain limit. It was great; you would get something really cheap, trawl the local supermarket for expensive receipts, and spend the rest of the money on beer and local wine. There was also a small camp shop on site with a really attractive girl behind the counter. After a while I got to know the inside of her flat very well.

There was only one occasion on that trip when we actually went up to the mountains to do some climbing. We packed all our gear and because we were in two man teams we decided to take two tents just in case. A decision that proved fortuitous! We took the larger, bell-type tents we had been using in the campsite and the smaller two-man tents. When we left the campsite we must have looked like we were going to the North Pole. We each had a Bergen on our backs and another one inverted on our fronts. We boarded a train that would take us through the tunnel that went through the Eiger and to a station at 12,500 feet called the Jungfraujoch. This train and tunnel appeared in the film *The Eiger Sanction*, starring Clint Eastwood. We then walked out through a tunnel and on to the glacier where we made camp. For some reason one of the blokes had brought a volleyball so we marked out a pitch and had a game. I believe it must be one of the highest altitude games of volleyball ever. The passing civvies were looking at us as though fourteen villages somewhere had lost their idiots!

That night the weather deteriorated and a storm began. We lay there listening to the thunder and looking at the lightning through the tent. At one point we had to get out to dig the snow away because the blizzard was starting to bury the tent. When we got back inside, we heard a loud bang and a rumble. We knew that there had been an avalanche somewhere and prayed that it wasn't on the glacier where we were. Suddenly there was a really loud bang and a bolt of lightning, and the tent collapsed.

Six out of seven tents had been hit by lightning and had collapsed. We decided to get out of there and reach the safety of the tunnels. We got our shit together, left the collapsed tents and started to make our way back to the tunnels. In the blizzard, a journey of less than 500 metres took about an hour and a half. By the time we reached the tunnel we were exhausted.

The whole of the next day was spent in the tunnel and restaurant waiting for the weather to abate before we went back out to the glacier. The decision to carry extra tents now bore fruit as we still had the small two-man tents. We went back to the glacier when the weather improved and it was decided that the next day we would attempt to climb the Jungfrau Mountain. You could also tell the amount of snow that had fallen that night because you couldn't see our original tents.

The following morning we got ourselves together and set off up the hill. Where it started to get steep and icy we put our crampons on and began to ascend the ridge. After a while I decided that I didn't like the exposure and this wasn't for me so I told my partner that I had had enough and that I was going down. He tagged on to another group and off they went. When the others returned there were no taunts of being a wimp because they realised that mountaineering is not for everyone. OK, I'd climbed Snowdon, done the Crib Goch ridge and abseiled 300 feet from a chopper, but nothing prepared me for that.

Some of these guys had been mountaineering before and went on to join the Mountain and Arctic Warfare Cadre, and became experts in their own right. In their company, I was a mere minnow. Since that moment, I have never been afraid to say no. I do not mean that a soldier should have a choice in operations or battle but he should in leisure pursuits. When you do turn round and say no, you might find that some of the people who take the piss are the ones who have achieved naff-all in their little lives. I will just look at them, smile and say, 'So fucking what!'

The ability to admit fear and to come to terms with it can sometimes be a braver choice than endangering both yourself and others. I found this out with one of the guys I worked with (although it wasn't fear in his case but common sense) who was put in the same position as Andy McNab in the Gulf War. He was the Patrol Commander who was dropped off by chopper, took one look at the terrain, said, 'No' and ordered his patrol back on to the chopper. After he got back to Hereford he was vilified and, I believe, was actually sent white feathers in the post. But even Andy has stated that it was one of the bravest decisions made during the war.

3

CIVILIAN INTERLUDE

Towards the end of my service in the Marines, I became interested in the police. I decided to make a career change and applied for the Metropolitan Police. I could just see myself as one of the Sweeneys (Sweeney Todd – Flying Squad) or some similar mob careering around London. I duly applied and was accepted and turned up at Hendon Police training centre. I completed the training course successfully and was farmed out to Norwood Green police station in the Southall district. I had found the training course to be hard work because it had been a few years since I had done any bookwork. The number of reports I had to memorise each night was often overwhelming and they had to be word perfect. Anyway, for certain reasons that I shall not go into I resigned and looked around for something else. Although I was devastated at the time, this proved to be the best thing that happened to me.

I applied for and was accepted on to the security staff with the British Airports Authority (BAA) at Heathrow airport, another new venture. To earn decent money it was necessary to do at least two or three double shifts a week, which meant a sixteen-hour day. I was involved in baggage and passenger search, which meant physically searching baggage and using the X-ray machines in the passenger terminals. The job wasn't physically demanding but sometimes the hours were long.

You'd be amazed at the things people carry in their baggage whether going on holiday or just going about their business. The worst flights were the African flights. I have never been aboard one of these planes but they must have the biggest overhead bins in the world because the size and quantity of some of the hand luggage was truly awesome. Imagine a big laundry bag packed absolutely full. Two of those per person were not unusual.

Contents ranged from clothes to fruit and anything in between. You couldn't help but laugh though because some of the people carrying them were so friendly and couldn't really understand the problem. The clothes people wore ranged from the sublime to the ridiculous, especially for those going on holiday in the summer. The blokes tended to wear daft T-shirts, shorts and hats whilst some of the women going in groups seemed to have a competition as to who could wear the sexiest outfit, which was great.

Security was supposed to be tight at these airports with announcements coming over the tannoy system regularly telling you not to leave baggage unattended as it could pose a security risk and would be dealt with accordingly. At Heathrow one time I saw how they dealt 'accordingly' with an unattended bag. Can you possibly imagine what it would be like to take the responsibility and close a terminal in the height of summer with the disruption and money it would cost? On this particular occasion there was an unattended bag in one of the terminals, and there was a huddle of BAA senior personnel around the bag. These guys were in charge of terminal security and had three and four rings on their epaulettes, so they were not junior people. The thought of shutting the terminal was obviously causing them some concern so after a while amidst much head shaking and hand gesticulation, one of them casually kicked the bag. As it didn't explode it must have been OK. It's nice to know that the security of the travelling public is in such capable hands! Perhaps the colleagues of these guys are also in charge of airside security, hence the big robberies that take place!

I can also say that I have been on Concorde. I have never flown in it but I have been on it. It's quite an amazing piece of kit but small. It's like a cigar tube with not an awful lot of headroom but I still wouldn't mind a trip in one even after the disaster. After a couple of months at Heathrow, I decided that the job was only a stopgap because I couldn't see myself doing it for the rest of my life. Although I hadn't decided what to do next, whilst in the police training school and out in the station I had let myself get unfit and now decided to get back in shape. Once I started training again I had an inkling in the back of my mind as to where I would be going next.

Working amongst civvies for the first time in my adult life had not exactly proved to be an outstanding experience. Compared to the military, their attitudes towards work and life generally were difficult for me to comprehend. I now looked at joining the Army and considered the options open to me. I wanted something where, straight after training or possibly a little while after, I would not have to wear uniform. My ultimate intention was to use the Army's time and money to get myself fit and motivated enough to go for SAS selection.

The two options I was considering were either the Royal Military Police (the monkeys) or the Intelligence Corps. After some hard thinking I opted for the Intelligence Corps (Int Corps or Green Slime).

I think what finally swung it was that I had a visit from Ken, one of my old mates from the Booties, who had just been badged into the Regiment (Special Air Service or SAS). He actually became Regimental Sergeant Major of 22 SAS and you can't do better than that. He'd left the RM at the same time as me because at that time you weren't allowed to go for SAS selection while you were still in the Booties. I suppose it was a natural progression because his dad was ex-SAS and his brother was also in the Regiment. It was around the time when we had two terrorist atrocities. Earl Mountbatten of Burma was murdered and the soldiers from the Parachute Regiment were blown up at Warrenpoint.

When I was in 40 Commando, I had spent two weeks in an OP in an ancient monument, which was right by the lay-by at Warrenpoint where the first bomb had been detonated. The OP had been put into place to watch for weapons being ferried by boat across the water from south to north. Unfortunately, we had never seen anything at all. With hindsight, however, I feel that PIRA had known we were there and had placed the bomb on the off chance. These two incidents made up my mind to get back into the forces where I could do something useful. Although my fitness was coming on fine, I knew that I had a hell of a long way to go. I went to the nearest Army Recruiting Office and told the recruiting officer that I wanted to join the Intelligence Corps. I said I wasn't interested in anything else so he agreed that I wouldn't even have to go to Sutton Coldfield to do the aptitude tests, which probably would have been a waste of everybody's time. If I had left things for a few months my life might have taken a totally different track. What I hadn't realised was that by then I was only just inside the age limit for joining the Army!

4

THE ARMY

I duly arrived at Templer Barracks, which was then the home of the Intelligence Corps, in Ashford, Kent. Although it is different now, recruit training then was done 'in house' by Intelligence Corps members. With the best will in the world, unless someone has actually served with an infantry unit or done the appropriate courses, it is very difficult to teach infantry tactics from what you can remember of your recruit days or from a book. At that time the only course you were sent away to do was the all arms drill course at the Guards Depot in Pirbright. Anyone who had any aspirations to become Company Sergeant Major (CSM) was obliged to attend so they could teach drill and take parades.

Later in my career we were obliged to go back to Ashford to do promotion courses and these included drill on the square. Apart from being sent to jail (I didn't even pass go) on day one, on my Senior Management and Duties Course (SM&D or promotion course), for not having short enough hair I was told not to bother applying for the Guards' drill course, thank fuck!

After a short period, it soon became obvious to all concerned that, with my background, I actually knew more than the instructors. I was removed from basic training and given the post of Company Clerk – whoopee! This had its advantages though, as I was able to put little ideas into the CSM's mind from time to time, which sometimes paid off. My best one was that, during their training, each recruit course went to the Lake District at some time for some adventure training.

Wouldn't it be an advantage, I thought, if I were sent on a Unit Expedition Leader's (UEL) course so I could assist the instructors, as they were always short of staff?

'Sir', I said to the Captain in charge of the detachment, 'I've been looking at the courses and know you're short of instructors.

With my background, how about sending me on a UEL course so I can help out?'

'That's not a bad idea' he said, 'let me think on it.'

I waited for a week and he came into the office one day and said, 'By the way, Private A [I was always referred to by my surname initial for some reason], about that UEL course…'

'Yes, sir?' I said hoping what was going to come next.

'I've booked you on the next one, OK?'

'Thanks very much, sir.' YES!

I was then sent to Twywn in Wales on the next course. A big part of the course was map reading but what I didn't realise at the time was that there are two Twywns in Wales, one on the north coast and one on the west coast. I duly arrived on the north coast and thought the place didn't lend itself to adventure training because it was flat and more like a seaside resort.

After some enquiries I found out there was another one and had to drive there. Initial map reading failed – shit! But it turned out to be a good week and I came away with my UEL qualification ready for the next adventure training course. During the firemen's strike, as I mentioned, I had gained my HGV 3 qualification, which give me more bargaining power as I was able to drive the four-tonner up to the Lakes and to ferry people around to the various locations. I actually did three trips in all and they were thoroughly enjoyable. Not only did it help me towards, at the time, my ultimate aim by being able to yomp over the hills with my Bergen but there was also a smashing pub in Ambleside where we always got a lock-in. The most incredible thing though about joining the Army was the close proximity of the women's accommodation, in Templer Barracks. Having come from an all-male Royal Marines barracks I couldn't believe that the women's block was only about twenty metres across the road and once again, I duly made the most of life before meeting the girl who was to become my second wife.

At the end of recruit training, I rejoined the rest of the troop for trade, or Corps, training, which basically entailed learning the nuts and bolts of Intelligence Corps work. This comprised two main subjects as far as I was concerned, which were Intelligence and Security. There was another side that I was keen to avoid and that was commonly known as 'The Dark Side'. This aspect was where the Intelligence Corps monitored Russian radio traffic and analysed what was heard, processing raw information into intelligence. Soldiers were required to study one foreign language – usually Russian – and would sit for hours each day with a pair of headphones on, listening to the radio traffic. Not for me, I thought! Everybody had to sit a language test that actually consisted of a bogus language and to my amazement I passed and dreaded the call to say that I had been selected for 'The Dark Side'. Fortunately, the call did not come and I went on to training in Intelligence and Security. 'The Dark Side' had, actually, very intelligent people, it just wasn't an environment I would have felt comfortable in.

Later on in my career we were required to go back to Ashford to take promotion courses and further qualification courses. With my specialisation most of us involved were from other branches of the Army who had transferred and we were almost all of the same mentality – fucking mad. On day one we would parade and we would eye up the opposition, mainly from 'The Dark Side'. After a quick inspection we would look at each other and wink with the knowledge that we'd be OK here.

The Corps training was actually split into these two subjects, with one or two others thrown in. The Intelligence side consisted mainly of the study of the Soviet Order of Battle as they were considered the main threat at the time. You would study from battalion through to Corps level, particularly the make-up of a Soviet Motor Rifle Regiment. By studying this and its component parts all the others appeared as add-ons or just larger formations. By also studying photographs and slides of equipment from different angles you could identify the equipment and attribute it to a particular formation. At the end of the training, by being shown a photograph or hearing of a piece of equipment that had been seen on the battlefield during an exercise, you could identify what formations you were up against and brief the commander accordingly. At the end of this phase you would do an exercise where you would be in a building for forty-eight hours, simulating running an Ops room. You would be hit with all sorts of information about small formations. Using what you had learned, you then had to make an assessment of the formations, which were up against you and brief the commanders accordingly.

After about thirty-six hours I was feeling a bit tired and briefed one commander on the formations he would be facing and the threat they posed. I think I made a bit of a fuck-up on this one because not long after I got his irate second-in-command (now the commander) on the phone to say that the commander had just been shot down in his helicopter. I'd forgotten to tell him that Soviet BMPs (armoured personnel carriers) carried shoulder-mounted surface to air missiles – shit!

The security side consisted of ploughing through the manual of military law. The main job was to conduct security investigations if documents went missing. You were also required to debrief serving or TA soldiers who had been to Iron Curtain countries in order to see if they had been approached or if someone had asked to take their photograph. If a member of a Foreign Intelligence Service (FIS) had taken their photograph it could lead to blackmail. We were basically looking for anything that might have compromised their integrity and could put them in a position for recruitment by a FIS.

Don't forget that at that time, popular tourist destinations such as Yugoslavia and Bulgaria were Iron Curtain countries. Other subjects included physical security inspections and surveys whereby you would go to a unit and ensure that physical security was up to scratch, the method of storing secret documents was adequate and if the method of storing arms and ammunition was correct. At the end of this you were required to write a detailed report in the military way, so instruction in report writing was high on the agenda.

Perhaps my biggest laugh in all of this was the typing training because we minions would never get a secretary and we would have to do our own typing. For this you sat at a desk with a typewriter in front of you watching a screen with a big typewriter face on it. A tape would then start and it would say, 'A now, B now' etc., and at the same time a light would flash on the appropriate letter. The idea was that you would have your hands on the keyboard watching the screen and you would hit the appropriate letter as it flashed. It soon became apparent that I was not going to pass the typing test using this method so when the instructor turned away it was eyes down to the keyboard and back to two fingers. I passed with flying colours. It must have done some good though because I am now up to three fingers. One other aspect of the course was interrogation training. This involved watching a demonstration of interrogation and then having a go. This only consisted of a day and I can say nothing more than the Corps has some of the finest interrogators there are. It actually takes a lot of patience to shout at someone doing the 'bad cop' bit and get no reaction. In the end it gets very frustrating and it's either a case of letting the 'good cop' have a go or get the interviewee taken back to his cell for him to think it over and for you to cool down.

There was one part of Templer Barracks known as Repton Manor, affectionately known as the Reptile House. I was not clear what the function of this place was but noticed that most of the people that went up there were in civilian cars and had long hair. One day, we were given a tour around the facilities there. I think a whole New World was opened up to me when I actually found out what was done in it. When I saw the covert cars, radios, cameras and all other sorts of goodies I thought, Yes, this is for me. These were some of the undercover soldiers that operated in NI. I had a long hard think about things and decided that I would like to give the covert side of things a try. Having matured from my time in the Marines when I felt I wasn't up to it, I now felt the time was ripe. So, I volunteered for Intelligence and Security Group (NI) (The Group) also known as 14 Intelligence Company (14 Coy), not 14th Int or any other derivatives commonly thrown around. There were two types of undercover soldiers in Northern Ireland and they were the Force Research Unit (FRU) and 14 Coy. The FRU were the people trained as agent handlers, who handled sources, or touts, in the province. 14 Coy were the surveillance specialists. Later on in my career I was asked why I didn't have a go at the FRU. My answer at the time was that I was fine following them but I didn't want to speak to or get emotionally involved with touts and their problems. I also find talking 'cold' to strangers pretty difficult, particularly as one of the tests at that time was to go into a pub and try to get someone's life story. Having talked to some of the lads who had done it, they agreed that going into a pub with three people in was a bit difficult. So I went to the headquarters of the Parachute Regiment in Aldershot for some tests and some pretty abrupt interviews. They asked if I knew what the unit did, what I was letting myself in for and if I thought I had what it took to pass the course. I must have given the right answers because I was accepted for training. Although I was accepted, I did not know when I would be allocated a place on a training course.

I was now fully focussed on this new goal in life and used to train every night by running around the Basic Fitness Test (BFT) route with a loaded Bergen. The route consisted of a half-mile circuit and I would run this for one hour per night. Part of the route had a slight incline that I used to dread every time I came around. One of the reasons I did this was because it was so boring and I was conditioning my mind to be able to switch off to any shit that was going to come my way in the following months, and come it did.

End of Corps training approached and we had to sit our final exams on everything we had done during the course. I knew I was going to be OK because I had taken in everything I had been taught and had passed everything so far, but you naturally take full advantage of every opportunity. Some people might call it cheating but I call it opportunism and for what I ended up doing in the future it served me well. I used to do my revision in the training wing where the secretary's door was always left open and it was she who used to type the exam papers. In those days typewriters and carbon paper were used and for those who don't know, when you type on to carbon paper it leaves an imprint and by holding it up to the light you can read what is on it. The secretary would type the exam papers out using carbon paper and then discard the carbon paper in the waste-paper bin, which wasn't emptied until the following morning.

It was easy to retrieve the carbon and see what was on it. There might be a load of other useless crap but you might just get an inkling of what the exam was about. Not very secure for Intelligence Corps HQ, eh! I passed out as top student! As I had done well I was told I was going to be given the plum posting.

Bloody great, I thought; Cyprus here I come. Instead, the Chief Instructor stood there with a cheesy grin on his face thinking he'd done me a big favour and said, 'You're going to Bulford security section.'

A kick in the bollocks or what! Bulford was one of the biggest army bases in the country with bosses flying about all over the place. I couldn't think of a worse place to go! Fortunately, I had already been accepted for training with 14 Coy, which coincided with my posting to Bulford, so I got out of that one as well. I was continuing with my training and got up early one morning for a run and twisted my knee. I went to see the doctor who suggested that I rest it for at least a month and told me not to do any physical exercise. This was a sickener, because the course was due to start in two weeks. I had two choices; the first was to go on the course, risk further injury and get RTU'd (returned to unit, or considered by everyone to have failed) or turn it down and ask for the following course. I chose the latter and was accepted on the following course that started in January. This left Bulford open but rather than send me there for a few months they decided to keep me on at Templer, teaching new recruits. At least on recruit training, my fitness wouldn't suffer, as it probably would have done if I were in an office in Bulford. That lasted for six months with training continuing once I was fit again. We broke up for Christmas with the next thing on my agenda being selection for 14 Coy. Christmas went like a blur with stacks of eating and piss-ups. I only managed to get one run in so I wondered what state I would be in when I got there.

I was told to report to a railway station in the Midlands, in January 1981, having previously removed all identification from everything in my possession and also all badges of rank and qualification badges. I was also told to ignore anyone I might know – not even to acknowledge them. You didn't know who was who and who might be trying to trip you up. When you arrived at the station and were waiting in the concourse you looked around and studiously avoided eye contact with anyone who looked as if he might be going to the same place as you. We were put into a truck and taken to a bleak training area in the middle of nowhere, known as Camp One, with a few buildings where all the hopefuls were unloaded and processing began. Everything that could be of use was taken from us: chequebook, wallet, money, credit cards and ID card. You were then given a number, which was yours for the selection course. Your number was your only method of recognition. Also during this period all your mail was censored to make sure you weren't giving anything away. If you wrote to anyone you would hand it in unsealed and it was sent out only after it had been read. Any mail coming in, at Camp One and Camp Two, if you made it, would have your real name blacked out and your course number written on. We then did the BFT, which consisted of a squad run to be completed in fifteen minutes and a best-effort individual run.

The rest of the day seemed a blur so at the end of it everyone was absolutely knackered and glad to get to bed. It seemed no time at all before someone was gently shaking you and whispering, 'Get out of bed and do press-ups.'

'What?'

'Get out of bed and do press-ups.'

As you began your press-ups you could see that the instructors were going to each person in turn saying the same thing, no noise at all. Suddenly the lights came on and the shouting began and we all had to turn all our kit out and everything was minutely inspected for the things I mentioned earlier that should have been removed. Anyone found with anything that could have identified him, his family, friends or which unit he was from was given a really hard time. We were then taken into a cinema and shown a really old film about the villagers of Mount Kinabalu, in the north of Brunei. All the windows were kept shut and with well over a hundred people in there it started to get stuffy and eyelids started to droop. At the end of the film it was question time so obviously those asleep didn't have a clue. Name ten things made out of bamboo – fuck me, guessing time? It was a really good film though because when I went back as an instructor seven years later we were showing the same bloody film.

Training continued at a hell of a pace and seemed to consist of physical training interspersed with classroom work. I say 'seemed to consist' because although the mind was active there was such a lot going on that things just seemed to blur.

During this time if you fucked up on something or were late you had your number taken and were put on what was called a 'change parade', which usually took place during lunchtime. This consisted of forming up outside the accommodation and the duty DS (Directing Staff) would call out a particular form of dress and you would have to disappear sharpish and reappear even more sharpish complete in that mode of dress. If you weren't on time or correctly dressed it would continue until you had it right. It was basically to fuck you about and make the point that you got things right and on time. My brother later told me that this had been one of the favourite ways of pissing people about when he had been a junior cadet at Sandhurst!

Sometimes it would leave you about five minutes to throw as much food down your neck before the afternoon training programme began. One session was usually enough for most people to get it right. Although it was a fuck-about and most people could see it for what it was, there were some that had reached their limit and even this bit of pissing about was enough to tip them over the edge and they would voluntarily RTU.

To encourage people to do this without losing face the DS would leave a tin in the phone box and you could go in and put your number in anonymously. There was no putting someone else's number in either because they would check. As you would expect there was no beer during this period – except for one occasion.

Part of the training was to develop the memory, to be able to walk through an area and then come back and then produce accurate sketches of what had been seen. There would be an immediate area sketch and a 500 metre sketch. Another sketch would be an internal sketch of a building. The building chosen for this was a pub – hoorah! The benefits of a pub were not only that it was a busy place with plenty of rooms but also that there were instructors inside to see how trainees reacted to other customers. To get all the information needed, you would have to change positions in the pub, without looking suspicious. The ability to look natural, as though you belonged, was essential and not a difficult thing for me to do in a pub. You would have to visit as many rooms as you could, to get an accurate picture of the place. Those places you couldn't go you would try to get into a position where you could see what was beyond the door when it was open. Although I didn't know it at the time, I was being trained to produce similar sketches when I gained covert access to properties in NI. Before entering the pub, however, it was necessary to do an external recce of the building and the immediate area. Once I had got all the information I thought I required, and after a few pints of course, I went back and produced the best sketches I could. Of course, not being a natural artist, I found this a bit difficult. It was a bit better than the sketch one of the girls did when we did a village recce and had to produce a sketch. She actually drew the bloody cows in the fields! Attention to detail is what they were after and it's amazing how that has stayed with me throughout my life. I piss my wife off sometimes saying things like, 'Do you see that car there? That was in Sainsbury's car park this morning.'

I might say this late in the afternoon in the opposite end of town. It does stick though, because even she's started doing it now. There might be just something that makes it stand out, such as an odd number plate or some slight damage. Attention to detail!

Another little aspect of the course was the so-called swimming test. We were lined up outside one freezing night with our towels and were marched away by the instructor for our 'swimming test'. On the way to the lake he stopped us.

'Listen lads,' he said, 'I know it's fucking freezing and I don't really fancy breaking the ice on the water either. How about we just go back and if you don't tell the Chief Instructor I won't either, OK?'

At that time, not knowing what to expect and being gullible bastards we just shouted, 'Yes, Staff.'

Of course we wouldn't! We right turned, stepped off and as we drew level with the gym the Chief Instructor walked out.

'Course, halt,' he shouted, 'Where do you think you're going with the course, Staff?'

'Er; we were just going back to the accommodation, sir.' He was obviously in on things.

'What about the swimming test, finished already? They don't look very wet to me, Staff.'

'Thought it was a bit cold, sir, gave it a miss.'

'Really, Staff. Best march them into the gym then so they can get nice and warm.'

So we marched into the gym, which was really a bare room with a raised stage at one end. As we walked in all the rest of the instructors were sitting on the stage with shit-eating grins on their faces and in the middle of the room was a makeshift boxing ring – fucking great, a set-up or what! You were then split into two teams and paired off with someone roughly the same size. Now this wasn't boxing, it was the army variation called 'milling'. Basically we stood toe to toe and when told to do so we would try to beat the living shit out of our opponent. If we turned away the fight was stopped until we were facing each other again and on we went. It only lasted for a certain period of time or until someone was badly hurt and couldn't continue. For the job we were hoping to go into it showed if we had any aggression.

I was put against a pipe-smoking Rupert and although the rest of the team and I thought I'd won it was given as a draw. When I went back as an instructor the students wore head guards, but in those days the only protection was to get in first. Thankfully, after what really were the hardest two weeks of my life the course ended. Throughout the course anyone could either RTU whenever they wanted or be forced to RTU. From approximately 140 who turned up on day one, we went down to around thirty. Some of the students had brought cars and we were split up into groups to travel to our next location by car and given directions on how to get there. We were elated by the fact that we'd come this far.

We were going to somewhere in Herefordshire and as we got closer we realised that we had plenty of time so stopped off for a pint in a pub in Leominster. We then drove to this place known as Ponty or Camp Two, and as we approached we drove down a lane on either side of which was a tall chain link fence with barbed wire on top and masses of radio antennae. Until now we had only seen the instructors in a variety of berets and badges ranging from Royal Marines, Parachute Regiment and Tank Regiment. The chief instructor himself had worn a Royal Engineers cap badge. As we approached the main gate to this new camp we were met and directed by the chief instructor wearing an SAS beret and cap badge. I think we now knew something of what we were really letting ourselves in for. The camp itself was more modern and a lot more comfortable than the previous one and even had a bar – deep joy! We were assigned four to a room but a couple of months into the course I ended up with the room to myself. We were still not allowed to hold our possessions, which had been taken from us at Camp One. So on the few occasions when we were allowed home for the weekend, you would draw them from the Admin office and hand them in on return.

Easter approached at one point during the course and we were going to get about ten days off. My girlfriend, who was also in the Intelligence Corps, was in Cyprus and I had told her about this leave but thought no more about it. I was expecting to go home to my parents and chill out for the Easter period. I received a letter from her a couple of weeks prior to the Easter leave and it contained what I thought was a pamphlet. I didn't really pay much attention to it because of all that was happening. I stuffed it in my locker and got on with the day's work. It was only when we had finished that evening that I thought I'd dig it out and have a read through. When I actually looked at it, it was only a bloody air ticket to Cyprus. It was a good thing I didn't do what I normally do with leaflets and throw it straight in the bin. I really couldn't believe that she'd bought me a ticket herself. The reason why I didn't recognise it as an airline ticket? Would you believe it, twenty-seven years old and I'd never even flown on a commercial airliner. I'd flown of course but it had been with the RAF and most times I'd never landed because I'd jumped out. My girlfriend and I had been going out for a while by this time and we knew we were both very fond of each other but I didn't expect this. I flew out and she met me at the airport along with a very good friend who had been in the same training squad as me and who later went on to be the best man at our wedding. We spent many happy times in Cyprus and it was one lovely sunny afternoon on the beach that I came to a momentous decision and asked her to marry me. We were both so excited by it and arranged a night out with friends to celebrate. The first thing we did though was to find a jeweller in Larnaca where we bought her engagement ring. It was actually a combined engagement/wedding ring that consisted of two rings that fitted together when they were matched. It was a beautiful ring and although a bit pricey she got it of course.

Back to the course. Training consisted of a series of phases and at the end of each phase there was a binning (sacking) session. This usually happened during lunchtime and took the form of the chief instructor coming in with his millboard. After the first one you knew what that meant. He would go up to an individual and just say, 'Go and see the training major.'

That's when you knew that person was history. He would disappear to see the training major and we didn't see him again. I remember one meal in particular where there were four of us sitting at a table when in walks the chief instructor complete with millboard. He spoke to a few others and then came to our table. The three other guys got the good news first and I thought it was my turn next. I was just about to stand up when he turned and walked to another table. My sphincter muscle was twitching like fuck.

We used to do a lot of situation awareness training which basically taught you how to recognise a situation that was building up and how to deal with it before it got out of hand. We also learnt how to react to a situation when you suddenly found that you had a problem, so that your first reaction was not to look like a startled rabbit. In some cases, the training involved reacting to an incident such as a bomb explosion and how to react when you arrived on the scene.

One scenario was that some of your fellow operators were in a house. You would approach it and there would be an explosion inside. Basically they were conducting a covert search and they had sprung a booby trap. On arriving at the scene you would first have to secure the room you were in, then assess the situation and deal with the casualties in order of seriousness. Quite often the casualties would involve the use of false blood, liver and gristle to simulate someone having their arm or leg blown off or their guts spilling out. There was one time where the casualty was made up to appear as if he had lost part of his arm because there was a lot of blood and crap where his arm should have been. He had in fact put his arm down a hole in the floor so that you could only see part of it.

OK, I thought, if that's how they play things, I'll look out for that one in future.

The next time something like that happened there was a guy lying there with what appeared to be part of his arm missing. Right, I thought, his arm's in the hole like the last one, piece of piss.

Imagine my shock when I came to treat him and as I moved his arm the rest of it wasn't in the hole because it wasn't there. I thought, chopping his fucking arm off is taking things a bit too far.

For this one they'd brought someone in from the Regiment who had actually lost part of his arm. That was a bit of a shock to the system! Invariably this sort of situation was always followed by crowd trouble and there were normally two ways to deal with it. If you were inside the building you would barricade yourself in and tell the crowd that you'd blow the fucking head off the first person that tried to get in the room. If it was outside it meant calling another guy in with a car who would scatter the mob. You would then pile in and drive off. In that situation it would have been perfectly acceptable to put one warning shot over their heads and then drop the ringleader with the second shot. Why waste an extra warning shot? This was all good stuff.

During our time at Ponty we were not allowed out of the camp except for training and this got everyone down after a while. The only forms of entertainment were the bar and TV. We were allowed out on special occasions to go to nearby Ross on Wye, where another bloke whom I got to know well and who was from the Red Devils free fall-team duly went on a pub and talent-spotting crawl. Towards the end of the evening we were both pissed and decided to go back to the car park and wait for the minibus. As we waited we laid down against a grassy bank and fell asleep and the next thing we knew there was a copper shining his torch in our eyes. He was asking our names but because we were still supposed to remain anonymous we wouldn't tell him.

Fortunately at that time the minibus turned up and the driver bailed us out. I think we would probably have ended up in cells that night if he hadn't.

At the beginning of the course we were issued with a Browning semi-automatic pistol and a magazine carrier with two spare magazines. We were required to wear this at all times, even when in the bar playing pool. The idea was that we would get used to wearing it and be able to pick the correct clothes so that it was properly concealed. We were also issued two blank rounds that were in the pistol with one up the spout and safety applied to simulate carrying it across the water. It was common to be sitting in a room and every now and again there would be a bang as someone practised his quick draw without unloading first. It was Voluntary Contribution (VC) time. In the regular Army, if you transgressed regulations, you were put on a charge – to civilians, it is basically the same as being put in court. In the Special Forces, Voluntary Contributions meant that there were no formal charges as in other units but we were 'invited' to pay a VC of a specific amount to the final piss-up fund. Great if you were one of those left!

The main part of our surveillance training took place in Bristol because it was the nearest big city to us, and the city was split into areas of differing hostility, as it would be if we made it across the water. The split indicated Protestant areas, soft Republican areas and hard Republican areas. The area chosen for the last area was the St Paul's district of Bristol. This was not a very pleasant area to operate in, especially for a couple of honkies in what appeared to be a covert police car. We got quite a few hostile looks driving around and sitting up when we had to. It was not long after the St Paul's riots, which made it doubly difficult. There was one particular incident a couple of courses before mine when one of the students was in a pub in St Paul's and went to the toilet. Someone from an ethnic background followed him in, produced a knife and invited him to part with his wallet. The guy instinctively drew his Browning and invited him to fuck off or else he'd give him a third eye. Fortunately the ethnic didn't know the student only had blanks. Bluff can be a great thing sometimes!

One particular exercise as we approached the end of the course taught me never to take things at face value and always to look beyond what I saw. Once again the exercise took place in Bristol and the scenario was that a terrorist was due to arrive from across the water and meet some people with the intention of forming an Active Service Unit (ASU) in Bristol. We picked this guy up at Bristol airport and followed him into Bristol and he went to a hotel.

Now at this point we thought we were stuck because up until now all our OPs had either been rural or in derelict buildings but here we were in the middle of Bristol with the target in a hotel. What do we do here? Do we try to book into a hotel opposite or what? We were, we thought, fucked. We then got the call over the air from the DS to lift off and go back to Ponty. When we arrived back we were debriefed on what had happened and how we thought it should go in the future. The general consensus was that someone should try to get an OP in a hotel opposite. OK, they said, should that be a single or a double. Obviously a married couple would stand out less than a single guy trying to book into a hotel on his own. And you'll never guess who got the job of one half of the couple! We went away and packed a suitcase with what we would need for the task. The suitcase had very few clothes in, as we couldn't fit many in with all the kit we had to take. There was camera equipment, weapons with spare ammunition, night viewing gear – the lot. The brief was that in reality we would turn up and try to book in but there was already a room booked in the front of the hotel that would give us a lookout on to the target's hotel. Fine, I thought, this should be a good few days. With us being in the hotel, we were not able to be part of the surveillance team because by the time we had given the target away we would not be able to get to our car in time, if we had one, to form part of the team. The hotel didn't have a car park so we were in fact dropped off. However, the theory was the same. Our job was to OP the hotel during the night in case of a standby and to watch the hotel during the day when the target was in. The rest of it was up to the surveillance team.

So, we turned up at the hotel in what was a bit of a run down part of Bristol and walked in to the reception and said we had a room booked in whatever name it was. The receptionist confirmed this and she led us to our room. At this point I started to get a bit concerned, as she led us out of the back of the hotel. I was expecting a room in the front of the hotel but she led us to a fucking annexe at the back. We were stumped! You could also tell the type of hotel it was as there were about eight beds in the room. We reported this over the radio and were told to try to get a room overlooking the front. This, we were later to learn, was to see if we could manage it and what excuse we would use to get it. I went downstairs to the reception and asked for a room at the front because the back was too quiet and I liked to hear the sound of the traffic. I was told that there wasn't one available that night but we could move the following day.

I went back to the room and reported this over the radio and was told that all we could do was go to the bar in the front of the hotel and try to keep an eye on the front door of the target's hotel. That sounded like an absolutely splendid idea to me so we secured our kit and went to the bar and tried to keep watch as we had a few – well more than a few – drinks. This was really to see if he came out because the team had lifted off for the night and we weren't due to start until the next day. Now, when we first picked the target up he was sporting a full beard so we thought this would be a piece of piss, as he was very distinctive. Anyway, we kept watch until closing time and didn't see a thing so we reported this and then got our heads down for the night. The next day, about mid-morning, we were moved to a room overlooking the front of his hotel which meant the rest of the team could stand off a bit, as up until now they had to be fairly close in to be able to take him if he came out. The room we now had was better except that the net curtains were filthy and there was no way that we were going to be able to take photographs through them. In the end we had to make a small tear in them so we could get a clear shot at the doorway. We set the tripod up and then prepared for the day. Obviously we couldn't stay in the hotel all day as that would cause a bit of suspicion and so would carrying the case out every time we left the hotel. That meant that the case had to have good locks on so we could secure it and put it under the bed with a couple of tell-tales so that we could see if someone had tried to get in. While we were out the team would close in and take the trigger on the target.

Although it may have seemed natural for a young (which I was then) couple to stay in the room all day, this may have started tongues wagging and the idea was to present an image of a grey couple (people who didn't stand out either by appearance or actions). Staying in the room while one went to breakfast wasn't a problem because the other one could always play the old hangover trick so we could keep the hotel covered. Sometimes one of us would stay in the room for a couple of hours while the other one went walkabout and vice versa. Other times it would be necessary for both of us to vacate the room so the team would have to come in and take the trigger while we were out.

We got to know the centre of Bristol quite well on foot and as we were fairly close to the university, in the summer, it gave me a bit of a chance to do some student watching of the female variety. This went on all day with not a sighting of the target and as the day went on we were becoming more and more worried that either we had missed him or he had got out a back way. We had people doing walk-pasts and checking for back entrances, but still nothing. At the end of the day we were convinced that he had got away and we had blown it so we were all a bit pissed off.

At 2000 hours that evening we were called to a local TA drill hall to be debriefed and asked what we thought had gone wrong. All sorts of scenarios were offered and at the end this bloke walks in and we were asked if we recognised him, to which everyone said no. He then admitted that he was the target but by now he was clean-shaven and had been in the same bar with us the night before. Shit, I thought, but it taught me a valuable lesson on not to take anything at face value and I actually used the same tactic a few times later in my career.

End of training approached and the group of approximately 140 that started on day one, six months earlier, was now down to nine, so we thought we were now all safely through. On the very last day a young Royal Marine Pig got the good news so that left eight. He actually left an Oxford Street Harris Tweed jacket and a decent pair of trousers behind that fitted me perfectly. I mentioned earlier that there are people whom you will come across time and again throughout your life especially in this line of work. One of the Ruperts, George he called himself at that time, was one of my brother's best friends and I had known him for a number of years. When I was at Camp One, you couldn't acknowledge people you knew but I saw this guy and I thought, as you do, I know you.

It actually got to the stage of everything being so secret that we were in the shower one evening and there was no one else around and we were eyeing each other up (but not in that way you understand) and I was feeling like a bit of a pervert, so I just said, 'Look, I don't want to blow your cover, but aren't you so-and-so and don't you know my brother?'

'Yes,' he answered, 'but I wasn't going to say anything either.'

He passed the course but when he got across the water considered that he had been fucked over and binned it.

The whole organisation was so secretive that I believe it contributed to the failure of my second marriage because perhaps I took things too literally. I reached the stage where I considered everything so secretive that I wouldn't tell my wife anything about what was going on. Obviously, she felt on the outside. Also, when we were engaged, I said – stupidly in hindsight – that if she wanted me to I would leave the Army. It got to the point at one stage that she asked me if I would leave the Army and I said I couldn't, not with what I was doing now. I suppose I was a bit stupid to have offered to in the first place but maybe she was also asking a bit much at that time. Having gone through everything so far, I couldn't give it up. I also felt that if she could ask that of me at that time she couldn't really have thought that much of me. What was I going to do, get some dead-end job that I wouldn't be happy in? I think that even if I had done the marriage would have ended anyway because of the resentment I would have felt. I still felt like shit when I took her back to England from Germany and dropped her off at her mother's house knowing that was it. Another chapter in my life had ended. She'd really done nothing wrong, it was just me. I also said goodbye to Ben (my dog, who I'll talk about later).

The final phase, as with most courses, took place that night with a good dinner and plenty of wine. It was actually quite sedate compared to some of the end of course dinners that I went to when I was an instructor a few years later. After that we had a bit of leave before deploying to the province, feeling like we could take on the world.

5

NORTHERN IRELAND

In June 1981 four of us were sent to North Detachment (North Det or the Det) in Londonderry based near Limavady. I still call it Londonderry; I won't use the abbreviated version, on principle. We arrived and had a bit of a social night before we started work in earnest on a three-week orientation phase, which was later extended to six weeks because some people couldn't hack the pace. During this period, apart from doing orientation runs (familiarity drives) we were not allowed out. This was absolutely right as we would have been a danger to ourselves and the other members of the Det if we had got lost or blundered into something that we shouldn't have, as two Royal Signals Corporals found out later on in 1988. The city, as far as the Det was concerned, was split up into different-coloured areas and we navigated by means of a spot system. Most road junctions in the city had a coloured and numbered spot on them and this is how we found our way around.

By the end of my first tour I probably knew the city better than anywhere I had been before and that included my hometown. I say 'hometown' but in fact I had been forced to adopt one because being involved with the Army all my life I didn't really have anywhere to call my 'hometown'. Despite this, I still knew the city better than anywhere I'd been before. I didn't know all the road names but I could get from spot to spot from one end of the city to the other either by the most direct route or by all the short cuts. The way the system was taught was simple but effective.

Taking one colour of spots at a time a route was devised that took in most of the major junctions and the route was videoed from the back of a van. We would then sit in front of the TV and one of the Det members, acting as teacher for the orientation, would run us through the route, calling out the spots and distinguishing features. Firstly we would learn the route as per the video so that we knew what to expect when driving it. Next, once we had perfected the basic route, we would be partnered with another operator to drive the route and call the spots and distinguishing features out as we went through. It was then back to the video for confirmation and some lateral thinking. For example, OK, we are now at white 5, what happens if we go straight, or left, or right or throw up (going back the way we had just come and not the obvious connotation)?

By doing this we built up an overall picture of that area of the city until we were taken out and could drive all over that section, spot by spot. The same was repeated with all the other sections, until eventually we tied all the areas in together with their relevant spots and we could navigate around the complete city confidently and safely. Before we passed the orientation, for the final phase we were taken out once again and we would be in one part of the city and told to get to a certain point by the quickest route calling off all the spots on the way. This could be on one side of the river at the outermost point and having to find your way across the river, through the town centre to the furthermost point on the other side. It certainly got the grey matter working especially as you were told to look out for any 'players' (PIRA members) as you drove through. Another part of the orientation had been to study mugshots of all the main players in the city so you could recognise them on sight.

Before we deployed to the Det we were advised on the sort of clothing to take over so that we wouldn't stand out like some dickhead on holiday. The most popular form of coat at that time was the snorkel jacket. This was a blue parka-type jacket with an orange interior and a hood trimmed with fur – height of fashion or what! So I went into town and got myself one of these and carted it off to the Det. When I arrived it was pointed out that the interior of my jacket, being new, was bright orange compared to everyone else's, which were dull. This, I was told, would make me stand out like a turd in a swimming pool so I had to do something about it. My answer was during the orientation period to throw it out of my window onto the grass. We had some dogs in the compound and they thought it was a great thing to play with. Coupled with the weather I thought that would do the trick.

So at the end of the three-week orientation I had a worn in, but slightly smelly, snorkel jacket ready for the streets. New jeans would also be a bit of a giveaway so I took an old pair across and spent the rest of the tour patching them whenever I got holes in them. I became something of an expert in sewing even if the stitches were more like 'homeward bounders' (big over and under stitches). Even in some of the hard Republican market towns people always said 'hello' and I put this down to the fact that I looked like a bag of shite.

During the orientation period we had it hammered into us that if we fucked up badly on the ground we were likely to end up dead. One of the main purposes of learning the spot system was that you didn't have to get your maps out to see where you were or where you were going. Would a native of Londonderry be using a map book to find his way around the city – I don't think so! Also most of the people at that time, unless they were going out for the night, looked scruffy and had long hair and stubble, so you had to look the same. This was one of the many times that my beard came and went on occasions. It's easy to shave a beard off to change appearance but harder to grow and you can't be walking the streets with the terrorists watching you grow a beard. So, if you had to, you would start a beard on leave and then spend some time doing choppers until it was OK. Some people in the Det preferred short hair but I preferred mine long as it used to hide my radio earpiece. PIRA weren't stupid, contrary to public belief, and they knew that we used earpieces so if they saw someone fairly young and fit wearing an earpiece they could put two and two together.

This brings me to a particular story about a Guardsman who had passed the course and been deployed not long before I arrived in the Det. He had passed orientation and then went on leave for a while. When he came back he had had his hair cut short so he looked more like a soldier than he should have done. He was on an operation, I forget which now, but he was covering an address on the Foyle Road. Along this road on each side were lay-bys for two or three cars. He started off in one and at one point thought he was attracting attention from the third party (you would be the first party, the target the second party and anyone not directly involved the third party).

What he should have done was informed the team that he was attracting third-party attention so that he could move out and someone else could take his trigger position, covering the target from another place. Instead he just moved further up the road from lay-by to lay-by. This might have been due to the fact that he was new and didn't want the other members of the team to think he'd cocked it up but no one will ever find out the real reason.

To the third party this would have looked very suspicious. The Guardsman was also not sure of the city and his map book was open on the passenger seat. To cap it all he couldn't find his earpiece so he had his speaker on. Someone had done a walk-past of his car, seen the map book, heard the radio and had reported this to one of the boys. Unfortunately at the time there was a van full of the Provisional IRA (PIRA) with weapons trawling the city looking for a suitable target. They were contacted and they drove along the Foyle Road and identified the operator's car. They pulled into the lay-by just in front of his car, flung open the back doors and riddled the car with automatic fire. He was killed instantly. This shows the importance of the orientation phase and how a catalogue of errors could end up with you paying the ultimate price. Apart from many other things you could have done to give yourself away, third-party awareness was the one thing that would probably get you every time. Even to this day, having been out of the system for nearly five years, I am still very conscious of the presence of any third party and I'm sure most other ex operators would be as well.

Our radio communications in the cars were done by induction, the same as foxtrot (foot) comms (communications), which meant that there would be a wire loop in the roof lining or in your seat. For foxtrot comms you would have an induction pad that would transmit the signals to your earpiece. My favourite was a wire loop that you hung around your neck as no matter where you turned your head you could always pick up the signal. This way you could wear an earpiece and hear what was going on but no one else could. There was one story, however, going around about an operator who was in a post office standing next to a pensioner who was wearing a hearing aid. When the operator received transmissions the pensioner would look startled and stare around, wondering who the hell was whispering to him. True or not I don't know, but if it were I would imagine it would have given the old boy a bit of a shock. I used to wear mine in my left ear so that when I was sitting up in the cuds (the countryside) I could crack my window and my right ear could hear what was going on outside. You can always spot a Secret Service Man by the curly wire leading from his radio to his earpiece but you will never see that on an operator as, as I have said, it is all done by induction. We had a speaker fitted to the radio but it was anathema to use it. Sometimes the bleeps (Royal Signals personnel) nearly got the shit kicked out of them because when they filled the radios with the new cipher (for secure comms) they would flick the speaker on and forget to switch it back again. Therefore when we were going out on a job the next day we would give a radio check and the fucking speaker would be blaring out.

Also during orientation you would choose a cover name so I chose mine and used it to obtain a Northern Ireland driving licence for cover purposes. Apart from disguising my real name I could use it if I had any traffic violations that added points to my licence. That way my real UK licence remained clean. I, in fact, picked up a £75 fine and three points on this licence but that was OK because on my next tour I could have a new name and a new licence. When we were stopped at an Army checkpoint they would ask to see our licence and I would hand this over. What most blokes used to do was put their cover ID card and a little note inside with words to the effect of, 'I am a soldier on duty; please treat me like any other motorist.'

This meant that if he were searching vehicles he would search ours as well. This was providing we weren't in a hurry or had some sensitive kit in the car we didn't want him to see.

At the end of the orientation came the inevitable piss-up during which a ceremony was held and we were presented with Det medals (a wind-up). This consisted of everyone being present in the bar and throwing as much beer down our necks before the actual presentation. The Det Sergeant Major (DSM) would then form all the FNGs (fucking new guys) up in a straight line and call us to attention (if you could still stand to attention). The Boss would then march in with a steel helmet and a Luke Skywalker light sabre. The DSM used to have an old greatcoat with a WW2 German Army helmet on and would be carrying a tray of beer. He would present you with your Army Spy Class 1 medal with one bar. On subsequent tours another bar was added. One of the guys from the Parachute Regiment there ended up with five bars and I've still got mine with two bars. He would also give us a pint and at the word of command we had to down it in one. If the steel helmets had puzzled anyone we now found out why. The rest of the guys in the bar pelted us with all the empty cans, and at least one full one, they had collected that evening. We of course retaliated and things degenerated until we got fed up and started drinking again.

We were now fully fledged operators although still on probation and we were allowed on the streets. When we first went out on the streets during a mobile surveillance job, you would always find yourself at the back of the team because the guys who have been there longer were quicker in the thought process and would take parallels to run alongside the target. They would then be at a particular junction ready to take control of him when he got there.

In the city you would probably not take him more than two junctions before you pulled off and let someone else take control. This is a great way to conduct surveillance because in most movies (especially American ones) you see the surveillance car right up the target's arse, following him wherever he goes. It must work in America because the target never seems to notice even if he is in the law enforcement business. It was good for the Det though because some targets expected the same thing; so by dropping the target every couple of junctions he had different cars behind him all the time and vehicles coming at him from different angles.

Anyway, I got my first Ops (operational) car and it was a Ford Fiesta 1.1S – brill! It was only a small car but it had enough legroom for me and it was just the right size for squeezing into tight spots when you had to take the trigger on the target. I was surprised because if I thrashed it, as I always did, it had quite a reasonable turn of speed. I spent my time at the back of the team as I was trying to handle everything but gradually found I was working my way to the front. Then one glorious day I was in a backing position, behind the guy in control, ready to take his place when he pulled off. We were in the Brandywell district, which is hard Republican, and there was a mini riot going on. We were trying to avoid the lines of bricks they had put in the road. Suddenly, just as I had said I could take control, I got a brick in my windscreen and had to pull off immediately. Anything that stands out on your car is a visual distinguishing mark (VDM) and that might attract the attention of the target. Bollocks, I thought, I was almost there. To say I was pissed off would be an under-statement.

It can probably be said that practically everyone in the Det, at one stage or another, has contributed to the Republican cause; I certainly have. Apart from the cassette tapes that a lot of the lads bought from Nutt's Corner we would also give money to people collecting in tins. The tapes of rebel songs were actually good to listen to and were certainly great to sing along to when you were pissed. The people collecting in tins were very difficult to ignore. On rare occasions you would find them on the streets in the city and to walk past with the attitude of 'Fuck you' was not conducive to making friends and influencing people, so you would put ten pence in the tin. The favourite place for collections was the crossroads just down the road from Castle Gate. Here the traffic would be slowed to a standstill and there would be people in the middle of the road with collecting tins 'inviting' you to make a contribution towards the cause. I think it would take a very brave, or foolish, man not to bung ten pence in the tin. There was always the thought at the back of your mind that they might just remember you or your car in another part of the city when you were on a job. Something might just flicker in the back of their mind and the whole thing could go to ratshit. Also you didn't know if your VRN (vehicle registration number) had been passed on for refusing to pay. So, although I spent quite some time fighting against them I can honestly say that I also contributed towards their cause. Thank fuck I never saw the round (bullet) that I had paid for!

There are a few operations that stand out during both tours that spring to mind. One was when we had the task of entering a flat that belonged to a known player. I was the No. 1 on that job (responsible for planning) and it involved people from Box 500 (security service) coming over to try to plant a technical device (bug) in his flat. One or two of the people from Box 500 weren't too bad but some others were scared stiff of even walking a few yards on the street, so we nearly always had to have someone walk with them as a babysitter.

I'd been in the Det for about nine months on my first tour when the Boss called me into the office. Up until this point I'd always acted as someone's No. 2 on jobs but now I was going to get the chance to do my first job as No. 1.

'OK Sam, you know about Mark McDade who lives in a flat near G26. Well we know he's involved with PIRA but we're not too sure of the full extent of his involvement. It's possible that he may be part of the Derry security team but that's just speculation at the moment. Interest in him is quite high though, because Box want to come over and try to insert a technical device into his flat. I know this will be your first job as No. 1 but you wouldn't be getting it if I didn't think you could handle it, OK? You'll have Pete 1 as your No. 2 so if you have any major problems he'll be able to help you out.'

If there was more than one guy in the Det with the same name, they would have numbers, i.e. Pete 1, Pete 2.

'Yeah, that's great. What time frame am I looking at for the initial CTR?' (Close target recce.)

'Well it's Tuesday now so we'd be looking to make the initial entry on Saturday night. We know he usually goes out on the piss on Saturdays and he's got himself a new girlfriend so he'll probably take her out. Just one thing to bear in mind is that some of the other flats in the block are occupied. A seaman rents one of them and the Branch [Special Branch] are sure he is away at the moment, but as for the others they're not so sure. Just something to bear in mind when you make your plan.'

'OK, what about entry to his flat? Have we got keys or do we need Ben for the MOE (Method of Entry)?'

'We've got a key to his flat and also to the communal front door courtesy of him being lifted last week and copies being made. It might be best to have Ben on the ground though just in case he's changed the locks. Any initial thoughts?'

My mind immediately went into overdrive, thinking of an initial plan. Ideally I'd have liked some time to think about it but it was a case of 'flip-flop off the top'.

'Well I reckon we're going to need three teams for this. One team will have to take him from the flat and keep him under surveillance while he's out. The second team will have to cover the approaches and junctions for the entry team to go in and out and the third team will be the entry team itself. The guy from Box will be part of the second team and they'll escort him to the door. Once we're in the flat and depending how far the Box guy is with his kit, if Mark looks like coming back we'll have to get the QRF (Quick Reaction Force) to stop him or arrange a little accident. Anything to stop him getting back to the flat.'

'Well that sounds fairly straightforward,' he laughed. 'What sort of accident did you have in mind?'

'Nothing too drastic, eh! Maybe just a small RTA (road traffic accident) but enough to get the police called and him lifted for drink driving or something like that. Better that than another form of accident if he made it back to the flat, know what I mean.'

'Yeah, roger that,' he chuckled. 'Just make sure you emphasise that point to the QRF when you brief on Saturday evening. Talking about briefing, what time do you want to go for?'

'Well I know he goes to the Bogside Inn quite a bit and they stay open until the early hours but if he's got a new girlfriend he might come home a bit early to get some shagging in. I reckon we brief at 1830 and after the brief the whole team deploys to the city. The surveillance team can stake the flat out ready for him to go mobile and the rest of us can lay up in car parks for when he makes a move and then we can move in.'

I went and found Pete 1 and put him in the picture of what my initial plan was and he seemed quite happy with that. Basically he was going to let me get on with it and would just make suggestions if he could see me forgetting something. At that stage in the Det you would be glad of someone like him available, to call on his experience if necessary. It's quite a big step in a new operator's career to be given your first No. 1, especially a job like this involving a covert entry and putting a device in. To say I felt a bit chuffed would have been an understatement. There were a number of things we had to do between now and Saturday and the main ones were recces of the target. I had a word with the pilot and arranged a fly-past for the following morning to get the latest air photos of the target area. If you like flying in helis then the Det was the place to be. You could arrange a trip almost every day if you were that way inclined with no questions asked.

The recces for any CTR, be it urban or rural, nearly always seemed to take the same format. You would try to gain as much information from any source available before you even put a foot on the ground. This would take the form of studying maps and available air photographs but normally you would fly the area and take your own. All this would be done to try to minimise your exposure on the ground. It normally went in the form of an air recce first, then a drive-past of the target and finally, if necessary, a walk-past. The following morning we went off for the air recce. Now air recces in the city are a different kettle of fish from recces in a rural environment. In the rural areas you would operate at a minimum of 2,000 feet, stand off from the target to get oblique photos and fly in a straight line there and back. In the city it was totally different because there was so much aerial activity that you could literally bank over the target's back garden to get a look in his back yard if you wanted to. It was aimed to try to maintain a height of between 1,000 to 1,500 feet, but hovering to get good shots was a piece of piss.

We got the shots we needed and went back to get the Brownie (photographer) to develop them and that afternoon had a good look in conjunction with the map of the area. What we were looking for were any alleyways that we could approach the target from that we might have missed previously. We were pretty sure there weren't any because, as I said before, we knew the city better than our hometowns by now. Because we had a good lead-in time to the job we didn't want to rush things so we arranged a couple of backing cars for the next day to do a drive-past of the area. As I say, it wasn't really necessary because we knew the area so well but there is a saying that covers all eventualities and that is the seven Ps: 'Piss-poor planning and preparation equals piss-poor performance.'

Sod's law states that if we hadn't bothered with recces there would have been an almighty fuck-up on the night.

Once we were happy with the drive-past we arranged to do a walk-past at a different time the following day. We also planned to do a confirmatory drive-past on the afternoon of the job just to make sure, because sod's law once again states that if we hadn't they would probably have decided to dig the road up or something. In between all this I was slowly putting my final plan together and writing out my orders for the briefing on Saturday night. By Friday afternoon I was fairly certain I had every eventuality covered and so was able to take it easy in the bar that night having run it by Pete 1 who had given his approval in his own way.

'Not bad for a first attempt, you wanker.' Praise indeed.

The guy from Box had arrived that afternoon and we got him into the bar for a few beers. Unfortunately for him it was his first time in the province and he had come across with a more experienced guy we knew although he was the one going on target. After a few beers we got the measure of this guy and started to wind him up with some horror stories of what could happen and what to do if the shit hit the fan, where to run to and so on. You could see the guy starting to get a bit agitated and you could see the other guy over his shoulder laughing his cock off and mouthing, 'Bastards.'

We thought it was fucking hilarious.

I think what we said must have worried him because prior to the briefing that evening he came up to me and said, 'Look Sam, I'd feel a lot better out there if I could have a weapon to carry.'

'No problems Colin, if it makes you feel safer of course you can have a weapon,' and I handed him a Browning 9 mm. 'Just make sure you keep it concealed with the safety on at all times unless you have to use it, OK?'

I'd cocked it previously and let the slide go forward so you could apply the safety catch. If he knew anything about weapons he would know that a weapon had to be cocked before you could apply the safety so as long as he could see the safety was applied he was happy.

'Yeah, thanks a lot.'

You should have seen the relief on his face. He might not have been so happy if he'd known it wasn't loaded. There was no fucking way I was going to give a loaded weapon to a civvy whose level of weapon training I didn't know.

Saturday evening and briefing time came and everyone packed into the briefing room. It was quite a crowded house that night. In all there must have been about twenty people including the three teams, the QRF, people manning the Ops room back at base and the Head of Special Branch, Mr D. He tended to look on us as his private army and quite often came to briefings and debriefings. On my second tour he had been replaced by TCG (Tasking and Co-ordinating Group) and that was when the jobs went downhill. Anyway the briefing went fine and there were no searching questions and after a final check we set off for the city. It doesn't matter how long you have been doing the job; final checks are a must. It might just be a little thing that you carry around with you all the time but you would be knackered without it. It's worth taking that extra couple of minutes to ensure you are fully booted and spurred. The surveillance team got into position and confirmed that his car was still static where it normally was and there were lights on in the flat.

At about 2030 we heard the call in our earpieces.

'Stand by, stand by. That's Alpha 1 and Echo 1 from Charlie 1 towards Bravo 1.'

In other words Mark (Alpha 1) and his girlfriend (Echo 1) had left the flat (Charlie 1) and were walking towards the car (Bravo 1). They were designated as '1' because they were the first targets seen that night. Things got complicated sometimes when you had Alpha 1 talking to Echo 4 at the door of Charlie 2 having been dropped off by Bravo 3. These were the codes on my first tour, and they had changed by my second tour. We were laying up in a car park about five minutes from his flat, ready to move in when called for.

'Approaching Bravo 1. Now complete Bravo 1, Alpha 1 driving, Echo 1 passenger.'

'That's Bravo 1 now mobile towards green 15 (G15), unsighted to me.'

In other words they'd got into the car with Mark driving and had driven off towards a junction (colour spotted for navigation and brevity). The car that initially had the trigger could not now see the car (unsighted).

'Golf, I have Bravo 1 towards green 15.'

'Roger that, Romeo backing.'

Now Golf has control of the target and Romeo is behind Golf in a position to assume control when he pulls off. Most of the handovers are done by radio but an experienced team will carry out mirror handovers. The guy in control will see the backing car in his mirror and rather than waste airtime will just pull off and let him take control.

We were following the take on our earpieces and he seemed to be going towards the Bogside Inn so we made our way to the general area of the target. Once he was housed in the pub we gave it about half an hour in case he'd forgotten something before the second team moved in to stake out the area. This meant that every junction and approach to the flat were covered by an operator who would give a warning if anyone was approaching as the entry team tried to gain access. As they got into position each one would call up as his option became clear.

'Delta, all clear.'

'India, all clear.'

'Hotel, all clear.'

'Mike, all clear.'

'Alpha, roger all that. Juliet, you're all clear in the target area.'

'Juliet, roger that, moving in now.'

We drove around the corner, parked the car and went foxtrot towards the target, listening out for any of the callsigns to report a not clear. If we had heard that, provided we were not committed into the gateway, we could have aborted, walked around the block and tried again. We got to the gate and everything seemed OK so we went into the garden and walked up to the front door. Everything was still OK so I opened the front door slightly, checked the hall was clear and then called for the team to bring Colin from Box in. He was pushed through the gate and was trying very hard not to run towards the door. I got hold of him as he reached the door to the block.

'For fuck's sake Colin, calm down will you,' I whispered urgently at him. 'If you keep on like this you'll wake every fucker up.'

'Yeah, sorry.'

Mark's flat was on the first floor so to save time and noise we all walked up the stairs together, having closed the front door, and got to the landing outside his flat. There was no movement in any other of the other flats. I put the key in the lock and it opened. Thank fuck he hadn't changed the lock, because some people did that automatically after they had been lifted. There was one guy in the cuds that stated that if he ever got lifted he would burn his bungalow down rather than risk having the security forces bug it. Once in, I put the snip on the door and also chocked it with a piece of wood I'd brought. I also told Alpha that we were in and secure and that the team on the street could lift off for now. It was pointless them being exposed out on the street for nothing. We were safe and Mark was under control in the pub.

The flat itself was very nice and consisted of a large lounge-cum-dining room, bedroom, bathroom and kitchen. We let Colin get on with what he had to do while we did our thing, which was, apart from providing back up for Colin, to obtain a panorama of each room with IR (infrared) photography in case we or someone else had to come back again (no sketches in the operational unit).

'OK Colin, if you need a hand just give us a shout.'

'Right, cheers, I don't think I should be too long.'

Now that he was getting on with what he was best at he'd calmed down and actually seemed to be enjoying himself. We got all we needed in about half an hour and Colin was still busy. After a while we got bored and looked around at what he had in his flat, as you do. There was nothing of interest in his bedroom so we thought we'd concentrate on his lounge. We also thought we'd get some happy snappies for the bar in the Det. We had Pete 1 sitting in Mark's chair with his hat on and reading a book. The snap that went on the wall was annotated, 'Me sitting in Mark's chair. Me wearing Mark's hat. Me reading Mark's book.' Childish stuff really but it was a good laugh at the time.

We then came across some photo albums that we just happened to glance through. We came across some topless photos of a youngish woman that seemed to have been taken in the flat – Mark's girlfriend? We just had to have some photos of her as well and for IR photography they actually came out quite well. We were then flicking feverishly through to see if he'd taken any more interesting ones of her but he hadn't. Shortly after that Colin came over.

'OK, I've finished for now. There was nowhere obvious I could put the quick plant in so I'm going to have to go back to London and make a special one.'

'Right, have you got all your kit with you?'

'Yep, all ready.'

'Alpha Juliet, we're finished on target now, can we have the cover back in?'

'Roger Juliet, all cover callsigns move back into position.'

We waited until everyone had got back to their cover locations and given the all clear before we left the target. We did a final check of the flat to make sure it was OK and I retrieved the wood chock from the door.

I cracked the door slightly to make sure it was all clear before we exited and made our way back to the car. If we had been compromised going in or coming out of the flat the only thing we could have done was to pretend we were burglars. In other words give whomever it was a good slapping, known as punch and run, and leg it. I was actually wearing some special gloves we had in the Det just for this purpose. They looked like ordinary gloves but the knuckle area was filled with lead shot. Anyone you hit with that would go down. We went out the front door and Colin came with us back to our car to save exposing his minder on the street for no real purpose.

'Alpha, Juliet's now complete and mobile; the cover can lift off now.'

'Roger, Juliet, all callsigns go complete and Swordfish [code for lift off].'

The surveillance team also pulled off from covering Mark in the Bogside Inn and we all went back to the Det for a debrief. After that we had the real debrief in the bar where all the little niggly points got brought up. We managed to convince Colin that now he'd done his first operational job it was traditional for him to get the beers in, which he did, to be fair. Once I'd made sure I'd got mine I turned to him and said, 'Oh Colin, have you got that weapon I gave you before you walk off with it? What did you think of tonight? It wasn't that bad, really was it?'

'No, it was good, but I felt safer with this thing, thanks,' He replied as he gave me back the weapon.

'Thanks. Oh by the way,' I said as I slipped the magazine and showed him an empty weapon, 'I really must remember to put some rounds in it next time; I'm always doing that.'

'You bastards,' he grinned.

There was another time in the Shantallow area of the city when we had information that there was to be a weapons move on the following Sunday. Now normally Sunday was a day off for the Det because it was very quiet and nearly everyone in the city went to church and consequently wore decent clothes. The only decent clothes the blokes in the Det usually had were clean jeans and a clean tank top. That night, after the evening briefing, the Boss said, 'OK there's going to be a weapons move in the Shantallow this Sunday. Now I know you fuckers are like bags of shite but does anyone have any what you could call Sunday clothes?'

There was no movement from anyone else so I put my hand up as I still had the jacket and trousers from the Royal Marines Pig who got binned at the end of the course. I had known they would come in handy some day.

'OK Sam, looks like you're the holy Joe for this one.'

Great! I thought.

Come the following Sunday, we staked out the house from where the weapons were supposed to move. Because it was tout information we also knew what the blokes looked like who were going to move the weapons. I was in the vicinity of the local church because that was where I'd pick them up.

'Stand by, stand by,' came the warning from the guy in the boot fit, 'that's a very good possible Alpha 1 and Alpha 2 foxtrot from the Charlie towards red 27. Alpha 1 is blue on blue (blue top and blue bottoms) and Alpha 2 is black on blue. Alpha 1 is carrying a blue sports bag, could be longs [rifles]. Can someone confirm?'

There were no church clothes for these two.

'Alpha, roger, Juliet acknowledge and confirm if possible.'

'Juliet, roger, static and foxtrot.' This meant I'd parked my car and walked towards the church.

When they emerged from the estate they were well covered both on foot and mobile. That was one of the things I used to love about the job. These arseholes thought they were doing a great job but they would have shit bricks if they had known that there were some of us good guys tagging on behind ready to take them out if it was necessary.

I went foxtrot through the churchyard just as everyone was going in for Sunday Mass. I had to loiter for a short while until they reached the area of the church but that wasn't a problem. There were plenty of polite nods from both sides, wearing decent clothes and all, but at that time I had my mind on other things. From a distance, I could see these two walking along the road in the direction that I had been given by the other callsigns from a distance.

'Alpha, Juliet, that's confirmed Alphas 1 and 2 with the bag foxtrot from red 25 towards red 18.'

'Roger that, Juliet.' Now by this time I'd had a slight head on with the two of them so normally I would have lifted off but at this point we were a bit stretched so I did a loop around a building and slopped on behind them.

'Juliet has, now from red 18 towards red 17 and they seem aware.'

'Roger Juliet, the QRF is slowly mobile ready to intercept.'

The plan was to house them and give it a few minutes before the QRF swarmed in and made an arrest.

As they approached red 17 they went into a house.

'Juliet, stand by, stand by, they've now gone complete at a Charlie, wait out for details.'

I was trying to give a description and also keep an eye on the front door at the same time in case they came out again. After about a minute, but it seemed a lot longer, the QRF screamed in and stormed into the house. At first I thought they had got the wrong one so I got onto the radio trying to put them on to the right one. Fortunately they went into the correct one because if they hadn't, those wasted couple of minutes could have been enough for the targets to get away and just leave the weapons.

They found half a dozen very shocked people sitting around the kitchen table having a weapon-training lesson with what had been in the bag. If only they'd gone to church instead!

On my second tour we actually did have another go at Mark's new house. By now he had moved into a small semi in a narrow street. I say a small semi because really they were terraced houses with just a small gap between them to make a back entry for each house. The narrowness of the street meant it was going to be difficult, because the rest of the street overlooked the front of the house. This proved to be a bit of a poser and all sorts of possibilities came up as to how to get round it. The idea was put forward to use a large box bodied truck to block the view of the entrance of the alley and because I was an HGV driver, courtesy of the fireman's strike in 1977/1978, I got the job. Obviously to try to get a truck into a street where cars were parked would have been a hit and miss affair so a couple of block cars were put in during the afternoon that it was decided to go in. A block car is a car used deliberately to reserve a spot for another vehicle in an operation later in the day. They wouldn't have attracted too much attention as we all had local plates on our cars and people used to park anywhere except in perhaps a cul-de-sac. This meant that the optimum position for the truck was now reserved. When the team deployed that night I stood off with the truck until it was time to go in. I would then drive in, co-ordinating my run with the guys that were going to lift the cars out, so that no other vehicle could get between us and take those spaces. Once in I would stay in the truck until the entry team had made the safety of the alley and then leave the truck, walk away and get picked up by another car. The truck stayed where it was during the time the team was on target because to start putting cars back in might have attracted attention with all the vehicle movement. When the team was about to extract I would go back to the truck, give them the all clear and they would extract. I would wait for a few minutes to see if there was any reaction in the street and also until they had made it to their car and we would all lift off and go back to the Det. We did this routine a couple more times until we had achieved our result.

In the Gobnascale, or Gob, area of the city on the grassy part that led to the Waterside below, there was a small building that gave access to the sewage system and we were tasked to search it one time because it was sourced that it was being used as a weapons hide. Two of us were given the job and I was once again No. 1. We did the usual recces and found out the make of the lock so that the CME (covert methods of entry) guy knew what he was up against when he went in to open the door for us. The night of the briefing arrived and we had the usual people in there. After the briefing we drove down to the city and to the area of the supposed hide. The plan was that we, as the search team, would be dropped off and wait hidden in the area until the CME guy had got through the lock into the building.

'Alpha, Juliet, we're now at the LUP (Lying Up Point), how's India doing?'

'Roger, Juliet, India, how are you doing.'

'India OK, towards the target now.'

India was a guy who was in the same Corps as me and had done a tour with the Regiment (SAS). He had got a bit of a reputation and was known as 'Barry the bastard'. He insisted it was 'Barry the brave', but he was the only one. We later worked together in the Det in Germany and he proved to be an OK guy, contrary to reputation. He actually thought he was body beautiful and in Germany someone got a picture of Charles Atlas, transposed his head on to it and put copies all over the building. He wasn't very impressed.

Anyway, he reached the target and within five minutes had got into the building.

'Alpha, India, I'm through, Juliet can come in now.'

'Alpha, roger, Juliet acknowledge.'

'Juliet, roger, foxtrot towards the target.'

We reached the building and went inside. The plan was for Barry to wait inside the door to give us some cover while we searched and also to secure the lock after we'd finished. As we stepped inside Barry leaned over and whispered, 'Have you seen this place?'

Up until now no one from the Det had been inside and we hadn't been told what to expect.

From the outside the building had looked about the size of a garage attached to a semi. No problem, I thought, it shouldn't take us long to search that – wrong!

What we didn't realise and no one had bothered to tell us was that once you were in this building the fucking thing went down about seven storeys. This was because, as we later found out, it had to be deep enough to go under the river Foyle. Two of us to try to search this thing – OK!

'Alpha, Juliet, we've been given a bit of a bum steer here. This thing goes down about seven storeys; it's going to take forever to do a proper search. The only thing we can do is to search the most logical places.'

'Alpha, roger that, we didn't know about that either. Just do what you can.'

'Juliet, roger.'

My No. 2 at this time was big Brian, a Royal Marine.

'OK Brian, the only thing we can do is to check all the shelves we can see and look for any tell-tales and loose bricks, usual thing.'

'Yeah roger that, what a load of shit.' I don't think he intended the pun on purpose, although he did have a good sense of humour and might have actually meant it, and I've spent all these years thinking it was a pun. There were all sorts of nooks and crannies on every level so we did our best and searched as thoroughly as we could but to do it properly would have taken a green army search team with all their specialist kit. We eventually got to the bottom, having found nothing. At the very bottom there appeared to be a tunnel that led under the river Foyle to the other bank, at least half a mile away. Apart from the time factor there was no way on God's earth I was going through that.

'Brian, do you fancy going through that? Because I don't. This has been a fucking waste of time.'

'You're not wrong. I reckon we should give it another once-over as we go up and then bin it.' I agreed with that so we checked again on the way up.

'Alpha, Juliet, there's nothing here that we can find so we're lifting off and going foxtrot towards the pick up.'

'Alpha roger that Juliet, see you when you get back.'

'Roger, I reckon someone owes us a few beers for that Int.'

'Cheers Barry, see you back at the Det,' I said as we walked out.

Barry wasn't left on his own though. He had his own cover and we loafed about until he was complete.

Covert searches are a great method of doing something without the sign of an overt presence but unless the Int (intelligence) is specific the chances of finding something are remote.

Dogs during CTRs can sometimes be an interesting experience depending on how they react. Very few are friendly but the ones that are tend to latch on to you and want to follow you around which can sometimes be off-putting and a bloody nuisance. You're better off with the nasty ones because you then know where you are and can work out ways of getting around them. In some cases it can simply be a case of coming in from another direction. In one job on a farm we did the initial recces because we were going to put a tracking device on a vehicle, a Mark 2 Escort. This can be quite a long and time-consuming process, because first of all you have to find a similar make and model of car. If there wasn't one available from your own resources you would go and buy one. In those days tracking devices gave off a signal so that the receiving station could see where it went. The only thing was that the device could sometimes interfere with the car radio and stereo system. With this particular car we were fortunate enough to have a similar vehicle in another Det. The first thing we had to do was to practise breaking into the thing without leaving any trace. A lever and a bent welding rod did the trick and we had it down to ten seconds – we were amateurs compared to good car burglars! The next thing was to find a place on the vehicle to plant the device in order to get the best signal. This was found to be at the back so the signal would bounce off the road to the receiving vehicles which had it under surveillance. Finally, before we went on target we did a test drive over different surfaces and some very rough and uneven ones to see if the bloody thing fell off, because unless it was a deep plant it would be held on by magnets. I really enjoyed that bit because as it wasn't my car I really put it through its paces and the magnets held.

Once everything had been tested we dropped off that night and made our way to the farm. As we approached from one direction we heard a growl coming from one of the barns and thought shit, was it locked up or could it get free? I didn't fancy legging it with a fucking great mutt bounding after me. We retraced our steps and came in from another direction and heard nothing, even though there was no wind at the time. We crossed the farmyard knowing that there were no security lights from previous CTRs and made the safety of the car. We tried the doors first because we thought why break in if they were open but they weren't and so ten seconds later we were in – no alarm! We had a look at the radio cassette and thought great, top of the range and duly got all the details. In cases like this it usually meant buying exactly the same make and model of radio for tests, because you can't exactly have his blaring out on target and after the tests one of the team got to keep the kit. At this time I didn't have a car so it wouldn't be me. We withdrew, did the tests and eventually deployed the device on the car and the job carried on from there.

There was one particular little tosser, who lived in the Creggan district of Londonderry, probably the hardest Republican area in the city. At the time he was a Sinn Fein Councillor. He was, however, heavily sourced as the driver in the car that tried to hijack the Det boss in May 1981 in which Charlie 'Pop' McGuire and George McBrearty were killed. During the attempted hijack he was reported to have shit himself, but we weren't really able to confirm that – not that I would've wanted to. Afterwards, the women in the Creggan gave him a hard time for being a coward, as he hid in the car while the others were getting the good news.

We were trying to get a device into his house and had been for quite a while but either someone was always in or factors just didn't lend themselves to an insertion. The Creggan was a funny place because you could be wandering around in the early hours of the morning, trying to do an honest job by breaking into houses, and there would always be someone around.

I have been in the Creggan at three or four in the morning and seen people washing their windows and digging their front gardens – very strange! Information came through one time that he and his family were going on holiday to the Isle of Man and would be away for a couple of weeks. The information also stated that the house would remain empty although sometimes in such cases someone would move in to house-sit. All the planning was done and this time I was No. 2 to another operator called Tom. On the night of the planned insertion we had the normal briefing but because the Creggan, as I mentioned, was usually a hive of activity we decided to go on to target in the early hours of the morning. Shortly after midnight the team drove into the city backed by the HMSU (the Royal Ulster Constabulary's Headquarters Mobile Support Unit). Before we even considered attempting the entry we did a drive-past, parked the car and did a walk-past. We could have got anyone of the team to do it to minimise our exposure in the area but it's always nice to have a look for yourself.

We parked the car in a small car park at the top of Lone Moor road because this enabled us to do a circuit of the target in Rathlin Drive and see front and back.

'Alpha Golf, static at blue 39 myself and Juliet going foxtrot.'

'Alpha roger.'

We walked up Rathlin Drive and it was fairly quiet. As we got level with the house it appeared to be empty and there were no lights visible so it looked like the information of negative house-sitter was accurate.

'What do you think, Sam?'

'Looks promising so far, let's try round the back.'

We walked on and turned the corner and had a good look at the back of the house. No lights! Another good thing was that there were no lights on in the houses either side.

'Looks OK to me, I think we'll go for it, yeah?' Tom whispered as we walked casually along.

'Foolish not to now,' I replied.

'Alpha Golf that's the walk-past complete we're now back to the Bravo.'

'Alpha roger. Give us an update when you're complete.'

'Click, click.' (Two clicks on the radio pressel – Det term for transmission switch – meant yes).

We were back at the car a couple of minutes later and went mobile out of the immediate area.

'Alpha Golf, the target appears empty. There are no lights on target and no lights either side. We're going to go static at green 25 for figures 15 and we'll get the team in to cover and we'll go for it.'

'Alpha roger that, just come up and let us know when you want to move in.'

'Golf, roger that Alpha.'

We drove to the car park at green 25 which was on the lower side of the bridge over the River Foyle and laid up for a couple of minutes. There were already a couple of team cars there as it was a popular, relatively safe spot to lie up in. After about ten minutes Tom was back on the radio.

'Alpha Golf we're going to go in now can we get the cover team in.'

'Roger Golf, cover team move into position now, over.'

The remainder of the team acknowledged and we gave them a couple of minutes to find somewhere to park and go foxtrot if they had to cover a particular position on foot. As we drove in we could hear the other callsigns reporting that everything was clear. We went static in a different car park a bit closer to the target and went foxtrot.

'Alpha Golf, that's myself and Juliet now foxtrot towards the target.'

'Alpha roger, all callsigns report clear.'

'Golf roger.'

We walked towards the target knowing that if anything moved in the area we would be warned by one of the team. At the back of the house was a five-foot wooden fence that we had to clear to get into the back garden. When we reached the fence we paused just to confirm there was still no movement in the other houses.

'Are you sure you can manage this, you stumpy little fucker?' I whispered to Tom.

I was all right being over six feet, but he could only just about see over it.

'Fuck off you long streak of piss. On three.'

He counted to three and then we both scrambled over the fence and went to ground in the garden bushes. We waited for a couple of minutes to see if there had been any reaction in the houses next door, which there hadn't. The cover team was still in position and would remain there until we were in the house.

This is usually the most heart-pumping, adrenaline-flowing time when you are trying to make the insertion, because even though the place appears empty you can never be too sure. Once you are in you can take a couple of minutes to calm down, but getting in is the pisser. I've actually tried to gain entry into a caravan, supposedly empty, to put an OP on a pub supposedly used by a high-ranking PIRA member and just as we were about to make entry someone inside woke up. We slammed the door and legged it like a couple of greyhounds. Anyway, I digress.

'Alpha Golf, we're in the back garden and now moving towards the target. We'll minimise until we're complete.'

'Alpha roger.'

Hearing that, the rest of the team knew that this was a critical period and would not come up on the air unless it was essential.

'OK, ready? The lock shouldn't take me long.' he said.

'Fine.'

We walked slowly down the garden towards the back of the house and as we were about halfway down we heard this very low but very menacing growl. We came to a shuddering halt and both came to the same conclusion at the same time. I think we both looked at each other and said simultaneously, 'Fucking dog, leg it.'

This was a double adrenaline rush coupled with hoping that you were fast enough to keep all your bits and pieces intact. Now on a normal withdrawal we would get to the back fence, stop and listen and wait for the all clear to be given by the rest of the team. Not this fucking time, even though we could hear one of the cover team reporting two Alphas moving past him towards the rear of the target.

As far as we were concerned we had a choice and that was to take on the dog or these two guys if we had to and we both knew the better chance we had. Besides we would have had to shoot the dog and that would have blown the whole thing. We reached the back fence and Tom, the stumpy little fucker, was over it like a high hurdler with me close on his heels. We'd just got out and calmed down a bit when we turned the corner and bumped into these two blokes.

'How're ya doin'?' I muttered in my best Derry accent as we tried to look nonch. As we walked past I heard one of them say to the other, 'Did he speak to you in your own language?'

'Yeah, he did.'

'Alpha Golf, we're now foxtrot back to the Charlie. We've aborted and I'll fill you in once we're complete.'

'Alpha roger, do you need the QRF?'

'Negative, once we're complete the team can lift off.'

'Alpha roger that Golf.'

Tom and I then casually sauntered back to Golf, giggling like fuck. Of course, once we were back at the Det the size of this dog we'd encountered grew to astronomical proportions even though we didn't even see the fucking thing.

Dogs are usually greedy creatures especially in the province because they never really seem to get enough to eat so one of the best ways of trying to get them out of the way is to use drugged sausages. To be honest the intention is not to kill the dog because at the end of the day they do you no harm. You try to see the dog to guess the weight and then give the details to one of the army vets who will then make up some sausages at what he estimates will be enough of the drug to knock it out for a while – great in theory. We tried it on a dog in the Gob when we were trying to put a device into a motorbike in someone's back yard. Once in it would only have taken about thirty seconds but it was getting past the dog that complicated things. It was difficult to guess its breed but Heinz 57 had nothing on this one. We had the sausages ready and I was acting as driver for the guys doing the job. They must have tried about four times but each time they approached the dog started barking so they couldn't even get near with the sausages. In the end the owner got tired of the dog barking and took it inside. The lads were in and out in no time, job done. Back to the Det for sausages and egg and a good day's sleep! Just before I arrived they had a similar thing on a farm and they tried the sausage trick. The dog wasn't having it and wouldn't eat the sausages. That meant they had to retrieve the sausages otherwise in the morning the owner would have seen them and twigged something had been going on.

They tried everything but with no luck and in the end had to shoot it with a silenced rifle and dispose of the body. The owner would hopefully think the thing had run off. Silenced weapons were not generally used in the province except in cases like these and also to take out street lights that might be an inconvenience if you were trying to work on a front door or something similar.

The Gob was the scene of quite a few operations and although it was on the other side of the river to the other Republican areas there were still some nasty bastards living there. We were covering an ASU in the Gob and because of the location it was impossible to sit in the area. We looked at all possibilities including either occupying a derelict or putting a covert camera in one. The only trouble with that was that we would have to go back in regularly to change the batteries, so the risk of compromise was too great. You also find that kids use derelicts in urban areas as dens so that also increases the risk of compromise. We got round this because one of the lads did a walk-around in the Gob, especially at the main point where anyone who was walking or driving out would have to pass. He looked for somewhere on the Waterside that was in line of sight. He realised he could see Ebrington Barracks, the main SF base, so he went in and found where he could see the Gob from.

He eventually found a flat roof that gave us an ideal spot. If we'd just put all our kit up there to OP it someone would have seen us and put two and two together. We tasked the Royal Engineers to build a wooden sangar on this flat roof so we could see them but they couldn't see us! The total distance was about 1,500 m to 2,000 m and by using powerful lenses attached to a video camera we could monitor the approaches to and from the Gob and trigger the players as they came out. We could also actually see one of the ASU's front doors. Even though it was a long distance we were able to identify them because we'd worked against them for so long and knew how they walked and what clothes they usually wore.

We'd had information, another time, that one of the ASU had a hide behind a coal bunker but were never able to get in and CTR it because of its location being so close to the house. There were occasions when we did enter the back gardens of occupied houses but in this case it wasn't worth the risk of compromise. In the end it wasn't necessary because the player in question was trying to remove the weapon one day by hooking his finger around the trigger guard – big mistake. He couldn't see what he was doing and must have hooked the trigger as well – bye bye, own goal.

On one other occasion I had dropped one of the lads off to do a walk-past and was lying up just outside the Gob, when the next thing I hear on the radio is that three blokes had confronted him. Now this guy wasn't exactly built like a racing snake but that night he'd have given Linford Christie a run for his money. I screamed into the area where he should have been but there was no sign of him but you could hear him giving a commentary on his radio as best he could in between the wheezes. Down the hill from the Gob on the Waterside was a road with an RUC station in it. By the time I'd reached there in my car he was sauntering along the road trying to look casual but making sure he was within sight of the police station. He actually did draw his weapon to warn them off but decided against wasting three unarmed blokes who might just have been out for a laugh.

In the Bogside area of the city, just outside Butchers Gate, was a row of shops and bars one of which was a place called the 'Rocking Chair'. This place was a PIRA haunt and so was avoided by the security forces. Just beyond that used to be a couple of blocks of flats called the Rossville flats and at a rough guess must have been about ten storeys high. In the days of the big riots the people used to get on top of these flats and pelt the security forces with missiles. It was also a favourite spot for snipers.

To try to catch one of these snipers would have been virtually impossible because by the time the Army had got up there the weapon could be in pieces in a number of flats and the sniper well away. To try to stop this a sangar was erected on the roof of one of the blocks, manned by the Army (not a place I'd have fancied). We had information once that it was intended to try to bomb the sangar by pushing a bomb up one of the rubbish chutes until it was under the sangar. Because the information came from a tout it would not be possible for the Army to go in and find it without risking compromising the life of the tout. At the time there was a guy called Eddie McSheffrey who was a PIRA Explosives Officer in the city and it would have been down to him to manufacture the device. Eddie was a small guy like John 'Shorty' McNally (described later), but quite fat and going bald. He used to drive a battered old Ford Transit. Although he was a known player we never actually mounted an operation specifically against him. The Det was tasked to go in and try to find the rubbish chute in question and to try to see if anything had been planted.

A big Geordie and myself were given the job with him as No. 1. Because of the urgency of the task we had to go in during daylight hours and I must admit I felt a bit uneasy about this one. We had to enter at the bottom of the flats and then go to the top of the block to try to locate this rubbish chute. We found what we thought was it eventually and to the best of our knowledge there was nothing there so we, thankfully, made our way down and out, much to our relief. Although we'd have taken a few with us if we had been sussed out, I doubt if we'd have got out alive. Although every operator was issued a PLD (personal locating device), in those days you physically had to switch it on if you needed it.

Once activated the signal would be picked up in the Det and everyone else warned off to look for whoever might have activated it. The chopper also carried special kit to pinpoint the signal, as did the cars. The only trouble about having to activate it yourself was that you were pretty likely to be stripped very soon after you were lifted so could you actually do it? With this in mind some of the lads didn't carry it. Also, if caught, they might have been able to bluff their way out claiming they were just ordinary soldiers in plain clothes. If PIRA had found a PLD there would have been no doubt as to who we were. I think the incident at the funeral in Andersonstown, with the two Royal Signals Corporals, disproved any theory we may have had about bluffing our way out of trouble.

Because of the different terrains we were required to operate in, I carried a variety of weapons around in my car to cater for different occasions. For example, if we were deployed in the city we would normally carry short-range weapons such as the Browning 9 mm and the MP5K. There was always the possibility that we might suddenly be tasked to go into the cuds where short-range weapons would be no good, hence my G3 rifle on the back seat. Halfway through my first tour and on my second tour, I used to carry a Remington Wingmaster shotgun in the boot. The first three rounds in the magazine were solid shot. The idea was that if one of the lads got lifted and I was one of the first on the scene, the solid shot would take the hinges off the door. The remainder of the rounds – nine ball shot – would help take out the occupants.

The only other time I felt a bit uneasy was when we had information that there was a weapons hide in a grassy area and two crossed swards of grass were supposed to indicate it. Looking at the air photos and having done the walk-past, this grassy area was surrounded on three sides by large houses turned into flats and was in fact behind Mark McDade's original flat. I just had this horrible feeling that we were being set up. Once we were inside that hollow square there was nothing to stop the escape route being cordoned off and a couple of blast bombs being lobbed from the flats or someone opening up with an armalite. Also, the crossed swards of grass sounded a bit airy-fairy to me. The planning went ahead and it was decided that while we were on target we'd have a couple of guys lurking at the open end of the square, heavily armed, to discourage anyone that had any ideas to have a go at us. We got into position and, while one of us searched for these elusive swards of grass, the other watched the flats on the other three sides. We must have searched the area three times thinking we must have missed it but in the end decided that either we'd missed it totally or it just wasn't there so we lifted off. We didn't get any comeback from that and didn't go back again so I think the info was duff.

Between Strand Road RUC Station and Fort George (a big Army base) was a small car park just up a hill and below the grounds of Magee College. The car park, which is slightly higher than and overlooks Strand Road, was a major route for police and Army vehicles. There was information that there was to be a shoot on one of these by PIRA so the Det was tasked to OP the area and watch for the hit team moving in. Our group was supposed to initiate the QRF to come in once we had identified them as carrying weapons but we'd decided that if they had tried to get away we were going to cut them off. Big Brian and myself were tasked with him as No. 1. The plan was for us to be passengers in a car but hiding in the front footwell and in the back so that it would appear that the car was only one up if anyone saw it. Because both of us were over six feet we needed a big car for this. One of the guys in the Det was driving an old style VW Passat so we went for that.

After we had briefed that night we drove to the city and as we got nearer the target we prepared to go into hiding. Mind you, for someone as big as Brian trying to hide in the footwell of a car, even a Passat, was a bit difficult.

'Alpha Papa, that's me at red 31 towards the drop off.'

'Roger Papa.'

Prior to this a cover car had done a drive-past and cleared the car park, as it was normally clear at this time of night.

'OK you two, into your little hidey holes and I'll give you a shout when to move.'

'OK mate.'

'Right we're just entering the car park now. When I get out for a piss you get out your side. Stand by; I'm just going static now.'

He pulled up and opened his door to go for a piss, to give him a reason for being there. As we were right up against the bushes we opened our doors and slipped out just pushing the doors to, so Papa could shut them properly later on. There was no interior light as the bulb had been taken out. We made our way into the bushes and got into a position where we could observe where the shoot was supposed to be taking place.

'Alpha Whiskey [Brian's callsign] we're in position now. OK Papa you can stop pretending now and go mobile.'

'Alpha roger.'

'Papa roger, going complete, I don't think I could have squeezed any more out.'

'Alpha Papa, now complete and mobile towards G17.'

As we settled down for at least the next five hours Brian turned to me and whispered, 'I wonder how long we're going to have to wait here, Sam.'

'Not too long I hope mate, it's going to get a bit parky later. You did bring the coffee, didn't you?'

'Hey, this is me you're talking to.' Although coffee has a distinctive smell, even in the open, we had considered the risk of compromise and decided that it would be negligible.

'Listen Brian, I know the SF have already been told not to move along here except in armoured vehicles but what if a soft-skinned one comes along by mistake? Just suppose it all goes to ratshit [I'd love to find out where this ratshit place is, because everything seems to go there] and one comes along before the QRF can get here, are you game to have a go at them?'

'If they fire first and there's no QRF in sight I reckon we should take them out, what about you?'

'Fucking right, fingers crossed, eh?'

So there we stayed for the next three hours with nothing happening. Eventually a car came slowly into the car park.

'Brian, stand by, stand by. We could have a possible here.'

'Yep, roger that. Alpha Whiskey we have a Bravo entering the car park, could be a possible stand by. Give the QRF a call to be ready.'

'Roger Whiskey, can you get a Pluto [registration number or VRN]?'

'Negative at the moment.'

'Alpha roger.'

'What do you reckon Sam; are they going slow enough to be having a recce?'

'Yeah, you're right.'

With that Brian got a good grip on his HK53 and me on my MP5K.

They swung round and reversed to where we had been dropped off, two metres from us and slightly lower. It was exactly the spot for the best concealment. Once again, adrenaline levels were starting to go up.

'Brian can you see how many up they are?'

'Yep, definitely two up but then maybe someone's doing the same as we did. Let's hang on and see what happens.'

After a while, still no one had got out of the car and then suddenly Brian turned around and said, 'Hey Sam, the car seems to be moving a bit. Have a look through the pocketscope [night vision device] and see if you can see anything.'

I got the pocketscope out and focussed them on the passenger window and nearly pissed myself laughing.

'Here Brian, take a look at this. Passenger window.'

He took the pocketscope and after a short while handed them back with a chuckle. 'Alpha Whiskey, you can stand the QRF down. We'll tell you about it when we get back.'

'Alpha roger.'

What we'd actually seen were the windows starting to steam up and this green arse going up and down. (Everything was green looking through the pocketscope.)

So for the next ten to fifteen minutes we took turns with the pocketscope because what we were looking at was a couple shagging. Little did they know they were in what could have turned out to be a killing ground. ('Did the earth move for you, darling?').

'Hey Brian, fancy putting your balaclava on and tapping on the window?'

'Fuck off you tight bastard, let them get on with it,' he sniggered.

If only they'd known that there were two heavily armed men just a few yards away watching every movement and trying hard not to laugh. I'm sure it would have put the poor sod off his stroke. We carried out the same exercise for the next two nights without a result and having read other books I think I now understand why.

Just around the corner from the Rossvilles was a small car park with a café opposite, G17 I believe. This car park used to be a favourite with the Det, before the incident I will describe, when they were working in the area. Ideally when laying up you would choose a place where there were other cars so you didn't stick out like a dog's bollock. Sitting in your car did, however, lend yourself to hijack attempts on occasion and one bloke in this car park did find himself in that situation. Two blokes approached him, one on either side of the car, and told him to get out, as they wanted his car. The normally one-way conversation would take the form of, 'Provisional IRA [or INLA], we want your car.'

Unfortunately for them they had picked the wrong bloke. At this point he had the option of drawing his door pistol and engaging them then but decided against it. The door pistol was a Browning with a twenty-round extended magazine ready for quick response kept in a holster clipped to the bin usually found on the inside of most doors and covered by a cloth. Two things decided him against this; the first being that the guy on his side had a weapon pointing at him (unloaded as was later found out but he wasn't to know) and the second guy on the other side would have seen the movement and alerted the other guy.

Instead, using his head, he got out of the car as if pretending to hand it over and as the guy with the weapon put it into his waistband and went to get in the car he drew his belt pistol, shot him dead and wounded the other one. He then pulled the body out of the car, casually got in and drove off to Strand Road RUC station. As with most incidents in the city this was attributed to the SAS but apart from reactive operations they never operated on a day-to-day basis in Londonderry. It was all down to 14 Coy.

The café also featured in another job I did involving a female RUC officer known as an RUC bag (as in rucksack). I was given a brief outline of what was going to happen in the Det and was told that I would be taking a RUC WPC with me. She came to the Det and was dropped off so we could use my car without having to drive into Strand Road. There was a woman in the Creggan who was suspected of terrorist offences but they didn't have anything on her. However, they had found some fingerprints, and wanted to confirm them. They couldn't just lift her for any reason, firstly because they had nothing on her and secondly as it might have alerted PIRA to some sort of tout involvement. She was known to go shopping on certain days and afterwards to go into the café for a cup of tea. The plan was to lift the cup she had been using and then dust it for fingerprints. The reason for the policewoman, apart for cover, was continuation of evidence. It was decided that the rest of the Det would impose surveillance on her while she was shopping and that once she was on her way to the café the female officer and me would go in and wait for her to arrive. People who have been involved in this sort of thing know how important it is to be in there before the target arrives. When they arrive they will look over who is in there but will accept them because they are already there. To go in immediately after the target is a no-no because they will be hyper towards anyone coming in after them. If you do have to go in after you have to wait until a few people have gone in first. Also by being in there first you can find the best place to dominate the room. Once I'd found out the full story I decided how we were going to play it. The policewoman's name was Bridget and she was married to an RUC officer.

'OK Bridget, we'll drive down to the city and we'll sit up in one of the car parks in the centre and listen to the team while they take her shopping. Once we see they are going towards the café we'll drive down to the car park and go in.'

'Right, is there anything I need to know? I normally just work in the office on the radio.' Fucking outstanding, I thought, they've given me someone who's non-operational, but being the perfect gentleman I didn't let on.

'No, don't worry about it; if anything happens just leave everything to me. When we get to the café just pretend it's you and your husband out for a cup of tea after a day's shopping.'

'If you'd have said pretend it's in a bar that would be more like it,' she laughed.

That's better, I thought. I could see she wasn't that convinced and I got the impression she was definitely a bit nervous but she had to be there. I have always wondered why it was me that usually got the women!

Before we left the Det I showed her where the pressel switches were in the car in case anything happened to me and she had to transmit on the radio. She had a pressel on her side but my favourite was situated in the horn. That way you didn't have to take your hands off the wheel to transmit. I also showed her where the arm and fire buttons were for my flash bangs. These were in a box under the car and the idea was if you were approached by an armed person you would hit the switches and this thing would explode with a fucking big bang and a cloud of smoke. It would disorientate the attacker and enable you to deal with him.

We drove to the city with the cassette playing and having a bit of a crack with me trying to put her at her ease and it turned out that she was not joking when she said that she had never really been operational but spent all her time in the office. I decided that this was to my advantage as if something did happen she wouldn't try to have a go. I know there is all this crap about equality and political correctness but I don't care what anyone says – if you are with another bloke you expect him to look after himself. If you are partnered with a woman, half of you is looking out for her and that goes against you. On the way to the city was a big roundabout known as 'one alpha' (1A), which was the switch-on point for all the Det members. On the way out of the city it was also the switch off-point where all the good tapes came out again and were played at ear splitting volume.

On my first tour the only way across the river was by the two-tier Foyle Bridge but by my second tour they had built another bridge that led from 1A over to the Shantallow. This made getting to some targets a hell of a lot easier and quicker. Anyway, we reached the city and parked up and went foxtrot to the shops and then back to the car after about ten minutes. If someone is watching there is something suspicious about a car parking up and the person staying complete. It's always best to go for a little walk and then come back and pretend you're waiting for someone. We got back to the car and listened to the radio as the team picked the woman up and took her around the shops. This is one situation where I will admit where it's handy to have a woman in the team because there's nothing more suspicious than a couple of hairy-arsed blokes in the lingerie department looking at frilly undies. Not only does it get other women a bit twitchy but it also attracts the attention of the store detectives. I remember a few years later when I was working on a target in Oxford Street, I was followed out of Mark's and Spencer's by a store detective and asked who I was working for.

After a while it seemed as if her trip was coming to an end, as they were moving in the direction of the café.

'Alpha, Juliet's going mobile towards the café.'

'Roger, Juliet.'

We were only about five minutes away from the café and found a parking spot when we arrived.

'Alpha, that's Juliet static at green 17, closing down and foxtrot towards the café.'

'Roger, Juliet, she's generally foxtrot in your direction, Lima has.'

'Roger.'

The first thing I did when I got out of the vehicle was to radio check with my body comms. I knew they worked because I'd checked them before I left, but you couldn't be too careful. If they had failed it would be back to the car and abort. That or get another member of the team into the area, to partner up with Bridget.

'Alpha Juliet, radio check.'

'Lima Charlie Juliet.'

I acknowledged that with two clicks on my pressel. This is a great way to communicate covertly. Alpha would ask you questions to which the answer would be either a yes or no. If your answer was no there would be nothing but if your answer was yes you would give two clicks. Once you had the hang of knowing what questions to ask you could find out everything that was going on without the guy on the ground having to talk. If you were in a situation where there was something you had to communicate urgently you would give a rapid series of clicks. This would tell all other callsigns to minimise and Alpha would start asking questions.

As we walked towards the café I turned to Bridget and said, 'OK, we want to try and get somewhere where we can keep an eye on the door and preferably at the back of the room but not in line of sight of the door.'

We walked in and the place wasn't that full so we had our choice of table and got the best one we could. When the waitress came, Bridget did the ordering, her with the accent and all. Mine was getting better but only in short bursts.

Anyway, there we were in the café having our tea and bickies and she walks in with a friend and sits at a table very close to us – great. Not only did it enable us to hear snatches of her conversation but also it meant that I could keep an eye on the cup she was using so that I could retrieve it later. I could also see where she was touching it so that when I picked it up I wouldn't smudge any prints.

Benefits of police training! Assuming it was a clean cup the only prints would be the waitresses, hers and probably lastly mine. Sometime later after we'd had to order more tea it looked as if she was about to leave and she called the waitress over to pay the bill.

'Right,' I said. 'When she leaves we'll sidle over to her table and you stick the cup in your handbag, OK?'

'When we do move just try to block the view of the waitress while I slip it in,' she said.

Good thinking I thought. As the waitress took the money the next thing that happened was she cleared the table and walked towards the door that led into the back – bastard! Once through that door we'd have no chance of getting hold of it. Luckily she put them on the counter near the door and went to collect another bill. I thought that if I didn't move now the opportunity might be lost so I still had my eye on the cup.

'Shit, I'm going to have to make a move and get that cup or we've had it. If it goes through the back we've got no chance.'

The toilets were also out the back so I made as if to go towards the back door and into the toilets. As I got level with the counter and when I thought no one was looking, I picked the cup up using my forefinger and thumb at the far side from where she'd been drinking, as she hadn't touched that side, and held it beneath the level of the counter. That way I wasn't going to smudge any prints. I think the waitress behind the counter must have noticed some movement because she gave me a funny look but I just flashed her my most charming smile and went and sat down. Bridget had a plastic evidence bag that I slipped the cup into and put it into her handbag. We stayed there for a minute then paid the bill and left – mission accomplished, back to the Det for beer and medals!

Sinn Fein centres in the province were some of the main targets for the Dets, as it was believed that these were where a lot of PIRA operations were discussed. There was one particular centre in Cable Street in Londonderry where the Det had tried for years to get a technical device into it. It was in a terraced row of houses and that made it particularly difficult to get into because of the close proximity of the other houses – a bit like Mark's house really. During my first tour we had unsuccessfully tried many times to get into it because it was believed the intelligence to be gained from it would be of tremendous value. Attempts were made to get in through from the front and the rear but it was not possible. At one point there was an extension being built at the rear and with all the building work it might have been possible to gain access through this point but once again it was a no-go. On my second tour special efforts were made once again to gain access because it was sourced that this extension was being used as a holding and interrogation centre for the PIRA security team. If an operation was planned in the city and it went wrong or if any of the players was lifted then there would be an immediate witch-hunt for the tout as PIRA were paranoid about informers. They couldn't believe that sometimes it was just through their own incompetence. Anyway the security team would be called in, either from Londonderry or Belfast depending on how badly it had gone wrong, and it was thought that the interrogation would take place in Cable Street. It was considered important at the time to know what was happening in the house, what was being said and to identify members of the interrogation team. It was also a place where useful intelligence could be gained for future PIRA operations. A concerted effort was therefore made to try to gain access.

We were given the identities of a number of possible key holders from source information and at different stages these people were put under surveillance to see if they actually had the key. From there it was a case of taking the person in question as he approached the door to see what lock he used and where on his person he kept the key. This was done by the guy in the sangar on the City walls watching the junctions as he was counted down to either junction at each end. There would be someone lurking in the Bogside ready to coincide his run to tag on behind him to see which lock he used. Once the correct lock had been identified and which pocket he had put the key in, it was a case of waiting until he came out that night and he was lifted by the RUC. He was then taken to Strand Road where he would be questioned and while this was being done copies of his keys – in particularly the one for the Cable Street door – were made. After that it was a question of planning the job and calling for the Security Service to come over with the device to be planted.

The job was tried on a number of nights in succession because sometimes the risk of compromise was too great to try. It was starting to get frustrating because everyone was hyper and all we wanted to do was get the bloody thing in. One night, everything seemed to go into place and entry was made through the front door by two of our lads and the Box 500 guy. They were in there for what seemed to be an eternity when in fact it wasn't that long. The fact that you are sitting there and feeling fairly vulnerable makes the time seem longer. You want to try sitting in your car in a hostile environment knowing that you can't move – at that time I was the drop-off car so I couldn't move in case they came screaming out. Eventually we got the nod that the team was ready to come out so everybody gave the all clear and out they came with no problems.

Once they got back to my car the whole team lifted off and went back to the Det for a big piss-up. After many years of trying we had finally succeeded. The Pilot's Row Community centre did not escape the Det's attention either but it proved to be a lot easier to get into.

The main police station in Londonderry was Strand Road and access was through a steel sliding door from the main road. Entry and exit from this gate is particularly hazardous as you could be kept waiting for anything up to one minute in full view of all passers-by who may be giving you the once over or taking number plates. This is one of the reasons why Det operators would not go in there in their Ops cars except after an incident. Plain clothes RUC officers were fired at a number of times when they came out and were also followed and shot at further down the road. If it were necessary for an operator to visit the station we would drive to Ebrington Barracks on the other side of the river and then get transported to Strand Road by armoured pig. Not a very salubrious way to travel but safer, though even then you would still feel nervous behind armour – so imagine how the poor old RUC guys felt.

There were a number of reasons to visit Strand Road and these could be just to visit the Special Branch, with whom we had a very close relationship, or to occupy a sangar we had mounted in the top of their lift shaft watching certain targets in the city. If certain players had been lifted we might also go down so we could look into the interrogation room to see what they looked like at the time – invaluable! It was also very good to gain up-to-date photography of all the known players in the city because they all used to sign on at the brew (dole office). Britain must be one of the only countries that pays its terrorists. There used to be a sangar in the corner of the station that overlooked the entrance to the brew office and every now and then we'd go and spend a day and photograph these nasty hypocritical people as they used to come and get their money from the British Queen. I, personally, used to find it infuriating that these guys were drawing their brew one minute and the next we would be imposing surveillance on them because we knew they were bad bastards.

We used to occupy the sangar on the city walls from time to time, especially when we had operations going on in the Bogside. It was equipped with a fuck-off pair of battleship binoculars that could see everywhere. You could even read posters on bedroom walls if the curtains were left open. Those and a long lens camera were especially useful for photographing people using the Bogside Inn. This was a staunch, hard Republican pub used by many of the players. One comic in the Det one time put a notice up in the cookhouse that read, 'Darts match Saturday night, North Det v Bogside Inn, names below.' Might've been quite interesting.

Talking of darts matches, at one point it was common practice to play darts in the bar using Walthers (pistols) as they were fairly ineffective. Also, one of the guys was a bit of an artist and drew some murals on the wall, one of which was Asterix the Gaul. It was quite a good work of art until one night in the bar one of the lads bet one of the Special Branch lads that he couldn't hit Asterix in the eye, expecting him to produce a ppw (personal protection weapon), usually a Walther. Unfortunately this guy had come straight from duty and produced this fucking great .357 Magnum and promptly blew Asterix's eye out. Fortunately it just impacted and dropped instead of whanging around the bar and giving everyone a headache. Weapons were banned from the bar after that.

When I was in the Royal Marines in Recce Troop I mentioned that we would gather information for other agencies to make more use of. While I was in the Det it became obvious that we were some of the people that would be making use of this information. It also became obvious that some of these poor bastards on the street were given very little information about the areas they were patrolling. I did get the impression that sometimes they were walking figure 11s (a figure 11 is the man-sized cardboard cut-out used for range work).

When not involved in surveillance serials or CTRs, you would conduct what were known as 'Hare and Hounds' (H&H) which basically meant that one of the lads would act as the target and the remainder would be the surveillance team. The target would work out a route around the city, taking in as much of it as he could. This would include both mobile and foxtrot work. You would be given a stake-out location either to see the static car, wait for him to return and pick him up or to watch a junction and pick him up as he passed through. They were quite effective and a good training aid for when you hadn't done a surveillance serial in a few days. We did get into a routine with the Boss and Ops officer at the time, which I strongly disagreed with.

The whole idea of being an undercover operator was to limit your exposure on the ground so that when operationally deployed you were 'fresh'. They also had us carrying out H&Hs in the morning and then we'd be operational in the city in the afternoon, doubling your exposure when there was no need. You actually did enough serials to be seen and recognised in some areas, even in the Creggan when working one up. The recognised sign here and in the cuds was to acknowledge someone just by raising your right middle finger off the steering wheel and you'd get the same response back.

I remember one particular incident in the Creggan when I was the hare. The route I'd chosen eventually took us into the Creggan where I'd planned to go static and foxtrot. The route went around the main church in the Creggan, past the Telstar bar and back to my car. The Telstar bar was where all the PIRA hard men hung out and it was not uncommon for people to be kneecapped or even topped behind the Telstar. As I was foxtrot I heard over my radio that I'd picked up company in the form of the OC Londonderry PIRA. Raymond Gilmour refers to him as

John 'Shorty' McNally so we'll stick with that even though that was not his real name. The way things are in the world I'd have thought he'd been called 'Lofty' as he was only about 5'2", but 'Shorty' it was. I wasn't worried because I had plenty of cover around me but he obviously wasn't happy. I casually made my way back to my car and drove off. After that I had to get rid of that car which was unfortunate, as it was a nice Opel Ascona.

Most of the blokes in the Det had little idiosyncrasies because I think if they didn't they wouldn't be there. Some were just a little bit more idiosyncratic than others. We used to be plagued with rats in the Det and one time this bloke came out of the Ops hangar and saw a rat outside the cookhouse so he drew his pistol and had a crack at it but missed. The round whanged around the inside the cookhouse before it hit the cook in the shoulder. It didn't do any damage because by that time it had expended all its energy but he was presented with a spoof purple heart at the next Det piss-up and I actually think he was chuffed to fuck. I also had this habit, apart from those mentioned later, of getting hold of the insecticide cans and spraying everywhere in the kitchen. It's amazing the number of cockroaches you can kill with a couple of cans. Another guy who was very intelligent but slightly eccentric had the idea of putting all the furniture in his room on bricks. His theory was that it would give him more floor space – sound really. He used to keep fit but would go for a run in his normal clothes. Once again, sound reasoning and his answer was, 'Well, if the fuckers come after me these will be the clothes I'll be running away in.'

We'd been out on a job one night and were having breakfast after having been in the bar for a few hours when that bloke walked in wearing his usual clothes and carrying a black bin liner. He was supposed to be going on leave that day to America so we asked him where his luggage was. To that he held up the black bin liner with a big smile on his face, no credit cards either, he just had £3,000 in cash.

He was actually a civvy from the TA Parachute Regiment who'd managed to get himself on selection and passed the course. He also became something of an expert in CME and used to teach the guys in Ashford. He'd bought a house in Ashford and it used to be one of the targets that the students had to break into. One night he'd forgotten his keys so he 'let himself in'.

He was seen and the police were called. When they were let in they thought he was squatting because he lived in the lounge. His clothes were in a display cabinet and he slept on the couch in a sleeping bag.

'Why use the whole house if there's only me here?' I believe was his answer.

I myself had some terrapins in a small tank on top of my TV and I was apparently told, although I could never remember, that when I was pissed watching TV I would put one in my mouth and try to blow it back into the bowl. Also listening to my Walkman with headphones on and singing, out of tune, at the top of my voice didn't go down well with the neighbours.

The deputy head of special branch (Arnold) at this time had a bee in his bonnet about a particular terrorist who lived south of the border and who was supposed to visit the north quite often and mostly at weekends. After a while this got to be a pain in the arse. Arnold would turn up at the Det, usually on a Thursday with this shit-hot information that the guy was coming over the border to a certain address, usually in the cuds, and he wanted us to put an OP in. No one minded the work but after so many times with the guy not turning up it got to be a standing joke. If we'd planned a function the proviso was always, 'Providing Arnold doesn't turn up and fuck it up.'

I'd been on leave for a few days and came back to the Det feeling pretty knackered. I'd no sooner arrived than I was told that Arnold had been in a few days ago and said this bloke was definitely visiting this time. We had an OP out and I was due to go out that night and replace one of the lads – shit, I could have done without that! I thought. I went out that night and we swapped and I found that we were in an OP in a running sewer. We had big, robust lilos to keep us out of the water but everything got wet anyway. The idea was that we'd be in the OP during the day and then a couple of us would move forward until we had eyes down on the farmhouse for the night then returning to the OP before first light. Needless to say that the guy didn't show but what it *did* show was the potential inadequacy of the weapons most of us carried at the time.

Most of us were carrying the HK53 (Heckler and Koch), which was a 5.56 mm rifle, it was handy because it was light. When we came out of this OP after a few days, even though we had tried to keep them dry, a couple of them had rusted up and wouldn't fire. Being in close proximity to the target made it impractical to strip and clean the weapons so all you could do was to try to wipe excess moisture off it. The popularity of the weapon went rapidly downhill after that except as a support weapon in the city. As a result, most blokes then opted for the 7.62 mm Heckler and Koch G3, which although heavier was more robust and had more stopping power.

My favourite weapon after that became the Remington Wingmaster shotgun. This was a pump action shotgun and as long as you could pump it, it would fire. Although we weren't allowed to shorten the barrel it did have a folding stock and I had a long coat so I rigged up a harness for slinging it over my shoulder and quite regularly carried it on CTRs, even in the city.

During the training course CQB (close quarter battle) had featured a lot. In fact it was said that during this ten-day period one student would fire more 9 mm rounds than a complete battalion would during a whole year. It was during this period that you were made familiar with the smaller weapons that would feature in your life for the next two years. The main ones we were taught were the 9 mm Browning and the Heckler and Koch MP5K. The MP5K (the K standing for Kurz, which in German means short) was designated because although it was a 9 mm weapon it was only about thirteen inches long and could be concealed in the car or underneath a coat. It had a very good rate of fire and if you fired it correctly was accurate over short distances. With a magazine clip you could clip two magazines together, which, in effect, gave you sixty rounds to play with. It was normally carried on the passenger seat of your car, hidden by a blanket. There was also a handy little harness that enabled you to carry it nicely concealed under your jacket. That, with the thirty-nine rounds you would carry for your pistol gave you considerable firepower. It was, basically, your urban support weapon, if you needed the firepower, backed up by the 9 mm Browning if it had a stoppage. The G3 on my back seat and my door pistol gave me more than enough firepower. I carried, all in all, 119 rounds on me and that's not including the shotgun. Normally, though, for day-to-day surveillance we would just carry the Browning on our person but have the other weapons in the car 'just in case'. Because we operated in the City and the cuds you couldn't really go back to the Det for extra weapons if a rush job came up so most blokes used to carry a variety. Weapon training continued in the Det and if we weren't practising on the range in Ballykelly we would go to the sand dunes of Magilligan Point where we could blast away at what we wanted.

We also used the range cars to practise what might happen if confronted by armed men whilst in our cars. One of the biggest problems that came to light was actually engaging a target through the windscreen of your car. As anyone who has been in this situation knows, firing through glass will deflect the trajectory of the round so you might not even hit the target. This is especially the case with laminated windscreens. Another factor was that the rounds we were issued with were encased in copper. We found that by trying to engage the enemy from inside the vehicle, firing through the windscreen was not successful, although the Det Boss managed it. Invariably the round, on hitting the windscreen, would strip the copper jacket and render it useless. The boffins eventually came up with a round that they assured us that would solve this problem. We were issued with a certain number of these rounds, which had a red tip to them. We were assured that these would penetrate the windscreen and anything in its path. After a few trials we were inclined to agree with them and from then on after we christened these bullets 'werewolf bullets'. In other words, as far as we were concerned they would kill fucking anything.

One of the range cars we had was a Ford Escort Mexico and although it was a powerful car, it was also distinctive. There weren't many in the city at the time, so it was relegated to a range car. It was common to take it on to the airfield from time to time and practise handbrake and 'J' turns. The handbrake turn is when you are travelling forward, spin the wheel and apply the hand-brake to swing the car through 180 degrees, and drive off again. The 'J' turn is similar except that you are reversing at high speed, spin the car through 180 degrees, change gear and drive away facing forward. We practised these as a counter to running into IVCPs (illegal vehicle checkpoints).

One time I was bored and thought I'd take it out for a practice. I'd done a few handbrake turns without a problem. Now the fact that the surface of the airfield was very dry might have had something to do with it but when I went for my first 'J' turn I rolled the fucking thing and ended upside down with the car on its roof.

Shit, I thought, I've fucked up here.

It's quite an eerie feeling rolling over and seeing the world spinning. I don't know how these fighter pilots do it. I had to walk back into the Det and get a couple of the lads help me roll it back on to its wheels and then drive it back. It was perfectly driveable, just a bit bent, and I really didn't get much stick!

Another town that featured prominently at that time was Strabane in County Londonderry, often called 'the Wild West'. We carried out a number of minor operations there but one in particular springs to mind when information came through that a new ASU was starting and our task was to identify them and monitor their activities. They used a mustard coloured Sherpa van that had a distinctive red door so it was pretty obvious even from a distance. By having a start point it was relatively easy to go from there, as with most operations, and develop a network of players, addresses and vehicles. One of the favourite places to drop off to move into a particular OP was the graveyard at the head of the town so that you could get eyes down on one of the player's houses.

It was on one of these, on a previous job, that the OP team saw a group of men walking towards them with weapons, so they took cover. As they drew level the OP team opened fire and killed at least one of the men. The lads had to go to open court (normally they, and anyone else from the Dets who had to attend court, would have been shielded from the public to prevent identification), charged with murder, but they were acquitted. To give a warning in situations such as that gives the terrorist a chance to return fire and could end up with you suffering casualties. It just wasn't worth the risk because they're hardly likely to just put their weapons down and say, 'OK it's a fair cop,' are they?

It really was a load of bullshit, when these people had declared war and seemed to think it was fair when they shot and bombed people but as soon as one of them was shot they shouted foul.

'Did they give a warning before they opened fire?'

Did they bollocks!

Let's not forget something before we have all of these Liberal do-gooders and the rest of them bleating. These people were hardened terrorists who would kill you soon as look at you and they didn't give a shit about human life, as the Omagh bomb proved. As far as the guys in the Dets were concerned anyone who walked around with a weapon at night in those areas was not just out to buy bread. They were out to kill someone and must have realised that, if seen, they should have been prepared to take the consequences of their actions. We were prepared to take our chances, and did do on more than one occasion, so what's the fucking difference? I may go on about the Republicans in this book but as far as I and the other guys in the Dets were concerned, a terrorist was a terrorist regardless of religion, and they would all get the same treatment.

Because the head of the town is such a difficult area to cover we would position cars as cut-offs to be able to trigger the ASU's favourite vehicle at the time – the old Sherpa van which I referred to earlier. We made a lot of use of the heli during this operation because our helicopters were fitted with a GOA sight that was used in Lynx helicopters as a missile-aiming device. This had a 360-degree capability and the ability to zoom in from a long distance. You could stand off miles away with this thing, zoom in until you had the target's front door filling the sight and then zoom out for when he came out and started walking and got into his car. Also by knowing where the target was in relation to junctions you could – and we did – use the heli at night to trigger the vehicle away and take it as far as the town before handing over to the car team. During this period the Strabane Golf Club was blown up but unfortunately we were not covering the ASU at the time. The operation was still continuing when I left but I heard shortly after that they had been arrested at a quarry in the

Republic with a dumper truck packed with mortars in the back. We actually used this sight as a trigger on a target in Rathowen Park in the city as well.

Because Strabane was a fair distance from the Det it sometimes used to take quite a while to get there, especially with heavy traffic, but we got around that on a couple of occasions. When one of the lads in the Det had been with his parent regiment, he used to provide a bodyguard for the Duke of Abercorn who had a large estate in the Strabane area. It only took a phone call from the guy to the Duke and we had our forward base all fixed up. I actually have a good photo of us sitting around the table having dinner with the Duke.

It was quite funny really because there was only him and the butler living in this big house so to heat it for the two of them would have been a bit ridiculous. What they did, certainly in the case of the dining room, was to build a room within a room so they retained the size of the actual house but they were only heating a slightly larger than average dining room. Very clever really; he must have been a Jock.

Socialising within the Det was difficult as the nearest 'safe' bars we were allowed to go to were about thirty miles away. Most of the guys were very careful about drink driving so if we went out for a particular night we would get dropped off and picked up. I think in two tours I must have gone out socialising about five times. Because of this we fully made up for it within the Det. Every now and again we would hold a function and the other Dets were invited along with the Branch lads. After a while we got a reputation as the North Det Animals and certain people were reluctant to come to our functions, especially as one time we threw one of the control clerks into the pond and he broke a rib. It was not uncommon to get very drunk on these occasions but that would only happen if there was no work the next day. We used to have a bar in a large room that was fairly basic and it eventually had a large concrete bar built with a tile top, so that it couldn't be wrecked. The rule in the bar was that if you wrecked it you repaired it and this happened on numerous occasions. With the job you were doing and lack of socialising it was really the only way of letting off steam. Better off in the bar where everything was under control.

We very often used to have theme nights and on one particular night we had a 'storm the bar' party. At a given hour everyone emerged and laid siege to the bar and gained entry however they could. Everyone had some form of makeshift weapon; I had my Wingmaster shotgun. I'd removed the shot from the cartridges so all that would happen was that you'd get a small bang. During the assault all the fridges were thrown out of the window into the yard outside and someone had put a jerrycan of petrol next to one of them as the gas was escaping. I thought that this would look good if it went up so I went back to my room and loaded up with some real cartridges. We got hold of a van and debussed as it was driven up to the bar and I let go a couple of rounds at the jerrycan and the fucking thing exploded in a fireball. The green army unit whose barracks we were in actually sent the QRF chopper up because they thought we were under attack. Oops, I thought, I've gone a bit far this time – but it blew over. They probably just put it down to those fucking muppets (as we were called) at the bottom of the airfield.

We surveyed the damage the next morning with a feeling of apprehension as to what we had actually done to the place. The fridges were a write-off, as you would expect. All the glass in the windows had gone as had the frames themselves. The plastic guttering had melted due to the fireball and the exterior paint was black. Ah well, we thought, it was a good night but we'd better get the bloody thing fixed. We got it done eventually but we never did ask where the new fridges came from – best not to!

The bar was the main form of entertainment in the Det and as mentioned, we got up to some pretty outrageous behaviour. It was quite common for some clown to throw a couple of smoke grenades in during a piss-up. Have you ever tried having a quiet beer in a bar full of smoke flares? As a hobby, myself and a couple of other guys were heavily into home brew and had taken over a couple of rooms in one of the Portacabins in the hangar. I used to make Irish stout from a Boots Homebrew can. One can made forty pints and it was good stuff. One day I thought I'd try an experiment. I still made a forty-pint barrel but this time I put two cans in and double the amount of sugar and eagerly awaited the end of the process. When it came out it was a bit thick, tasted good, but was fucking lethal. Four pints and you were all over the place – I never did it again. There is a drink in Ireland made out of potatoes called poteen which is in fact Irish potato whiskey and also illegal. Quite often the Branch guys would come along with a couple of bottles of this stuff and pass it around (I never knew where they got it from!). The normal stuff was like firewater and the first time I tried it I went straight outside and threw up but the flavoured stuff, such as apricot poteen, was very nice.

You hear many stories about the Irish and most of them are just stories but this one just sums up everyone's idea of them. There was a Branch guy called Martin who decided to demonstrate how you could tell the good stuff from the bad stuff.

'It burns with a blue flame,' he said, and with that pours some into a metal ashtray he's holding and sets light to it. It looks good and it's burning away quite happily, but he's still holding it, OK! After a while the ashtray gets red hot, but he's still hopping around and juggling with the ashtray in his fingers, going, 'Look [blow, blow] it's got a blue flame.'

Only the Irish could do that.

On my second tour we were taken to the Bushmills distillery by some of the lads from the Branch who told us it was certainly worth a visit. I wasn't too sure about this because the last time I had drunk whisky (Scotch whisky that is) we hadn't exactly seen eye to eye. It was during one of the piss-ups that we had at the RMR. Normally, when I was younger, I could drink beer all night without a problem but that night someone had persuaded me to try a horse's neck (whisky and dry ginger). The first one didn't taste too bad so after that I was throwing them down my neck, which was a bad move.

I suddenly found myself feeling as though I was on a merry-go-round and wished the room would keep still. This is it, I thought, it's time to get home. Somehow I managed to get the bus home in one piece and staggered off to bed. The next morning I woke up and thought, thank fuck I'm still alive. I then went to get out of bed and there was a big pile of puke on the carpet. Could have been disastrous.

Anyway, since that time I have never drunk Scotch whisky. It's funny though because I must have an inbuilt homing beacon

– no matter how much I have had to drink I always seem to find my way to my bed.

So, off we went to the distillery and as we arrived we were given a ticket for a drink in the bar. The Branch lads had told us that, once the tour had finished, it was into the bar and get wired into as much Bushmills Whiskey as you could drink.

'Excuse me love,' I enquired politely, 'What's the ticket for?' (knowing full well!)

'Oh, it's for a drink in the bar afterwards.'

'But I thought we could have as much to drink as we wanted.'

'That's right,' she said, 'that used to be the case but sometimes there was too much trouble.'

'That's terrible,' I said in all innocence, 'and who used to cause that then?'

'The bloody Peelers, they were terrible,' she answered.

Peelers are what the Irish call the police and here we were with the Branch. Nice one lads!

Anyway it wasn't as bad as all that because after the tour it was into the bar and you handed your ticket over for a large glass of Bushmills Whiskey. Now compared with the last time I had tried blended Scotch whisky (I'm sure it was the ginger ale that made me throw up) this stuff tasted like nectar and I have been a fan of Irish whiskey ever since. Bushmills Malt Whiskey is one of the smoothest things you can taste. So, after you'd handed your ticket over the barmaid would put it on the counter below the bar. Well you just have to don't you?

When the barmaid had her back turned one of the Branch lads just reached over and grabbed a slack handful of tickets. That was repeated more than once so we ended up having a very enjoyable afternoon especially as we kept the Branch lads in order!

We used to have a special Army Air Corps flight (G flight) that supplied us with helicopters and with pilots trained in assisting us to put surveillance on cars and buildings. They knew where to position the chopper so that the target would not be able to see it in his mirrors or be able to hear the engine. We had one in the Det at all times and sometimes had two. On this particular occasion we had one on the pad and we were in the bar having a beer (surprise, surprise) when we heard another one coming in so we thought, OK, he'll land on the grass. Next thing we heard a bang and the pitch of the engine rising before it landed. Although the choppers had landing lights it was common practice not to use them but come straight in. What the pilot didn't realise was that there was already another chopper on the pad and he lowered his chopper onto the other one. As soon as he realised he'd made contact he hit the throttle and pulled the stick back before landing on the grass. He looked a bit sheepish when he'd shut down and got out and with good reason – it was only the guy in charge of the flight section. After that we put a light at ground level so that it wouldn't happen again. Choppers are pretty difficult to see at the best of times anyway!

During my second tour with the Group we had a couple of SAS guys join the Det, one of whom was Andy McNab. For a while the SAS guys were a bit concerned about coming to the Det because it did not matter which branch of the forces you came from – if you couldn't hack it you were sacked and that included both SAS and SBS. In fact, the very first SAS guy that came to the Det was sacked at the end of orientation. He was a nice enough guy but just was not covert enough.

I'll just digress slightly and say that the guys that came to the Dets were usually the more natural guys. There was a troop of the Regiment based in South Det and when they weren't deployed they would spend their time weight training and eating everything in sight. Some of these guys were built like fucking gorillas and would not have made covert surveillance operators but were good for scaring the shit out of someone. A little while later the Regiment actually started to put more and more people through the course and if you said no or failed the course you were RTU'd. I thought that was particularly unfair as these guys joined the Regiment for a purpose and that may not have been to become a covert surveillance operator in NI. I actually got on quite well with Andy and recall one night in the bar recounting how many marriages we had between us. I was on my second and I believe that at that time he was on his third.

There is one thing I will contradict Andy on and that is something he mentions in his book, *Immediate Action*. He

Author being presented with the MBE by Her Majesty

Author exchanging pleasantries with Her Majesty
'I couldn't tell you what she said, I was just blown away by the whole experience.'

Group photograph before 'storming the bar party'
Note the faithful hound with shoulder holster

Fridge exploding prior to fireball

*Author (left), before change of appearance,
with a good friend from a previous SBS course
Note the cool tank top*

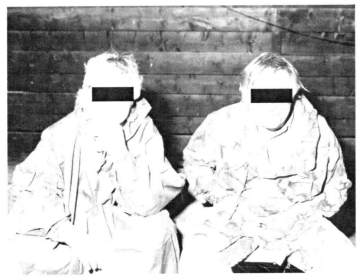

The aftermath

Pelting the FNGs with Asterix in the background

Author debussing (right) with a Remington Wingmaster

Caribbean theme night (author second from left)

Author after change of appearance, with 'shoulder holster' dog

Author in the Duke of Abercorn's living room sipping Earl Grey tea

Having dinner with the Duke (at the head of the table, with the author to his right) Note the radio bottom right for a crash out (weapons discreetly hidden)

Author going foxtrot, photo taken from Strand Road Police Station sangar

Author going complete in Ops car

Driving away

*Author's eldest son on his Passing Out day, with medal presented for best shot –
a proud moment*

describes an operation where the covert search team inserted via Gemini raiding craft on Lough Neagh. There was indeed a hide that was found but what he omits to say is that he wasn't in fact the No. 1 for that job; I was and he was my No. 2. I was called into the Boss's office one evening and sauntered across after I'd just got out of the sauna and my nightly session on the sun bed.

'Sit down Sam, there's a job just come up that I want you to No. 1 and I want Andy to act as your No. 2. He's on a serial in town at the moment and I'll brief him when he gets back. I just wanted to give you a 'heads up' so you can maybe get hold of a map from the spooks and do an appreciation before you get stuck into it tomorrow.'

'Yeah OK Boss, what is it and where?'

The Boss at this time was a Rupert in the Parachute Regiment although you wouldn't have thought it to look at him. At the time most of us wore tank tops because the top kept you warm and it didn't have arms that would snag if you had to draw your weapon in a hurry. Mine were bad because I just used to cut the arms off my jumpers but his were in a class of their own. They looked as if he had brought them at Moss Bros, so mister fucking sensible had nothing on him.

'TCG have got information that there is a hide with some weapons in near an old farm close to the shores of Lough Neagh. They want us to go and have a look and see if we – or should I say you – can locate it. They must be fairly sure of the information because if we find something they want to remove the contents with a view to bugging them. There will be a team from 7 SCT (Special Collation Team) running with you ready to take the contents away, do the business and return them so you can replace them back in the hide. After that we'll be monitoring the hide waiting for a move. Apparently the marker is a tree stump but take that with a pinch of salt.'

This sounded promising, as we hadn't had a covert search for weapons for a while.

'I'd imagine you'll want the chopper in the morning for a fly-past so I've warned Dave that you'll probably have a chat with him in the bar later.'

'OK, roger that. Have you seen the chief spook lately? He'll probably know where the maps are and if we've already got existing air photos of the area. I'll want to take my own anyway but I'll be able to get a feel for the area if I can see it first.'

'Last seen he was in the collation office but that was a while ago. If you need anything give me a shout.'

'Yeah, OK, see you in the bar later for some home brew?'

'You must be fucking joking, the last time I drank that stuff you make I puked my ring up the next day.'

I left the office with a little chuckle, thinking, these Ruperts have got no fucking stamina.

'Oi slime, got any maps and photos of Lough Neagh?' I shouted as I found the Chief Spook.

I found this amusing because I was 'slime' myself.

'Shut the fuck up wanker, and let's see what we've got.'

Things were always informal in the Det and there was always a bit of friendly banter going on.

'Which part do you want? Because it's a fucking big place in case you didn't know.'

'I'm after the north-east side showing the lake and the nearest roads in the area.'

He gave me a map first and after I'd orientated myself to it I said, 'That's the place, got anything on that?'

While I was studying the map he was looking through the old air photos but after a while he said, 'No, 'fraid not, nothing on that, looks like you'll have to fly it yourself.'

I took the map away with me and found a quiet corner to have a good look. The place was fairly isolated and the nearest road suitable for a drop-off and pick-up was about three kilometres away. We were in the middle of summer now and the hours of darkness were few and far between. To move tactically over three kilometres, find the hide, extract the kit, call in 7 to do the business and replace the contents would have taken most of a good night in the middle of winter. I had a quick think about it and went back to the Boss. 'Look Boss, I've had a quick look and got some thoughts. Let Andy know I'll be in the bar when you've finished the debrief and we'll have a chat then.'

'Yeah, OK Sam, no probs.'

I walked over to the bar with the map to wait for Andy. 'Bar' sounds a grand word for what in fact was an old low building with a solid concrete structure that served as a bar. The picnic tables that we used had long gone during the mayhem of various piss-ups but what always puzzled me were the optics. In the two tours I did there was a row of optics behind the bar and in all the stuff that got thrown around the place never once did an optic get broken.

'All right Dave,' I said as I walked into the bar, 'landed on any good helicopters lately?'

Dave was the guy who had landed his chopper on the other one. He was always getting stick after that.

'Fuck off twat, what do you want?' This was accompanied by the finger.

'Well, a drink would be nice first and then I'll tell you what I want in the morning. There's a new job come up and I'm No. 1 on it.'

'What do you want,' he asked, 'beer or what?'

'No it's OK mate, I've got a new batch of home brew I'm going to try, fancy one?'

'No ta, maybe later. What's this stuff you've made?'

'Ah, this should be a good one; it's a little experiment. You know those cans you get from Boots – put the sugar in and add forty pints of water? Well what I've done is get two cans, put double the amount of sugar in but kept to forty pints of water, should be good.' I poured myself a pint of this stuff out of the barrel and it was jet black and poured like very liquidy treacle.

'Jesus H Christ.'

I'd drunk about half a pint before coming up for breath and when I did I felt as though I'd already drunk a couple of pints.

'You'll like this Dave,' I coughed. 'Trust me, I'm a soldier.'

'That's what I'm afraid of. Anyway, who's your No. 2?'

'Andy. He's on his way back from a serial in town and I've said I'll meet him in here after the debrief.' We chatted about things in general for a while and after about an hour Andy walked in with his usual cheesy grin on his face.

'All right, get the home brew out then and tell me about this job. The Boss has filled me in on the basics but what else have we got?'

'Here, get this down your neck first and then we'll have a

chat,' I said as I poured some home brew for the three of us. I had to chuckle as I watched their faces; it was pretty powerful stuff.

'OK,' Andy said, 'what's the plot?'

'I don't know what he's told you but all I know is that there is supposed to be a hide near the shores of Lough Neagh that possibly contains weapons. I know it's TCG Int so we'll take that for what it is – normally bad. The only thing that makes me think there could be something there is that they're running 7 [7 were the technical people responsible for technical devices within the Group] with us. Now normally they wouldn't commit them unless it was pretty hot stuff. There aren't any air photos so I'm going up in the morning with Dave to take some. Now looking at the map the nearest DOP [drop off point] is about three clicks away for a walk in and I reckon that with the light the way it is it'll be too long. Now it's up to you. You can either come in the heli tomorrow to have a look at the ground or you can drive it and look for a possible DOP. I've looked at the map and because I was a Bootie my first thought is to go in by boat. Barry 2 is SBS [from my aborted SBS course] and Gerry is Raiding Squadron so all we need is a boat and I reckon we should be able to do it ourselves.'

'Well looking at the map I think I agree that it's too far for a tab in so I'll come up in the heli.'

'OK, Dave, is that route on a normal flight path or do we have to deviate and put a bit of deception in?'

The deception would be required because suddenly putting an aircraft in an area where they normally didn't fly might attract attention. So what you would do is perhaps have a word with the flight and ask them to start using that route for a few days to build up a routine. Once the locals had got used to seeing choppers, you could do your fly-pasts. You would fly in one direction to get the photos from one side, stand off for about ten minutes and then do a return run on the other side of the target so you had what photos you needed.

'It's not on a normal flight path but down there a chopper can normally get away with it because it's not too far from Aldergrove. I wouldn't recommend a fixed wing in that area though.'

'Right, we'll go for a fly-past tomorrow morning, what's the met like for tomorrow, Dave?'

'It should be sunny with very little cloud and if you want to do it in the morning I'd recommend leaving here about mid morning, say 0930. That should get us over the target at about 1015.'

'Sounds good, we'll go for that then. OK, now we've got the serious business out of the way, let's get down to the home brew.'

Dave had a couple of beers and went to get his head down as he was doing the pilot shit in the morning and that left me and Andy and a couple of the others in the bar. The talk eventually got around to our personal lives and I said that I had been married twice and divorced twice but would probably be getting married again.

'Ha, beat you there – I'm already on my third.' So between us there were five marriages. It shows somewhere along the line in both kinds of work the pressures that are put on relationships. Most of the people we worked with at the time were either divorced and remarried or were once bitten twice shy. Life in the Regiment and in the Dets was not conducive to settled long-term relationships. Certainly in the Det, apart from two weeks leave per year, the routine was that you had the choice of working five weeks and having five days off or working eight weeks and having seven days off. I opted for the five and five but it wasn't a particularly good time. Life in the Regiment could be much worse with the guys being away for months at a time and their wives not even knowing where they were.

By this time I was living with the woman who was to become my third wife. I used to find that it took me at least a day to calm down when I got home and then the day before I was due to go back I was already back there in my mind and completely withdrawn. So really we only had three good days together.

I know Andy had just had a little girl but at this time I didn't have any kids so perhaps I wasn't feeling it that much. My family came later when I went back to Ponty as an instructor. After a few more treacles we wove our way down to the cookhouse for bacon sarnies before bed. One of the good things about the Det was the cook used to leave a night tray in the fridge packed with bacon and sausages so you could feed your face instead of having to get up for breakfast. The only difference to this was when the Troop

(SAS detachment) used to come up from its base. Then everything was locked away because those fucking gorillas would eat everything in sight and we wouldn't get a look in.

The next morning I got up feeling a bit woozy and wondered who'd shit in my mouth and thought I must have had a good night until I remembered what I had been drinking. That was the one and only time I made the home brew like that. I'm afraid I went back to being a wimp and just made normal strength from then on. I went over to the Ops room and bumped into the Boss, and so I put him in the picture about what was happening that day and my initial thoughts of how I intended to go about it.

'OK' he said, 'sounds good to me. Have a look at it and let me know what you think when you get back.'

I prepared the camera and got the lens I thought would be good enough for the job and some spare film. I decided I'd got plenty of time for a couple of cups of tea before we took off. I left the Ops block and walked towards the cookhouse and something caught my eye in the outside toilet at the back of the cookhouse. It was Andy having a dump with the door open and his head in his hands, looking a bit the worse for wear. He had this habit of going for a dump and leaving the door open so he could see what was going on.

'All right Andy, take-off in about half an hour.'

'Twat.'

Fucking charming, I thought.

He came in about ten minutes later and we shot the shit for a while and then walked towards the helipad, putting on our combat smocks as we went. Even though we were wearing jeans you always wore a combat smock so that if PIRA were looking at the chopper with binos they would think it was a normal soldier in the passenger seat. I briefed Dave on what we wanted and off we went. When we got to the area we made one pass over the target then flew on for about ten minutes and just stooged around for a bit, for the reasons I mentioned earlier. I took photos of the target, the surrounding area and possible routes in from the shore of the Lough. We got back to the Det around lunchtime and gave the films to the Brownie to develop.

Once they were developed we had a good look at them and more or less came to the same conclusion that the best way in would be by boat across the Lough. We had a chat with Barry 2 and Gerry who were more than happy to take us in provided we could supply the boat. We couldn't really see much of a problem with that as there was a Royal Engineers base on the Lough shore and they used to patrol the Lough in small boats. Great! It seemed a simple case of going down there and saying, 'Give us a boat for a few days.'

This was when things started to fuck up in the planning as far as I was concerned. We went and saw the Boss and put the plan to him; it was at this point that he thought he would get involved. I don't know whether he could see something in it for himself but he stuck his oar in.

'That place is a bit remote, isn't it, and we don't know how good this Int is. How about if I organise an IRLS [infra red line scan] for you just to be on the safe side.'

An IRLS is a special camera mounted in a Beaver aircraft that when the film is developed will show any heat blooms in the ground – for example, if PIRA had booby-trapped the hide and run a buried command wire to a detonating point.

'No way,' I said. 'It *is* remote and it's not on a normal flight path so anything flying over that area would attract interest. Besides, Dave has already said that he wouldn't recommend putting a fixed wing over that spot, so thanks but no thanks.'

I thought that would be the end of the matter because normally the No. 1 has the final say in the planning and preparation of a job. I thought nothing more of it and went away to get kit together and to make a start on my orders. Also thinking of our stomachs, as we might have to stay out overnight, I went to the cookhouse and found the cook.

'Hey slop,' I shouted – the cooks were affectionately known as 'slop jockeys' or 'slop' for short – 'Andy and me might be out in an OP on Thursday, could you make us up a pile of snarlers [sausages] that morning and maybe a bit of chicken? I just want to give you plenty of notice.'

'OK, no problems. Is it just for the one night?'

'Yeah. If it's any more we'll just make what we've got last two nights.'

'Right, they'll be ready at lunchtime that day.'

'Cheers mate.'

Snarlers are great things to take into an OP because if you cook them right and wrap them tight in cling film they will last for days. All you need is a jar of Coleman's mustard and it's just like having a picnic. Apart from them being nutritious I also find that they bung you up. I found that with snarlers and Mars bars I could manage up to five days in an OP without a shit. While I'm on the subject, cling film is fine for normal stuff but if you've got the shits it goes everywhere. You can't beat the old black plastic bag to collect the whole lot, but that is only personal preference.

The reason for using either method is that if farmers found human excrement anywhere on their land they would come to the obvious conclusion that there were security forces somewhere around, probably in an OP. Some farmers would actually come out each morning checking their hedges for them. There was a story going around at the time about a Regiment OP that was in position when the dog from the farm came sniffing around and found them. They had two choices – to kill the dog or grab it and hold it 'hostage' for a while, which they did. After quite a while a young lad came from the farm down to their bush and said, 'Hey mister, we don't mind you staying in our bush but can we have our dog back, please?'

As I said, I don't know how true it was but we all found it bloody hilarious.

The rest of that day was spent sorting kit out that we thought we'd need and making sure that if we didn't have it we'd be able to get it in time. Because it was a covert search of a hide there were certain things you'd need to protect the integrity of the hide and to be able to record the contents. Because it was in a rural area I'd need a sheet or some hessian to lie directly outside the hide so I didn't leave any sign. I'd also need a blanket to cover my head, as I'd be using white light from a small torch to look into the hide. A pocketscope would be no good as it was too bulky and wouldn't focus close enough. Besides, despite all the technical gear, you can't beat the mark one eyeball. I'd want an IR camera with film to record my progress into the hide and once in I'd need a hook with a long length of cord. The theory was that if there was anything in the hide I'd hook it, pay the line out to a safe distance and yank it. If there was no bang it meant that PIRA hadn't booby-trapped the hide. Better to be safe than plaster myself all over the nearest bushes.

The following morning I was up fairly early with no home brew-induced hangover and went across to the Ops block to finish off my orders and to prepare the board for the briefing. That meant that if anything came up the following day I wouldn't be running around like a blue-arsed fly.

Everything was going great until lunch that day when the Boss said, 'Sam, can you come over to the Ops block after lunch? There are some things we need to discuss.'

'OK, will about 1400 do?'

'Fine, see you then.'

I thought no more of it so I went back to my basha (a basha was what a shelter in a jungle was known as, but it became common terminology for wherever you laid your head), watched the news and got my head down for an hour. At 1400 I went back across to the Ops block and into the Boss' office.

'OK, I've had an IRLS flown and I've been in touch with Hereford and they're sending some of boat troop across with a couple of boats to do the insertion tomorrow night.'

I just sat there, gobsmacked, then went ballistic.

'You've done what!'

'You heard. I didn't think your idea of self insertion would work so I've organised boat troop to do it.'

'I don't give a fuck what you think. I'm the No. 1 on this job, why didn't you talk to me about it? And as for the IRLS, I fucking told you I didn't want one flown and I gave you my reasons. If my plan and what I want isn't good enough why don't you go and do the fucking job yourself?'

'Being on the ground isn't my job. Are you going to do it or not?'

'Of course I'm going to do it, just keep your fucking nose out in future.'

I then did my normal storming off trick. I was absolutely fuming at what the stupid twat had done and the risk of compromise he'd introduced into the job. The rest of the day I was like a bear with a sore head and couldn't get it out of my mind but there was nothing I could do about it now except try to focus my mind on it. Half a barrel of home brew that night helped but the Boss was noticeable by his absence in the bar. It was probably a good move.

Thursday afternoon was briefing time and everyone involved in the job was there except for the boat troop lads who we would team up with in the SF base on the Lough. I gave a full briefing and that included the fact that once we had successfully inserted the technical devices into the weapons we would need a team forward mounted at South Det along with a chopper with tracking kit as well as the kit in the cars. We drove down to the SF base with all our kit and met up with the boat troop lads; I was surprised to see my mate from the Booties.

'All right Sam,' he said, 'are you the No. 1 on this? If you are give us a brief 'cos no one has really told us what's going on.'

'OK Ken mate, if you get your lads together I'll give you a full brief as far as it concerns you and try to answer any questions you've got.'

I gave the full brief and then took him to one side after and explained what had happened in the Det with the Boss.

'Twat! They just can't leave things alone can they? What do you reckon?'

'I think we should be OK. We've got a pocketscope for the walk in and stacks of firepower if the shit hits the fan. My main worry is a booby trap but I've got a pull cord so we should be OK.'

'Don't worry about it, break a leg. We'll get together for a beer after it's all over.'

'Roger that, sounds good. What time do you want to set off, bearing in mind we need as much time on target as possible?'

'Well there's still quite a few people on the opposite bank so we'll set off as soon as it starts to get dusk, OK?'

'You're the rubber dinghy man mate, you call the shots.'

'OK, we've just got a bit more preparation to finish off and I'll give you a shout when we're ready.'

That gave Andy and me another chance to go over the air photographs and memorise the route in. We weren't taking anything that might identify the target and any RV points. We'd already sanitised ourselves by taking out all personal effects, wallets, diaries, etc. We'd also given a kit list of everything we were taking to the chief spook. This was standard practice so that when you came back you went through the list to make sure everything was there. If it wasn't, you had a problem because you might have dropped it on target and compromised the operation. No big problem, you might say, because you've got back safely. The problem was that some of the information that got you to the target might have been tout information. If it came to light that the SF had been poking around a hide there would be a witch-hunt in PIRA as to who knew where the hide was and who might be the tout. The security teams sometimes weren't that selective in whom they picked up and in the punishment that was handed out. A Black and Decker drill through the kneecap is a fucking hell of a way to go to prove your innocence.

Dusk fell and we piled into the boat. Andy and me had a big Bergen each with all the stuff we'd need for that night's search and also our own kit in case we had to stay over the following day. It was actually bloody nice going out on to the Lough at that time of night. It was summer so it was still warm and the sun was just going down on the left-hand side of the lake (west side) as we went out. The water was calm and if you took your mind off the job for a minute you could almost imagine you were going for a jolly. Even some of the people on the other bank waved at us. You then looked back in the boat and took in the Bergens and weapons and came back to reality. Stupid twat, don't go getting sentimental.

The further we went out over the water the darker it got and the safer we felt. Having studied the maps and the air photos we didn't actually need to navigate because that area was so sparsely populated that you could actually navigate by relating the lights on the bank to the houses on the photos you had in your head. After about an hour the cox cut the engine right back and turned towards the shore. Ken and another lad slipped over the side of the boat in their dry suits and weapons and swam towards the shore. Once they landed they would recce the shoreline and if it were clear they would signal with an infrared torch that we would pick up with our PNGs (passive night goggles). After a fairly short time we saw the signal and the cox opened the silenced engine up slightly and took us in. We shit ourselves at one point when the throttle stuck and the engine raced like fuck but he soon got it under control and we carried on. As we got closer towards the shore he killed the engine and we covered the last bit using paddles. As we reached the shore Ken and his mate, being good eggs, were there to pull us in and we stepped ashore without even getting our feet wet. There's nothing worse than starting a job or an exercise with wet feet. We then grabbed our Bergens and moved off.

'Cheers Ken,' I whispered. 'See you either later or tomorrow night.'

He gave me the thumbs up and we took up covering positions for them as they moved off. It's at that point that they are most vulnerable and that's why Ken and his mate went ashore to cover us.

They waited until we had established comms with base and then they got into the boat and paddled off. We waited until we heard the engine start up before we hoisted our Bergens on and started our move in. We moved along the hedges towards the target area, pausing at our prearranged RVs, to listen and to observe the ground in front with the pocketscope. It was quite an easy route and definitely a lot quicker than using the nearest road. As we approached the target we stopped short and went to ground, observing and listening. There was an old farmhouse and barn but they both looked in a bad state of repair so we decided they were derelict and moved forward looking for the tree stump. When we were near the barn we noticed a prominent tree stump.

'What do you reckon?' I whispered to Andy.

'A bit obvious, don't you think?'

'Yeah, let's have a look around further on.'

After my little search for the swards of grass in the city I too couldn't believe it could be that obvious. However, what you have to remember is that it might not always be someone coming to the hide that has been there before so sometimes the marker has to be fairly obvious.

We carried on searching but couldn't find any other tree stumps in the area.

'It's got to be that one,' I said. 'Let's go back and have a closer look.'

We told Alpha that we were on target and were going to have a look at a possible hide. I took out the hessian from my Bergen and laid it at the entrance to the possible hide. Fortunately the ground was dry so we wouldn't leave much sign. I then got the blanket out and put it over my head while I shone the torch into the stump. At the base was a large hole and when you looked inside there were some sticks and some quite large rocks that could have come from the shore. They didn't get in there on their own. Each step I took getting into the hide I took an IR photo so that when I put it back together again I would be able to see if I had got it right or had fucked it up. Ideally this would have been done with a Polaroid camera so you could instantly see if you had made a mistake when putting the stuff back, but we didn't have one at that moment. I took all the rocks out and carefully laid them down on the hessian in order so I'd know which ones to put back first. I suppose you could liken it to taking an engine apart. You would put all the pieces in order so that you could reassemble it after you'd finished. As I took the last ones away I could see that there was an even bigger hole inside and I could see the butts of some weapons and some plastic bags.

I turned to Andy and said, 'Bingo'. He relayed this to Alpha and said that we were going to go further in. You could just picture everyone back in the Det and the guys in TCG doing back flips around the Ops, room as we'd got a result.

I checked my watch and by this time it had taken me about an hour to get into the hide, so the team from 7 wasn't going to have enough time that night to come in and do the business on the weapons. We decided to have a look at what was inside the hide so at least the guys could gear themselves up for what they had to do the next night. I looped my hook around one of the weapons and fed the line out to a safe distance and then took cover. When I yanked the line I didn't know if I was really expecting a big bang, but I breathed a sigh of relief when nothing happened. I wound the cord up again and we went back to the hide. I extracted the contents and had a look. We'd found two G3s, an Armalite, two sawn off shotguns, a couple of hand held radios and some balaclavas. Not a bad night's work!

We passed all this information to Alpha and said that we would spend the night and the following day on the shore out of the way. We'd considered trying to OP the hide in case anyone came looking but decided against it because time was running short and the area was pretty exposed. I replaced the kit in the hide, once again taking infrared images, and closed it up. I'd also given details to the 7 guys so they knew what to expect the following night. We then cleared the area of all our kit and made sure that we had everything before we moved back to the shoreline. We found a nice secluded spot and settled down until it was time to go back to work the next night. The plan was that the team from 7 would start to move in by boat and stand off on the Lough to wait for dusk. As soon as darkness fell we would move back to the hide and extract the kit while they came ashore and moved up to join us. We quickly settled into a routine of working two hours on and two off, with radio checks every hour. The day itself was really good, nice and sunny and warm. Apart from a bit of sleep we spent the day eating our picnic of snarlers and chicken and watching the people on the Lough sailing their boats.

As evening approached we packed our kit and got ready for the move back to the hide. As soon as we thought it was dark enough to move we informed Alpha. He told us that the team from 7 was already on the Lough and would land and move in when we said we were back at the hide, ready to come and take the kit. We retraced our steps from the night before but were just that little bit more cautious this time in case anyone had visited the hide and found anything disturbed. I looked at the hide when we reached it and decided it hadn't been touched because I'd put two tell-tales at the entrance that would indicate if it had been disturbed from the previous night.

One disturbed might be an accident but two, no! As far as I was concerned it was OK so we informed Alpha and I went in and took the kit out. I'd just finished when Ken 2 and Paul from 7 turned up to take the kit away.

'All right lads,' I whispered, 'there's the kit; how long do you reckon you'll be?'

'It's going to take us a good hour to get back and then we have to put the kit into the weapons. We've had a practice today from what you told us last night so we should be OK on that score. I reckon four hours tops.'

I checked my watch. It was now 2230, which meant that they would be back about 0230. Taking time to put the weapons back in the hide and to replace all the camouflage would be another forty five minutes to an hour so with the boat trip included we would be getting back about daybreak. 'OK Ken, be as quick as you can otherwise we'll run out of time and I don't want to be stuck here at daybreak with no weapons in the hide.'

'Right, we'll fuck off then and see you later.'

They left and we stayed on target so that we could observe the hide in case anyone came to visit. I kept checking my watch every few minutes, wishing we'd get the call to say they were on the way back. Eventually Andy leant across and said, 'They're on their way back.'

'Great!'

They turned up at the hide and I took the weapons off them and put them carefully back in the hide. I had all the stones and sticks laid out in the right order and hoped I was putting them back in the right place as I sealed the hide up again. Once finished and satisfied that it looked just as we'd found it, we all moved back to the shore where my mate Ken was. We all got into the boat and paddled out into the Lough before the engine was started and we went back to the base. It was just starting to turn light as we entered the jetty area of the base, so it was straight into the boat shed with big grins all round. Someone produced a bottle of rum; hot tea and rum at that time of the morning went down a treat. By now the banter had started flying around about boat troop and their 'live insertion'. I was speaking to Ken and he mentioned that he wasn't sure but he thought that was the first active insertion that boat troop had done since the Second World War.

'Do you know what, that's got to be at least a Military Medal for me,' Ken said, 'and what about you Tom?' he shouted to a mate. 'A Queen's Gallantry Medal for you or what.' All good crack.

After I had been back in the Det for about eighteen months I was asked if I would like to go back to Ponty as an instructor. I jumped at the chance. Det life was good but at that stage things were starting to get stifling. On my first tour we had had a lot more freedom to get things done. The head of Londonderry Special Branch at the time was a man called Mr D and he used to take a very keen interest in us because he knew what we were capable of and used to come to the Det sometimes to brief us personally. He used to give us some good jobs and we used to get the results for him. During my second tour all our tasking now came from TCG. There were British Army elements in there including our own LO (liaison officer) but it was predominately RUC-dominated. They had been in control in Belfast for some time but this was the first time I had come up against them. It soon became apparent that we weren't getting the sort of work that we used to. The RUC had their own surveillance unit called E4A who were ultimately trying to take over the surveillance in the city. It became quite apparent that there were certain areas in the city where they would not operate, namely the hard area of the Creggan. That was left to the Det who could, and would, operate anywhere in the city. The Creggan is the place where, only a few months before I joined the Det there were big headlines in the papers with one in particular reading, 'Lone SAS hero kills two IRA gunmen.' This was the Det Boss, described earlier. Also as far as TCG were concerned, it had been agreed that E4A would not operate in the city at the same time as us and this was an agreement that was broken several times. I remember one particular time when we heard that they were in the city and the team leader said that if they didn't pull out then we were lifting off the target we were on. They went.

My first intro to E4A had been in Ashford during the last few weeks when I was waiting to start my training for 14 Coy. They used to send their volunteers for E4A over to Ashford to attend a two-week OP course in which they would be taught urban and rural OPs and also photography. We would also take them on a certain amount of fitness training – or not, depending on how much vodka they'd consumed the night before! Just behind the barracks in Ashford was a small wood and one particular tree that was used as a punch bag. The area that was used for punching had been used for a long time and was relatively soft. One morning we ended up there and we duly punched fuck out of this tree and invited the RUC guys to have a go.

One particular guy gave it one or two light taps and then walked away as though he was bored by the whole affair. It was that and his general attitude on the course that led me to believe that he was a wanker and wouldn't pass the E4A course as long as his arsehole pointed down. Imagine my shock when he walked into the Det bar one night, now a fully accredited member of E4A. When they came across they also brought an LO (Liaison Officer) with them whose sole job was to keep track of their overtime and to keep the bar stocked with vodka – of which they drank plenty.

On my first tour we used to use the green army as a QRF, which meant that when the Det was deployed in the cuds or in the city the Army would act as the cavalry in case of an emergency. Whenever this happened one of the Det would drive to the barracks of the 'cavalry' unit to act as LO. If it wasn't feasible to send a LO they would be given a sealed envelope with a codeword on the outside and full details of the OP, how to get there and whom they should expect to meet. If something happened we would phone their Ops room and give the codeword. They would then open the envelope and react accordingly. At the end of the job, if there had been no incident, the envelope would be returned unopened. This system worked on at least one occasion when the lads got burnt out of a building, but most blokes preferred to have one of the Det as a LO. When the Army had a LO turn up they would obviously know something was happening because when we operated in those areas we would impose OOB (out of bounds) areas. This meant that the Army was not allowed in those areas while we were there. This was so that we were not disturbed while we were going about our 'legal' business and also so there were no possibilities of friendly fire incidents. I'll never know why they call it 'friendly' fire. I would imagine that regardless of who was shooting at you, if you were on the receiving end you wouldn't consider it to be fucking 'friendly' fire at all.

'I'm sorry you've had your leg blown off but don't worry about it my boy, it was "friendly" fire after all.'

'Thanks a bunch, I feel so much better knowing that they didn't really mean it. Maybe I'd be better off on the other fucking side.'

So anyway, when you turned up with perhaps long hair and a beard in uniform and with a Bergen they were obviously curious. You would introduce yourself by your Det name (not necessarily your real one, for reasons of security) and park your arse in their Ops room. You would then put your earpiece in and listen to what was happening on the ground.

If anything had happened, you would then go with the lead vehicle and direct them to where they were needed. At the end of the operation you would just stand up, thank them and walk out, leaving them to wonder what the fuck that had been all about. Most of the older hands used to accept it but you would always get some curious young Rupert being nosy and trying to find out what was going on. Some of them got a bit pissed off when you ignored them. Because you didn't wear rank you would always assume a higher rank than them if they got snotty unless it was the Commanding Officer, whereby you would just tell him that he didn't need to know, end of story.

On my second tour the QRF role was taken over by the HMSU (Headquarters Mobile Support Unit) of the RUC and they would normally operate in armoured Ford Cortinas. We would again supply an LO on each job and this used to get a bit unnerving in the city. You would put on an RUC uniform, minus shoulder identification badges, and sit in the back of the car. In some places, anyone walking by could have seen you and the following day you would be back out on the street minus RUC uniform. At least being LO for the green army it would be at night or in a barracks out of the way. These guys, much to the chagrin of Det members, used to make a fortune in overtime payments. There was one time where we had bugged a bomb and we, and them as the QRF, were living in an RUC station waiting for the thing to move. The only difference was that they lived in the RUC station and we lived in a garage at the back for forty-eight hours at a time. The job went on for a couple of months and one particular time we were sitting watching TV and they were discussing their payslips for that month. I think the conversation went something to the effect of, 'Well, that's another holiday in the Bahamas for me this year, how about you?'

I think that if the guys in the Det were on overtime payments I'd be a rich man now. The HMSU lads were also quite handy to know because of their contacts – for reasons I'll describe later. In the end the whole job went tits up because we got a stand by from the guys monitoring it, saying that it was being disturbed. It was being disturbed all right because PIRA had found the device and were busy separating it from the bomb. So when we reacted and crashed out we ended up following the device, which went across the border while the bomb went the other way. You win some, you lose some!

There was one time when I had been there for a while that it was my turn to take the FNGs around for their orientation. This was one thing nobody liked doing but it was essential. Normally we worked one up and that normally didn't raise any eyebrows but two guys in a car in certain areas of the city just made people look and in some cases do other things.

There was one particular bloke in the Creggan with a wooden leg who 'blew' (compromised) more guys in the Det than anyone else. If we could have got rid of him it would saved the Army a fortune. I don't know how he got his wooden leg but he was rumoured to be a vicious bastard and was supposed to have killed a police sergeant but avoided being jailed by the judge because he was a cripple. We were in the Creggan and him and a couple of his mates, who were on foot, saw us drive by and must have twigged straight away because when we reached another junction they were there in a car and tagged on behind us. I called it in on the radio and the other cars stopped orientation and loosely tagged on to the back, waiting for the contact. We drove around for a while because I was quite happy but I wanted to see if he was tooled up and had the bottle to have a go. Eventually I thought I'd better get out of the city but he still wouldn't have a go and even in static traffic he stayed a fair distance behind. Little did he know that apart from me there was another Det car two cars behind him and two cars on parallel roads either side of him! I guess he was worried that if he got too close I could initiate the contact and claim that I thought my life was in danger. As it was there was a flyover on the Lecky Road and I went over this towards the Protestant sector and he just gave a toot of his horn and drove on – bastard!

At the time I had very long brown hair and a beard so I decided a change of appearance was in order. As he had only seen my top in the car I thought a new jacket and jumper would do for clothes. The army was very understanding about this and had no hesitation in giving you money for a change of appearance – not! I asked one of the HMSU guys if they knew a safe hairdresser so I could get my head sorted out. One of the guys had a sister who was a hairdresser in Coleraine. I asked if she would do it for me and he said no problem, he'd put her in the picture and arrange an appointment. In the meantime I stayed in the Det and did heli jobs as and when required. I shaved my beard off and eventually went for my appointment. Up until then I had always been fairly conservative apart from looking like Grizzly Adams. Just to digress on that point, when my current wife came out to see me in Germany at one time I met her at Hanover airport looking just like Grizzly – she was a bit shocked! She got to work and when she'd finished even I had trouble recognising me.

I now had fairly shortish hair swept back with blonde streaks – height of fashion or what! I went back to the Det and the boss just walked straight past me without a glimmer of recognition so it must have worked. I also got quite close to the guy (who had blown me) a short while later in the Shantallow area with no recognition. Shortly after that I went home on leave and phoned my current wife when I arrived home for a pick-up. She arrived at the station and said that she couldn't see me but saw this bloke standing there with my bag. It was only when I walked up and got in the car that she realised it was me. It took her a while to get used to it and wouldn't even kiss me at first, but I can now streak her hair.

I arrived back at Ponty in June 1988 and I instructed there for two and a half years until December 1990.

My stay at the training wing this time was a far cry from when I had been there as a student, although at times the work was just as hard. For two years I taught CTR skills both urban and rural and for my last six months I went on the surveillance team prior to my going back to 28 Section. To anyone who has done the course I think they will admit that the CTR phase is the most intensive phase of the course. At the time it is very demanding and tiring with the students probably getting on average three hours' sleep per night over a ten-day period. The instructors didn't do much better either. After a while this will weed out those people who cannot hack it either physically or mentally. Apart from the physical side of actually planning the operation they would have fly-pasts, drive-pasts and walk-pasts to do during the day. While in the operational unit this could be spaced out over a number of days they did not have that luxury, because it was only a ten-day phase. Therefore they would have all this to do before giving their orders for that night's operation and then going to do the job. Once they had finished the job they would have to return to the camp and write out a report on what had happened before starting the whole cycle again. I have actually seen grown men from elite units burst into tears because they couldn't take the pressure and constructive criticism.

With the orders, the Ruperts were always the worst, because they thought they knew how to give a set of orders because they had been taught at Sandhurst and had maybe done so in their unit. Our orders here were totally different because in a normal unit you had a large group of men and a large back-up readily available. Also, you knew that at one point you were likely to engage the enemy. Although by the end of the course you would be more than capable of taking anyone out, that was not the official function. We were in effect a passive, covert, intelligence-gathering organisation. The fact that we were able to draw our pistols, engage three targets with a double tap, reload and engage a further two targets all within six seconds was irrelevant, though handy!

Part of my function within the CTR team was teaching the students what was required to give a good complete set of orders. Our orders proforma was about thirteen pages long and covered every eventuality you could think of so that if something went wrong on the ground you knew that everyone was singing off the same sheet. I would go through each section and explain what was required in each part and how to think a problem through to its logical conclusion. The best way to approach this is to decide on a course of action but then you say, 'But what if…?' OK, you then follow that course of action, but what if…? As an example, the best explanation would be to go through a team dropping off for a rural CTR. All their planning and preparation has been done, they have given a radio check at base so they know all their radios are working. They would usually have a mains set in their Bergen, a spare in the drop-off car and their own covert radios. They would drive to the DOP, which would have been previously cleared by a lead car. The DOP would be in a dip or on a bend so it would be a natural point to slow down and probably next to a gate so they could get into the fields quickly. As you approach the DOP you can feel the adrenaline build up, especially on a proper operation. On the approach you would have applied camouflage cream, as you can't drive around built-up areas with blackened faces.

The same would go for after the pick-up. The driver would make sure he had wet flannels in the car so you could wash the cam cream off. On the approach to the DOP, you would have discarded your jacket, as once again you can't be seen in a civvy car in uniform where the public could see you. The team is ready to debuss the car as soon as it stops. If it is a small operation the Bergens might be in the car so they can be removed quickly, but larger Bergens would be in the boot.

On the approach the driver would pop the boot to keep the noise to a minimum when he stopped. The team would also have popped the doors for the same reason and the interior bulb would have been removed so the light didn't come on. The driver would also apply his brake cut out, which would disable the brake lights so that anyone in the area would not see brake lights coming on. When he came to a halt the team would debuss and quietly push the doors to without slamming. They would push them on to the first click so they would still be half open but they would hold until the driver got to his LUP (laying up point) where he would fully close them. If the Bergens were in the boot they would have to be careful when they retrieved them so as not to walk past the rear light, for the same reason as applying the cut out switch. If it was possible to reach them from the side they would do so, otherwise they would have to roll on the road under the level of the lights, retrieve the Bergens and then roll under again. This is providing the driver remembers that the Bergens are in the boot and doesn't drive off as has been done before. Once that is done the team would gently tap the car to let the driver know he is clear and he would drive off to his LUP ready to return for a pick up when called for. Just for deception purposes also the driver would always move away in second gear, as this would lessen the signature of the engine. To pull away in first you always get the scream of the engine that, to anyone listening, would mean a car had stopped and pulled away.

Once dropped off the team would then move into the cover of the field and give a radio check. This is where the detail comes in with the orders and does not only affect the communications side but also every aspect of the operation i.e. what if? If the radio check failed the drop-off car would have been briefed to return to the DOP point after a certain period of time to change sets, but what if? If the set worked, fine; the team would continue on its task. If that set failed the drop-off car would have been briefed to return to the DOP to pick up the team and abort the mission – 'what if' carried to its logical conclusion in one scenario. The set is OK and the team continues and there are radio checks every fifteen minutes initiated by Alpha because the team might be focussed on something else and might not realise the time. One missed radio check was acceptable but after two the lost comms procedure would be initiated. If the team realised they had lost comms they would try their covert sets, but what if? If they had comms the decision would then be taken to either continue on covert comms or return for a pick-up, but what if?

If it was just a CTR they might go ahead but if it was an OP insertion they might decide to go ahead, insert, then get another set dropped off the next night (only if it was absolutely vital to insert) or abort there and then – what if? The reason they might go ahead and insert using covert comms is that on the original CTR to find an OP position they would have tested their covert comms in the OP site so they would know if they worked, what if? During the walk to target they would have given a time of how long it would take, so in the event of complete lost comms if they were within a certain time frame they would make their way back to the drop-off point for a pick-up.

The drop-off car would have been briefed to drive the route and look for cats' eyes at the DOP. These were cats' eyes dug up from the road (apologies to the County Council) and mounted on wood that would be stuck at the side of the road. To an ordinary driver it would seem to be a cat but to the Det driver it was a sign that the team was there.

If the cats' eyes were visible he would stop and the team would get into the car. If the team weren't there, then the QRF would be called and sweep towards the target looking for a firefly (powerful blue strobe light). By this stage there would probably only be one or two reasons why the team wasn't there and that would be a contact or an injury. This lost comms procedure would apply on the walk in, on target and the route to the PUP (pick-up point) and that would only be one – what if? At the end of the day you would never deploy or go through with an operation without comms. Not only would you be a liability to yourself but also you might put other members of the team in danger if they had to come and look for you. If you were in an OP and all comms failed during the day the last resort would be to place something prominent outside the OP. This would be so that when the chopper was sent over, briefed in your orders as part of the lost comms procedure – what if – they could see it and know you were OK. That way you could stay where you were until nightfall without compromising the OP. In other words it stopped the QRF from having to be deployed. Come nightfall you would either move to a prearranged point and either pick up another set or extract. If the chopper did not see the marker the QRF would be alerted and come in for a rescue. If you consider all the other eventualities that had to be considered, it was little wonder why the orders were so in-depth and took so long to write and give. The actual orders lecture used to take me about three hours to give with it culminating with me giving a full set of orders as an example.

When the students used to give the orders one of the instructors always sat in and usually tore them to pieces in the first instance because there would always be so much left out. As I mentioned earlier, the Toms would accept the constructive criticism for what it was and would try to improve next time. Some of the Ruperts could not take it and started to get lippy until you told them to shut the fuck up and learn something. After a while though most of them got the hang of it and they were passable in most cases. The thought behind it was if someone can't sit in the quiet of a classroom and think through a set of orders how the hell was he going to think things through on the ground if things went tits up?

We were very lucky in and around Hereford with OP locations. There were quite a few farmers who would let us use their land during the OP phase; the only trouble was that some of the bushes had been used so many times that it was a struggle finding a decent place. This was overcome most of the time because we had so many to choose from that you could 'rest' the bushes for a while and let them regrow for the next course. Usually it was just a case of paying a visit to the farmer and asking if it was OK to use the farm during the coming couple of weeks. Most times it wasn't a problem but if it was lambing season he might say no or just ask you to keep away from certain fields or from the farm buildings. I had quite a good night one night when it was the lambing season. I would be in the area of the farm watching the students doing what they were supposed to do – or not, in some cases – through a pocketscope. This one time I'd sneaked up to one of these open-sided mesh type barns where all the sheep were and spent about an hour watching all the lambs being born. I thought it was absolutely brilliant watching this, especially when they didn't have a clue you were there. Sometimes the farmer used to forget to warn his workers not to do certain things around the farm and this had some students panicking a bit and on one occasion resulted in me having to go out to the farm to speak to the farmer. They had got themselves into an OP in a thick hedge and thought they were bulletproof, as they couldn't be seen. During the next day we had a panic call come over the radio that they were in a bit of bother. One of the farm hands had decided that the hedges needed trimming so he'd got a tractor with one of those fuck-off big hedge trimmers on and at one point was slowly moving down the hedge towards them. They didn't know that we had the farmer's permission and were a bit worried as to what would happen if they were discovered. After speaking to the farmer he told the other guy to finish off next week. Sighs of relief from the hedge!

Urban CTRs and OPs were an interesting part of the course and also took place in Hereford. Once again the Special Branch approached people they knew in the city and they thought would be 'on side' to having people hiding in their premises for a few days at a time. Once again, when this part of the course approached the people would be contacted to see if it was OK to use their premises and to collect the keys to save us breaking in and also to get them to switch their alarms off. Some people actually felt that their premises were more secure with people in them at night. At one time the students saw a shop being broken into so they alerted the Ops room on the radio which in turn contacted the police and the arrest was made. I bet they wondered what the fuck they had done wrong to get caught. The students would be given the target they were supposed to watch and they would do walk-pasts to try to locate the best position for an OP. More often than not they would choose the right location but if not they were pointed in the right direction. Their first CTR would be a fairly simple one, to look at the lighting system around the target and to do a locks recce to see the type of lock on the entry point and if there were any other entry points.

When they reported the type of lock they would be told that the key holder had been lifted and we had a copy of the key. The next CTR would be to see if the key worked and to gain entry to see where the best OP position was. The owner of the premises would have agreed to leave the alarm off during this period. When entering a building on an urban CTR there are certain things that differ from a rural setting. You might, for example, be entering someone's nice carpet and if it were raining outside you wouldn't want to leave dirty footprints. You would therefore take a cloth or towel to put inside the doorway to step onto. You might also consider taking a spare pair of trainers to change into. Climbing stairs can be a problem as well because they tend to creak. The way round this is to step on the very outsides where the joint is because that is the strongest place and least likely to make noise. Once the CTRs had been carried out the insertion would take place. The orders would be as detailed as a set of orders for the rural phase. There were a couple of very good OPs we used, covering a betting shop and a bank. The targets would visit these and this would be reported and photographs taken.

The OP covering the betting shop was very realistic as it was on three floors and office workers occupied the building during the day. The staff toilets were also on the same floor as the OP so the team had to be ultra quiet during working hours. This was a realistic scenario as some OPs had, in the past, been in the attics of occupied houses. We also had another situation like that on the farm. Another OP was in a derelict factory near the railway and bus stations in Hereford and had been used for a long time. On this occasion the team inserted and was watching a weapons hide that had been serviced. They had been in for just over a day when we got a call for help. The demolition people had moved in and were knocking the place down, so we had to go and rescue the students and the weapons. The workmen thought it was quite amusing.

Towards the end of the course we would combine an urban OP with a rural OP and surveillance thrown in as well. The scenario was of an ASU constructing mortars in an old farm, with its progress monitored by an OP. This went on for a period of time with the OP carrying out CTRs to monitor the construction.

There was one point in the phase where I was monitoring the students in the Ops room and I heard the control room giving instructions for a resupply of food. The guys in the OP obviously didn't know I would be there at that time and I heard, 'Can you also bring me out some of the obvious.'

I had an idea what this was so I quizzed the guy in the Ops room and he eventually admitted that 'the obvious' were cigarettes. Here was a guy wanting to be a covert operator across the water and he was smoking in a fucking hay barn. One dropped match or a cigarette end might not only have blown them but, as I've said before, a good long-term tout might also have gone up in smoke. Once again, I went ballistic because I was thinking that this bloke was hoping to serve in the same organisation as me and he was possibly fucking up a whole operation because of sheer negligence. I got straight in a car and went out to the OP and confronted him and he admitted it. I then told him that if possible I would get him sacked for his fucking stupidity but it never happened. At that time the Dets were so short of people that we had to grade people that normally would have failed and the highest-grade failures got through the course. When I went through the course there used to be an open forum with all the instructors and the Training Major as to who was considered suitable and then the decision was made. The instructors were allowed to voice their opinion if they considered it a good or bad choice. Now we just had to write down our comments and opinions on the students and hand them to the Training Major and Chief Instructor. We would grade them 'A' – automatic pass; 'B' – marginal; 'C' – fail. We would also have to grade the 'C' grades one to five, and so on. We would then leave the room and be called back in and given the results of who was going through to the next phase. These would inevitably include some of the highest grade Cs, so in effect you were passing failures. As I said before this all came down to numbers required for the Dets so you would have someone documented as a failure that eventually got through the course, and in some cases they came back as instructors.

Anyway, the exercise came to a close by some of the instructors acting as the QRF and using an armoured Granada, as they would do across the water. The idea was that the surveillance team would take the targets from the farm towards Hereford with the QRF tagging on behind. They would gradually make their way up through the team until they were in a backing position. The control car would then lift off at the next opportunity and the QRF would overtake the target car, forcing it to a halt. It caused a few double takes from other motorists to see three guys bale out of this armoured Granada and run to the target car dressed in RUC uniform.

Another part of the training course was the driving phase, which I absolutely used to dread every time it came around. Because there was a requirement for the students to employ progressive driving techniques they were taught this on the course during another ten-day phase. The unfortunate part of it was that the instructors had to take their lives in their hands and teach the students. This started off as an assessment during Camp One and then went on to actual instruction at Camp Two.

There were actually one or two nasty accidents in which people were quite badly hurt and that is why the instructors were wary of this phase. Before you were able to instruct on this phase you had to do a two-week progressive driving course with the

South Wales Constabulary. The usual instructor was a big Welshman called Mick who had a terrific sense of humour as well as being a bloody good instructor. The car we used for this was a Colt Gallant Turbo and it went like shit off a shovel.

The first week was spent with us driving, and Mick pointing us in the right direction. If we weren't doing it right he'd correct us and also give tips on how to position the vehicle correctly on the road. I enjoyed this part, especially having already done the Police Advanced Driving Course in Preston. During the second week we would act as the instructors and Mick would drive. Whatever you told him to do he would because that was what the students would do.

If you said, 'Take the next right,' he would. It didn't matter if it was into someone's drive or on to a dirt track, you had told him to take the next right and he had done. If you had meant take the next A class road you should have said so.

If you said, 'I want you to stop the car,' he would jam the anchors on and throw everyone forward. What you should have said was, 'I want you to bring the car to a controlled stop.'

It might sound petty but to be honest, with some of the students you had to be very accurate.

The cars we used for the course were ordinary cars without dual controls. So although the student was driving, you were watching the road and in your mind you were driving for him. You would be reading the road and talking him through it. Some of them actually got to the stage where they used to rely on you to think for them during the first stages and if you let your mind wander for a second you could end up in the shit. For example, if the road was clear you would tell them to get their speed up so they might be doing 80–90 mph. They would continue to do this unless you told them otherwise, although you might think they could think it out for themselves that they wouldn't make a bend that was coming up at that speed. It might start off as you saying in a quiet voice, 'OK, brakes on a bit, slow down.'

Nothing! Next would be a slightly raised voice with a tinge of anxiety coming in; 'OK, brakes on, slow down now.'

This would usually be accompanied by a glance across at the student who might by now have white knuckles from gripping the wheel, a kamikaze stare and this maniacal grin on his face. After that it would be a case of, 'FUCKING BRAKE NOW YOU TWAT!'

It made me laugh when I sometimes thought of what could have happened (usually in the bar that night with a few stiff drinks) but it was no joke at the time.

After my tour as an instructor I returned to 28 Section. While I was at Ponty I had married for the third time. This was to the girl from college who used to pinch my arms black and blue but I loved her to death. She had a son from her first marriage and by now we had two beautiful little boys of our own. I was fortunate enough to be given time off during these periods and had the privilege of being there when the two of them were born. They were two of the most memorable times in my life. You can do all sorts of things in your life that you might think are good or important but nothing stays with you more than being there to see your own children being born and having them put into your arms. I remember watching a film years ago about the young children of the Czar who were killed in the Russian Revolution; one of the bodyguards in it turned around and said, 'I should have been there.'

That's my attitude with my kids. I worry because if anything happened, it's the thought that, 'I should have been there.'

During this period my dad died, ten days before he would have seen his first grandson born. I will never forget that time because for me it was a time of immense sadness and immense pride. There was the immense sadness because of my dad and the immense pride because of my son. I cried like fuck and I'm not ashamed to admit it. We might have had our ups and downs, but at the end of the day he was still my dad and I loved him. We had him cremated because he didn't want to be buried. For a year after that I used to keep the urn with his ashes in my garden shed. It used to be a talking point, as I would take friends into the shed and say, 'I'd like you to meet my dad.' It might seem heartless but it would have appealed to his sense of humour.

Towards the end of my time at Ponty I was wondering where my dad should go. I had thoughts of scattering his ashes on the River Mersey, from a small boat, as he was born in Liverpool. I decided against that one, because when I had been in the RMR years before, I'd nearly been washed away to sea in a Gemini raiding craft, so I gave that one a miss. It also might not have gone down too well if I'd scattered them from a Mersey ferry. In the end I had a small ceremony on the training area at Ponty, just him and me. I'd asked my brother if he would mind this and he had thought it was a good idea. I said stupid things like those a son would have said to his father and things I should have said before. I then took his ashes and scattered them on the high ground where I thought an old soldier should be buried: on military ground with honour. He might not have made Special Forces like his younger son but I think he was proud of me, although I don't really think he knew what I did for a living. I think that at last, I'd laid a ghost to rest from all those years ago. I loved him and gave him a bloody good send off. He had spent thirty-one years in the Army in the Lancashire Fusiliers, the Royal Artillery (including being a gunner on the Icelandic convoys) and finally the Pay Corps. He had also been a heavyweight boxing champion in the Army, but couldn't turn professional, as he had wanted to, because he broke his hand.

At the time the Int Corps had the remit for all surveillance operations conducted by the Army throughout the world except for NI where they were controlled by the SAS. However, as there weren't many other surveillance operations in the world I believe the SAS wanted to bring all covert operations under their wing. While I was at Ponty there was a dispute between what I wanted to do for my next posting after the Group and what the Int Corps wanted me to do. I wanted to go back to 28 Section in Germany and the Int Corps wanted me to go off and do some naff posting that I can't even remember. I went and saw the CO at the time who was a Lt Col in the SAS and told him my problem.

He got on the phone there and then and spoke to someone in Ashford and his words at the end were, 'We have bigger guns to bear,' and obviously they did!

6

OTHER TASKS

My first tour with 14 Coy was close to finishing in December 1982 and I was asked where I wanted to go to next as everyone had to return to their unit for at least one year before another tour with the Det. You were normally guaranteed your choice of posting and I asked for and actually got Hong Kong – marvellous! My wife at the time, however, didn't want to go so I very reluctantly said I didn't want to go. Somebody else somewhere must have thought that all his or her birthdays had come at once. I then asked for and was sent to the North-Western Security Section in Preston. My wife's parents lived in Blackburn and Preston was within easy commuting distance. Because of that we also bought a small cottage just outside Blackburn in a place called Dandy Row in Darwen. It was only a small two up, two down but it was my first house and I was chuffed to fuck with it.

DIY never came naturally to me, as I found out years later in another house, but this was one of those places where I had to do it because money was a bit tight. Take plastering for example: I had never done it before but I'd seen it done on TV and it was amazing how well it worked out. It had no central heating so we survived on a gas fire downstairs and a calor gas heater upstairs. In the winter, thick ice on the inside of the windows wasn't uncommon but you got used to it. Say to someone now, 'If you're cold, go and put a jumper on,' and they'll look at you as if you've just arrived from the planet Zanussi because that's what central heating is for. I know that a jumper will keep you warmer but now it's, 'Let's just whack the central heating up a few degrees and I'll stay cold for the next hour or so until it kicks in and heats the house up.'

Out of eighteen years in the Int Corps this was the one and only 'real' Int Corps job I did. It really consisted of everything I described we did during Corps training except that this time you were doing it for real. I'd bought a golden Labrador pup, Ben, by this time who was an absolutely smashing dog and I really loved having him with me.

When we bought the cottage it had a lean-to at the back and one time I decided to take it down but with it being made of a lot of glass I had to be really careful where I trod when I got to the top. The back bedroom had a really big window so you could see right into the house. Now can you picture this? I'm on top of this bloody lean-to trying not to go through the glass and Ben sees me from the landing. With him being a playful dog and full of fun, I saw his little face turn into a big doggy grin and his tail start to wag. He hadn't got a clue what he was about to do but I did, because I could just imagine his thought process: There's Dad, I'll go and say hello.

Our eyes met and at that point I was doomed because I knew exactly what was going to happen. He started running with his big grin. All this time I'm on the lean-to, thinking, Fuck me, no.

He charged through the back bedroom like a good-natured demon possessed, still with the grin, and came straight through the fucking window into my arms. By good luck we managed not to go through the glass of the lean-to but I said a few choice words to him afterwards, I can assure you of that. That was also my one and only attempt at glass replacement.

It was very difficult to come down to a normal job after the excitement of 14 Coy but I was lucky as the Int Corps took the fact that you had done it as a bonus and at that time I suffered no ill effects as far as promotion was concerned. I have known other blokes to go back to their units and be treated like shit. There was one particular Royal Marine who was the Operations Officer during my first tour and basically the 2ic (second-in-command) of the Det (even though he had no rank, being just a basic Marine, but he was the best man for the job). He went back to his unit and was stuck on main gate sentry the next day. Many people thought, OK, you've had two years swanning around being a cowboy, now I'll bring you back down to earth. These arseholes couldn't have been more wrong. The guys who volunteered for and served with the operational unit were intelligent people, otherwise they wouldn't have been there. What they did was, by their own choice; take themselves out of the Army/Royal Marine/Royal Navy/Royal Air Force system to do a job that needed doing basically because most of the other lazy bastards couldn't be bothered getting off their fat arses and having a go themselves. Some of the animosity came from people who had tried the course and failed for one reason or another but for others it just seemed like their mission in life to be a twat.

I remember I did a short tour with the Recruiting and Liaison Team when they went to Germany while I was instructing at Ponty, because I could speak German. At one particular presentation, some fairly senior officers were present as this was geared towards a large headquarters. Before the presentation I was told to give direct answers to direct questions and I did: big mistake on behalf of the Rupert in charge. I was asked a number of trivial but well-meant questions. Then this Colonel asked a question and I couldn't tell if he was being sarcastic or was serious but I thought his attitude was more sarcastic. I noticed he was wearing parachute wings, which meant he must have been around a bit.

'Sgt Major, could you please tell us why so many soldiers who have served with your organisation volunteer for subsequent tours or just leave the Army?'

'Yes sir, I can. You have some of the highest quality people in the Army coming back to your units and you are just wasting their talents. These people have given up two years of their lives and instead of treating them like cowboys, you should give them the education and promotion courses they need to enable them to get back on a par with their colleagues. They have planned and carried out – and in every case commanded – highly detailed and sensitive operations and then they are put on a back burner – and you wonder why they want to do subsequent tours. If you gave them the opportunity, sir, you might actually keep them.'

I don't think I was asked any more questions after that.

After the presentation the Rupert in charge of the team came up to me and said, 'I know I said give direct answers but take it easy, eh!'

Crap; those people needed to be told the truth.

There are two passages that, I think, sum up the attitude of 14 Company. The first is a passage from St Luke's Gospel which appears at the front of this book and the second is a framed text headed by the Argus bird (the bird with a hundred eyes). To me this typified the attitude and dedication of the people in the Company. It is:

It is not the critic who counts / Nor the man who points out how the strong man stumbles or where the doer of deeds could have done better. The credit belongs to the man who is actually in the arena; whose face is marred by dust and sweat and blood; / Who knows great enthusiasm, great devotion and the triumph of achievement. / And who, at the worst, if he fails at least fails whilst daring greatly – so that his place shall never be with those odd and timid souls who know neither victory nor defeat.

You've never lived until you've almost died.
For those who have had to fight for it
Life has truly a flavour
The protected shall never know.

Anyway, back to Preston. I'd been there for a few weeks and I got back to the office one day and I just sat on the desk and thought, what the fuck am I doing here? At that time I couldn't see the point in going to some of these places and, in effect, rattling padlocks. I had reached a point where it was sink or swim, make the most of it or pack it in. I also nearly made a big mistake because the Rupert in charge at the time was a young Captain and I went in to have a moan.

I think that remembering where I had just come from, and being so pissed off, I just turned around and said, 'I'm bloody well fed up of being told how to do my job by young officers who've got fuck-all experience.'

We looked at each other for a moment and I think we both realised what I had said because he cocked his head and asked, 'Well, just how young do you mean, Corporal A.'

I did a quick double take, as you do, and realised that he had been in the Parachute Regiment before he transferred to the Int Corps and therefore was not exactly green and just said, 'Look sir, there was no offence intended but even you can see some of these people are incompetent.'

He took a moment to think then said, 'Yes Corporal A, I know exactly what you mean. No offence taken.'

'Thank you, sir.'

I had a lot of respect for him (for a Rupert) after that and we got on really great from then on.

When Ben was old enough I brought him into the office during the day because my wife worked. He was definitely one of the things that kept me going. After that I decided to plan my schedule so that I had at least two or possibly three days out of the office each week. I think some people must have wondered why I kept making appointments to visit them – well, now they know. Our area took up the whole of the north-west, so it was fairly easy to organise a day out, because there were always people that needed interviewing or units that needed inspecting or surveying and follow-up surveys. In the whole of that area we actually only had two regular units to take care of and the rest were TA units, University Officer Training Corps and Cadet Units. It was basically anyone with an Army connection who held documents with a confidential caveat or higher or held weapons. It could be a Cadet Unit that held two obsolete .303 rifles but if they could still be fired they had to be inspected to ensure they were stored correctly. Part of the frustration of this particular job was that you could carry out the survey, make all the recommendations to bring them up to scratch and then go back the following year to carry out the follow-up survey and find nothing had changed. When you asked why, the stock answer was always lack of money. So Ben and I used to get in the car and troll off to visit these units. Because we covered such a large area we visited such places as the Lakes and other places in Cumbria. Apart from being nice to get out, it used to give Ben a good run. He got quite used to going out and about and a lot of the people looked forward to seeing him. Unfortunately, when my second wife and I split up she kept him because I couldn't. When we did split up though, I took Ben out for a last run and then drove off. It was fucking heartbreaking considering all the times we'd had.

During my time in Preston I went and did a parachute refresher because I was supposed to go on an airborne exercise with 5 Airborne Brigade, but this didn't materialise. This course took place at RAF Brize Norton and some of the sights I saw there floored me. I went into one of the junior ranks' dances one night and nothing would have persuaded me this was a forces base. Apparently, at that time in the RAF, as long as no one could see what you had under your cap, beret, hard hat or whatever, you could have what hairstyle you liked. Some of these young lads had their heads shaved either side so it came to a point at the back, some had patterns cut into their hair and the girls were just as bad. Call me old-fashioned or a traditionalist but what a bunch of wankers!

Towards the end of my first year in Preston I was informed that I was being sent to the Falkland Islands as this was part of 9 Intelligence Company's commitment to the manning there. I set off in October 1983, with some trepidation and having to leave a fairly newly married wife, and flew down to Ascension Island from RAF Brize Norton. I only spent a short time on Ascension but it wasn't a place that I would have liked to be based. From there we caught the *MV Keren* (formerly the MV Norland), a converted ferry down to the Islands. I'd heard quite a bit about the place from some of the guys in 40 Commando who had served down there, so I knew it was a bit bleak. I had a look at the place where the guys were accommodated – it was shot to pieces. I was surprised at the lack of casualties which I think goes to show the professionalism of the Royal Marines. When I first arrived, the Int Section lived in a house in Port Stanley itself and we were entirely self-contained. We were given rations but it was up to us to cook them which worked out quite well.

At this time all the main headquarter elements were based in Port Stanley in a small building that I believe was an old school and this was known as Headquarters British Forces Falkland Islands (BFFI). I have always had a dislike of main headquarters because they are usually full of bosses each trying to outdo the other to get themselves noticed to gain brownie points. This place was no exception because although the General lived in the former Governor's house, he had an office not far from ours. When he came to the Ops Room he would pass through our office. This meant that everything had to be tidy all the time so we were always cleaning the fucking place just in case he walked through.

The General at the time was a guy called Spacey and he was OK actually; well mannered and pleasant to us minions compared to the arrogance of some of the other bastards. When I was on the parachute refresher a couple of months before, I received a phone call that gobsmacked me. My Company Commander on the other end of the line said that he wanted to be the first to congratulate me because I had been awarded a Mention in Despatches (MID), a minor Gallantry award, for my service with 14 Coy. It was General Spacey who presented it to me while I was down there. I also didn't do too badly with the cleaning side of things, because he used to pass through the main office where the clerks were. The Intelligence side of things was in an inner sanctum, accessed by a simplex lock to which only a select few had the combination.

In this office was the J3 staff (Army Captain level Intelligence officers), who were responsible for plotting enemy shipping/troop/air movements. In a normal Army headquarters the designation would be G3 but because this was a joint HQ it was J3. Every morning, the J3 staff produced a briefing for the senior officers about the events of the previous twenty-four hours. From information they had been given and plotted on their various maps/charts they would then make out slips of paper commonly known as 'babies' (God knows why) which they would then pass to me to enter into the computer to build up a database and the big picture. This is probably where my dislike of computers arose. I can use them now because they are an essential part of working life but I am by no means fully conversant with them. If I am doing anything really complicated at home I get my kids to show me. They think it's great!

This is where I also found out that with the security classifications attached to documents and information that 'Top Secret' is not in fact the highest classification. With my vetting I was allowed unrestricted access to Top Secret material but when I was attached to the Int Cell in BFFI, I had to be vetted to a higher level. It was not so much that the actual information was any different; it was the source which the information came from. You would therefore have a separate caveat, or codeword, for the Top Secret information. It might be given the caveat Top Secret 'Bambi' (made up). The codeword itself would also be Top Secret so a higher vetting was necessary simply to be allowed to see that codeword and handle the information. That's enough said on that because, as I have said, it is not my intention to give away secrets.

The headshed (what we called the people who made the decisions – i.e., the Ruperts) in the office usually tried to let people have some time off each week and it would usually be a Saturday afternoon, not that there was much to do if you had time off. We would finish work on Saturday lunchtime and this was celebrated with an office 'cheese and wine' party. These actually got a bit of a reputation in BFFI and some of the officers from other departments used to angle for invitations, but we were very selective. As the Int Corporal at the time it would be my job to organise and present the cheese. Now we're not talking restaurant cheese board standard here; far from it. Sometimes it might be possible to get some cheese from the galley (cookhouse) but these times were few and far between.

In the Forces then you got a small tin of processed cheese in rat (ration) packs (affectionately known as 'cheese possessed') and that was the main constituent of our cheese part of the cheese and wine. The wine was real enough, from the Islands stores. So, towards the end of the morning I would throw a white sheet over one of the tables and arrange everything for that lunchtime. It is amazing how many ways you can actually present 'cheese possessed' if you really put your mind to it.

Talking about rat packs, the worst thing the Forces ever did was to take out the tube of condensed milk that everyone loved. This was only a small tube but it was a damned sight better than packets of dried milk substitute. Not only did it taste nicer but if you needed a quick energy burst you could just empty the whole thing down your neck and it certainly did the trick. I'm really into healthy eating but removing those tubes was a big mistake, as I think most blokes of my era would agree.

Part of the Int cell's task was to visit the outlying areas where troops were based to give a 'Roadshow', which was basically an Int presentation to new arrivals and also to update people who had been there a while. Normally when the ship arrived we would go on and do the presentation as they arrived but there were always those who slipped through the net. It was good to get out and about and to see some of the places you had only heard about on the news. One place I found particularly poignant was Goose Green, where a memorial had been erected. I always get a bit emotional about things like this, including Remembrance Day, so I took a few moments to pay my respects and saluted before I walked away.

As part of the Roadshow we had quite a few captured Argentinean weapons and it was my job to cart these around and let people handle them and to try to explain the characteristics of the weapons as best as I could. Having taught weapons recognition at Camp One as an instructor, I became quite proficient at this. There was some kit there I would have loved to have brought home but if I had been caught, I would have been in the shit.

I have mentioned about time off and not having much to do but on one occasion a few of us did make the effort and arranged a short trip. Towards where the new airfield was being built, we'd seen a lake on the map that wasn't too far from where the road ended, so we thought we'd go there. We got all the kit ready, including fishing rods, and set off Saturday lunchtime and were due to be picked up on Sunday afternoon as this was our R&R (rest and recreation) for the tour. We got into the back of the Mercedes truck, courtesy of General Galtieri, and drove as far as we could along the road before we were dropped off and started to yomp towards the lake. We took our time because there was no real hurry. We each carried a Bergen but mine was definitely a lot heavier than the others were. The reason? I was carrying the wine and beer for the evening's entertainment! At least it meant it would be lighter on the way back (but I would still be carrying all the empties). We reached the lake and set up our one-man bivvy bags, which were excellent pieces of kit. We then went fishing and caught some grey mullet for our tea. Those and the beer and wine made the whole thing a very pleasant evening. It might only have been twenty-four hours but it made all the difference. I might not have been too chuffed if I'd known that there were bloody minefields in the area that no one had informed me about!

I spent Christmas and New Year on the Islands and by this time we were in the Portacabins in Lookout Camp. They weren't too bad except that because I was the only Int Corps junior rank, I was put in a cabin with all the other odds and sods. However, this had its advantages at Christmas. It was a tradition in the Army for the officers to bring 'Gunfire' to the troops in bed on Christmas day if you weren't on leave. 'Gunfire' is hot tea liberally laced with rum. This meant that with all the odds and sods in one cabin we were visited by about four or five different officers that morning, all bearing Gunfire for their soldiers. Once they had dispensed it to their guy it was a case of, 'I suppose you'd like some as well, Corporal?'

'You're too kind sir; but yes, if you insist.'

We were half pissed by the time we got out of bed. The Argies could have come over in a couple of rowing boats that day and taken the Islands back.

I keep saying throughout the book that it is a small world and, in fact, one of the other odds and sods in the cabin went off and became a pilot in the Army Air Corps and was one of the pilots flying for the Det when I went back for my second tour with the Group.

Other forms of relaxation were sparse. When we lived in the house we had a small bar and when we moved to the new camp at Lookout Point there was a NAAFI bar. I quite often used to go to the pubs in Stanley and actually got used to Penguin ale. I also got to know some of the islanders quite well. There was one couple I got to know there who would perhaps say that they would be out for the day but that there would be Sunday lunch in the oven and that I should go and help myself. The main meat there was lamb, for the obvious reasons, and they would leave a note in a box outside as to what they wanted and it would be delivered to the door – all free.

I got to know the Naval Provost Team (Naval police) quite well while I was there and they had a very nice bar that I was invited to quite regularly. Within the Navy you have different ratings such as seaman, radio operator, etc. The Naval policemen are known as Regulators or more commonly as 'Crushers'. There was one guy there I got on well with and that name fitted him to a tee. He was about my height but he was built like a brick shithouse and had his head shaved. He was a fucking fearsome sight and someone I would not have liked to meet in a dark alley without my friend Mr Browning, but a nicer bloke you couldn't have met. When in their bar, after quite a few beers, we nearly always ended up playing the same stupid game. We would give each other a line from a song or a movie and you had to guess what it was. As I said before, it's amazing the daft things grown men come up with to amuse themselves when they have to.

I will just mention one more group of people I came across when I was down there and they were the Submariners. I actually spent a day on board one of their diesel-powered boats (you don't call them ships). I was airlifted to it and winched down from the chopper and was given a guided tour starting with the sail and then into the control room and all the workings of the boat. We then submerged and spent a few hours underwater before surfacing and I was winched back up to safety. Amenities on board are basic to say the least. Unless I am wrong – and if so I apologise – there was only one toilet on board and showering facilities were limited. The only person on board who had any privacy and his own cabin was the Captain. The rest of the guys were limited to pulling a curtain across their bunk. The officers lived together, as did the crew.

If you consider a good-sized living room then this was where approximately twenty men ate, slept, watched videos and did any other form of recreation they had. This would go on for weeks at a time. It was a bit disconcerting when we submerged to hear all the creaks, and every now and again there would be the sound of air escaping and one of them would dash off and turn a valve. With it being a diesel boat they were very quiet and this had the advantage of being able to stealthily approach Argentinean ports such as Ushuaia, observe enemy shipping and aircraft and report their movements. The food on board was good and the blokes were sound but I can now understand why they go fucking bananas after a trip. I was glad after about six hours to get off it and back to fresh air. I think perhaps because of the stress of this existence the guys, as I said, go a bit wild after a trip – but not in a nasty way. They just want to go and enjoy themselves and forget the shit they've had to put up with for so long and this goes for the whole of the Armed Services and some of the civilian services.

People who have never been in situations such as this will never understand the need to unwind and just let your emotions out. Try to bottle them up and you'll end up as nutty as the proverbial fruitcake. We did, however, have one boat come in and unfortunately one of the guys went and got himself absolutely shitfaced, fell off the jetty and drowned.

During my second tour with the Group we actually had a Submariner in North Det. I wouldn't think of myself as particularly claustrophobic but I don't think I would be able to take that for weeks – or in the case of nuclear boats, months – at a time. I take my hat off to you guys.

We also went on one of the battlefield tours and had some sites of the confrontations pointed out. I, personally, found these interesting having been in the Booties and considering some of the distances that had to be yomped – or tabbed, depending who you were – across before any fighting took place.

For the Booties and the Paras, fitness and mental attitude obviously paid off. Perhaps if other units had made the same preparations some of the disasters wouldn't have happened but ceremonial duties obviously come first. I explained to my brother once that having joined the Royal Marines I expected to have to fight and felt a bit disappointed when I didn't. My war had always been the silent war and I just wondered what it would have been like to have been in a full-scale firefight and to have been involved in hand to hand combat. Part of me thanks God that it never happened but the other part, having been a combat soldier, always wonders just what if? But then again, the war I was involved in was just as important as any face-to-face conflict. At the end of my time there we boarded a C130 which, thankfully, flew us all the way back to Brize Norton. The only thing was it was so packed that once seated you couldn't move. Twelve hours without even a piss; not that it mattered one little bit.

While I was at Preston I also went and did the course for 28 Intelligence Section (28, or the Sect), the army's surveillance asset in Germany. I passed that and waited for my posting in January 1985. The actual surveillance techniques used were almost the same as in the Det except that at this time you were training to go up against the Soviet Military Mission in Germany.

There were a few slight differences, mainly because they would carry out overt anti-surveillance drills to try to catch you out and put you off. For example, you would read well ahead on the map, always trying to leave yourself a way out if they suddenly threw up and came back towards you. When they did that they would flash their lights at every car they passed as part of their overt anti-surveillance drills. Had they seen you or not? You could never be too sure. All of this was practised as well as normal surveillance techniques pertaining to the Section in Germany.

One of the main exercises was carried out in Brighton and because we would be going up against different targets with a relatively small team we had to have enough jackets etc. for a number of changes of appearance. The main difference between surveillance in the Det and the Section was that across the water you might do a two-hour serial and then bin it or change teams, and also you were working in a hostile environment. In Germany you might have the same team up against the same target for ten to twelve hours per day for maybe ten days at a time. The exposure to that target was high and changes had to be rung throughout the team constantly. With this in mind one of the first things we did on arriving in Brighton was to raid all the Oxfam and Age Concern shops. For about ten pounds you could get your changes of appearance for a week.

We also had to find ourselves accommodation and that proved to be really difficult, because it was the time of the Tory party conference. Normally we would all try to get into the same hotel for ease of debriefs and logistics. This time, however, by the time we had all found accommodation we were strung out all over Brighton. I was the driver for the person who was acting as the surveillance controller (SC or Sierra Charlie) because I had been across the water and was considered to have the most experience. The Sierra Charlie is the person responsible for controlling the team and taking notes as well as doing the map reading in the car.

With everything going on, especially when things are happening quickly in a town, this can be a bit hectic, as I found out in Germany. This is the main reason why the Sierra Charlie never gets out the car unless absolutely necessary. The Sierra Charlie this time was a young female Rupert called Sal and because the car crew stayed together, once again I was sharing a hotel room with a female member of the course. I think if things hadn't been so tight on the accommodation front we would have had separate rooms. Sal was quite short and a bit plump and not that attractive but she had fucking enormous tits. I was informed by a reliable source at a later date that they were very firm as well but I didn't find out for myself. Brighton was quite a good place to do surveillance and when we weren't working the nightlife was good.

We were supposed to keep a low profile while we were there and not to attract attention to ourselves. This was fine until one night when we were out in the Lanes having a few drinks. Most of us had already made a move back to the hotels but we had a young Rupert called Dan with us who hung on for an extra pint. As he was on his way back there had been a bit of trouble and this young lad was running away from this bobby who had no chance of catching him. Dan did his good citizen bit and as this lad got level with him swung his elbow out into this guy's stomach – just by accident, you understand! The guy went down like a lead balloon and wasn't allowed to get back up again until the bobby had caught up. There was one other story that concerned Dan on the course and that was when we took a target to Gatwick airport. Our people went into the terminal after him but I was driving the Sierra Charlie, and we made for the top of one of the multi-storey car parks. By gaining height you were able to get better comms with the team on the ground. This applied to multi-storeys in shopping centres. I've spent many an hour in a multi-storey car park in Düsseldorf, Germany while the team was swanning around the *Altstadt* (old town). Anyway, Dan was one of the ones in the terminal and I was doing the radio as Sal was trying to write everything down. I was desperately trying to raise the team on the ground, because Sal was doing the notes, but wasn't getting anything.

I had tried Dan for ages and I was getting a bit threaders (threadbare – hacked off or annoyed) by this time so I thought I'd get a bit sarcastic and came up with the call, 'Earth calling Dan, Earth calling Dan.'

'Yes, go ahead,' he answered straight away.

I've always thought some of these Ruperts were from outer space. Just after the exercise finished and we left, the Grand Hotel was blown up and I did wonder at the time if some suspicion might have fallen on us from some of the hotel owners as we kept strange hours and probably seemed a bit strange ourselves.

After Preston I went to Germany to start a tour with 28 Section and on my first tour our only role was to impose surveillance on the Soviet Military Mission (SOXMIS). Due to the agreement after the Second World War and the division of Berlin amongst the allies and the Soviet Union, each country was allowed to keep a mission to conduct tours in the opposition's field of interest. This meant that the British were allowed to have access to the Soviet side (East Germany) and vice versa. The Soviets (Sovs) were called SOXMIS and the British equivalent was called BRIXMIS, but this wasn't our role. Therefore the Sovs maintained a compound in a place called Bünde.

Bünde is situated in Nord Rhine Westphalia, fairly close to a town called Herford where 28 were based. Our task was to impose selected surveillance on the vehicles and occupants when they left the compound and wherever they travelled all over the British sector in Germany.

To this end we mounted a twenty-four-hour telephone watch and were informed by the watchman at the Bünde control post whenever one of the tour cars went out. This could be a bit hit and miss, as you would get a phone call from the guard post to the effect of 'Wache Bünde' (guard post, Bünde).

At that time you could tell that he was pissed. He would then tell you what car and occupants (he thought) had gone out. The common theory was that he used to place some sticks in the road and when he looked, if they were broken, he knew a car had gone out. No use if you are on five minutes' reaction time. During the day this was reinforced by another source that used to ring in on a special phone provided for him, and his information was a lot more accurate. When you answered this phone you always answered in German and to this day – and I'll bet it applies to others who were there – I can remember the phone number in German but I have to think twice for what it is in English.

Because it was not known what radio equipment they had in the compound in Bünde it was decided that we would not sit around that general area and not transmit when in the Bünde area. Even if we had control of the target and were transiting the *autobahn* that ran near the compound it was radio silence. The common practice was for S3 (a department in our HQ in Rheindahlen responsible for collating information and tasking) to predict a tour and then we would deploy to an area where we would hope to pick them up. Different areas in Britain have number plates attributable to that area, so that you are able to see if a vehicle doesn't really belong in another area. Because the tour might cover a large part of the British sector the same number plate would stand out in another area. The same goes for Germany except that it is much easier to identify a car out of its own area because the first letters of the VRN might be the first two letters of the town. For example, Herford would be HF and Bielefeld would be BI and so on. We had the ability to change number plates quickly by adapting the housing to where the number plate was fitted. Therefore by unscrewing the old plate it could be quickly replaced by another set of plates. We had hundreds of sets of plates covering most of the areas in the British sector, so prior to the deployment you would select a number of sets of plates. All of these plates were legal and we had the necessary paperwork to support them so if stopped by the police we were perfectly legal.

In Germany there are different areas called *Lands* that are much the same as counties in England. The only difference was that although there was a federal government the *Land* also governed itself and controlled its own police in that area. Because of the nature of the operations we carried out it was sometimes necessary to 'bend' the law slightly, mainly by speeding and other road violations. We therefore carried our own paperwork issued by the government in each *Land* that we would show the police if stopped. It was not a get out of jail free card as such but it was enough to show the *Polizei* that we had the backing of the government in that *Land*. It was great when you were stopped to ask the *Polizei* in which *Land* you were. They would tell you, but you really knew already and were just doing it for effect. You would then produce your wallet and make a point of flicking through all the *Bescheinigung* (*scheins*, or papers of authority) and produce the *schein* for that region. It was petty really but we used to have a giggle when we got away with it. The times that I was approached the production of the *Bescheinigung* always worked.

There was a British Liaison Officer (BLO) who lived just outside the compound and his task was to provide liaison between the British military authorities and the Sovs. When a new member arrived in the compound they had to inform the BLO who would then provide the necessary authorities. His deputy was the ABLO (Assistant British Liaison Officer). It just so happened that the ABLO's house had an attic that overlooked the Sov compound and it became apparent that this provided an ideal location for an OP to photograph what was going on in the compound. This OP, nicknamed George, was frequently manned in order to gain good up-to-date photography of new arrivals and to update our records. If it were necessary to go in we would phone the ABLO and say that we would like to visit George on a particular date for a number of days. We would then arrive after dark and occupy the OP. Mrs ABLO must have known what was going on but didn't say a word. Video footage was invaluable because it showed their mannerisms and the way they walked. It would also show any modifications they were making to their tour cars. Their main tour cars were Opel Rekords that had curtains in the back windows so that you could not see in but there was usually a gap in the back that they could look out of to try to see if they were under surveillance. This was similar to one of the PIRA targets in Belfast years back. His method of anti-surveillance was to have his wife in the back seat looking out of the back window. He would then drive to the roundabout nearest to his house, go around it twice and then go on his route.

After a couple of times the Belfast Det got wise to this and just used to let him run and then picked him up as he left the roundabout. As far as he was concerned he had done his anti-surveillance drills and so his arse was clear – little did he know.

Although outwardly their cars appeared normal they were easily picked out as they had a large yellow plate on the rear where the registration plate should have been. This had the Soviet flag and the number of the tour car. This made surveillance a lot easier, because we could stay a couple of hundred metres behind them on the *autobahn* with a lot of other cars in between, making it very difficult for them to pick out the surveillance car. When we knew that an exit was coming up, we used to close up on the target, so that if he decided to leave the *autobahn*, we were close enough to maintain control. We also used stabilised binoculars to keep the target in sight. Normal binoculars used to shake too much, but these were mounted on a gyroscope, which made it much simpler to keep the target in sight. They had been developed from a type normally used in choppers. The only trouble with them was that if you looked through them too much the movement of the car and the movement of the gyroscope made you want to throw up (the correct connotation this time).

Everyone in the Army in Germany was issued with a card that had the number of the SOXMIS sightings desk. This desk was manned twenty-four hours a day and in theory anyone who saw one of these tour cars was supposed to phone the desk and give the location of the sighting, the direction of travel, any interest being shown to military convoys and the number of occupants. What the vast majority of people probably didn't realise that the SOXMIS sightings desk was run by 28 because when answering the phone you would use a cover name you had given yourself to protect your identity and also the identity of the sightings desk. The reason for the number of occupants will become apparent later. We would receive these sightings and the following morning we would send these by secure telex to our HQ in Rheindhalen, which was also British Army HQ.

During my first tour, the method of sending these telexes was antiquated. We had a box that went into the code machine and inside this box were ten wires that you plugged into sockets. There was a one-time code pad for that day telling you where to slot each wire. The box was probably no bigger than about four matchboxes and to relate where these wires would go to what was on the code pad sometimes got a bit confusing; manual dexterity played a big part. When you consider that the guy in S3 also had to make a match with your box, it was understandable that there were mistakes. You'd go through this bloody process and send the telex and the next morning you'd get a phone call with that well-known cry, 'Let's check our boxes.'

Oh fuck me, not again. The message at the other end would

have been garbled because someone hadn't put his wires in the right place.

We also had a really efficient self-destruct mechanism for the code machine in case we were 'overrun' by the Sovs. There was a fuck-off sledgehammer next to it, which we were ordered to use to beat the shit out of the machine to break the code. I think I'd have been more interested in getting the fuck out from there than worry about something they probably already had.

Anyway, back to the plot. S3 would then collate these sightings and add them to information they already had. By doing this they could build up a picture of tour practices. There were certain times of the year, during the exercise period, when tour patterns were predicted quite accurately. This enabled S3 to task us so that they could deploy the section in order to pick up the tour car and place it under surveillance.

In Germany at that time there were certain areas that the Sovs were not allowed to enter at any time called permanently restricted areas (PRAs). These would be areas of particular sensitivity to which access to them was felt not to be in the interests of the allies. Other areas called temporary restricted areas (TRAs) were put on during exercise periods when obviously the allies did not want the Sovs snooping around. Part of the reason for surveillance was to try to identify any acts of espionage on their part and also to see if they violated any of these areas. If they did, although we would have it on record we could not really challenge them about it because that would reveal that they had been under surveillance. Just to have it on record was good enough.

There was one particularly large military area where there was a lot of armour called Fallingbostel which they used to pay particular interest in. This was a PRA and the limit to the PRA was just off the *autobahn* so an operation was mounted to try to photograph them violating the PRA. This area was great for surveillance because we knew the bastards would try to fuck us about. They would go past the Fallingbostel turn-off and come off at the next one. Then they would either rejoin and go back south or go for a couple of hundred metres down the road, U-turn and rejoin. They might do this a couple of times until they thought they had lost their surveillance. After a while we got around this problem.

As soon as we reached this section of the *autobahn* we would send a car ahead to cover the next junction and leave a car at the Fallingbostel turn-off so that when they went up and down there was no need to have anyone behind them. This worked fine until the bastards decided to go straight to Hamburg, which meant that the team was strung out all over the place. This was where the good driving skills came in. As I said about PIRA though, it would have been great to sit down with these guys, have a beer and discuss our tradecraft. I can just imagine Ivan saying, 'Da, I saw you on the docks at Hamburg but I just thought hee-hee, there is the stupid English spy again.'

I'd be sitting there thinking, Bastard! He'd seen me because I'd made a mistake. However, the other part of me would be thinking, Yeah, but you didn't see me in the woods did you ya bastard?

Anyway, a place was found where a town sign for Fallingbostel marked the limit to the PRA so that if they crossed this sign they had violated. Another guy and me were given this task and I was the one to go into the OP and try to get the photographs. We deployed numerous times to try to achieve this but either the car wouldn't turn up or it would stop short and rejoin the *autobahn*, which led to a lot of frustration. They say patience pays off and one day they actually did violate the PRA. I was there doing mental back flips and thinking, fucking great, because here I was watching these Sovs commit, in their terms, what would either have been in some cases a shootable offence or certainly one that would have got them deported – and I had it on camera! Bloody brilliant! Anyway, fuck-all came of it because as I explained, to say we'd seen them would have admitted liability and we couldn't be seen to do that, us being the good guys and all. I got the car and one of the tour officers getting out of the car and as far as we were concerned it was fucking priceless.

There was more than one occasion when the importance of the number of occupants in the car became apparent. We would perhaps get a report of a sighting near a PRA or TRA with, say, three occupants and the next might be with two occupants. In that case, where had the third one gone? Had he been dropped off to have a closer look at some of the formations in one of the prohibited areas or had he just ducked down on the back seat? The Sovs knew, however, that if they were caught 'spying' (as they would put it) on materiel or a location they would be detained until they were handed over to the ABLO – all very civilised! On the other hand, when on at least one occasion an American officer was caught engaged in similar activities, things were not quite so civilised. The bloke was near a Sov base in East Germany when he was seen and shot. At this point you may think that they had made their point and would at least give him first aid and call a doctor. He was left to bleed to death. No wonder people see the Western democracies as a soft touch. Can you imagine the outcry if a British soldier did that? The guy would be arrested and charged with murder because that is what civilised democracies do. Things may have changed now with the end of the Cold War but this was definitely the case before that.

When I joined 28 there were two further courses I had to attend and the first was a colloquial German course, for obvious reasons. Normally you would attend a basic German course to give you the background before you went on the more difficult colloquial course. I arrived at the section on the Friday and was told that there was a colloquial course starting on the Monday.

When I pointed out that I had never done German before I got the old, 'Don't worry, you'll be OK.'

'Yeah, OK. Thanks a bunch'. Now where had I heard those pearls of wisdom before? There was another guy called Mac who had been on the training course with me and he was on the German course as well although he'd done the same course a few years ago. He actually looks like Rowan Atkinson and if he reads this he will know who he is. He was (is) a great lad and I also used to work with his wife, who is a lovely lady. Because of the bad weather we didn't arrive until late Monday afternoon so we thought we'd go for a few beers and start the course on Tuesday. The trams back to the camp had finished by the time we had left the bars so we got a taxi back. In fact we got on a bloody tram that took us in completely the wrong direction and it was only when we reached the terminus that we realised we had fucked up. I put it down to him, as he was the German speaker. So we had to get a taxi back and I was cleverly nominated to pay for the taxi so as we pulled up at the camp gates, Mac said, 'Give him a DM20 note.'

I did so, and as I handed it across Mac said, 'Stimmt so, Mein Herr.'

'Danke sehr, Güten nacht,' answered the taxi driver.

As we were walking away I asked, 'Hey Mac, what does "Stimmt so" mean?'

'Keep the change, mate.'

Welcome to Germany, sucker!

On Tuesday we turned up at the classroom and took our seats, having apologised at the reception centre for being late. After a short time the instructor came in, rambled on in German, then looked at me and said, 'Yes.'

We looked at each other for a short time, him expectantly and me with this blank, startled rabbit look on my face.

In the end I said, 'I'm sorry, but I don't know what you're talking about. I've never done German before.'

It was his turn then to wear the blank startled rabbit look.

We commenced lessons going through the book with me trying to make up weeks of work in one day. We had a load of vocab to learn that night and I scored well the next day so it was decided to keep me on for a while to see how things went. I passed the course but there was only one way I did. I cheated again. Mac had, as I said, done the course before so he had his own book as we had to leave all of our textbooks in the classroom. I used to borrow his book and spent about five hours every evening revising that day's work and learning the next day's lesson. I actually used to dream in German and on more than one occasion each night I'd have to get up and look at the book about some bloody word or phrase I'd been dreaming about. Improvise, overcome, adapt.

Because we were required to drive at high speeds on the *autobahns* – as fast as the car would go in most cases and on my second tour that was 240 kph (150 mph) – we all had to attend the police advanced car-driving course at the Lancashire Police HQ at Preston. The reason for having to drive at such high speeds is a simple case of mathematics. If you have a Sov vehicle under surveillance and he is driving at 180 kph and the time comes for you to change plates or refuel you have to drop out of the chase.

You then have to find somewhere quiet so no one can see you change and then try to get back into it when the target could now be perhaps fifteen kilometres away travelling at the same speed.

Driving skills were therefore very important, especially when taking calculated risks such as driving on the hard shoulder. It got the adrenaline going when you were doing over 200 kph on the hard shoulder and a truck just gives his wheel a little spin and swerves over because he doesn't like what you are doing. The worst part for time was refuelling. On my first tour the cars were registered as British Forces Germany (BFG) vehicles and carried the distinctive black and white registration plate.

Before deploying on operations you changed to German plates but you carried fuel coupons to be used only on BFG cars. This meant that before you could refuel you had to change back to BFG plates, refuel and then change back to German plates. You got to know areas where there were places you could change plates, or 'scrub', but if it was unfamiliar territory it wasn't so easy and was a long old process. On my second tour we used German plates all the time (but still changed for operations). This way you could draw some money before you left the Sect and pay at the pumps, a much quicker method.

The driving course itself was four weeks long and was time well spent as I thought it was one of the best courses I had done in the Army. There were four Army people on the course and the rest were police officers who had to achieve a class one pass to progress on to the career they had chosen, traffic. Before they got to this stage they had done a basic and an intermediate driving course and were well versed with the police way of doing things. For example, on day one they had their normal parade after which we all got into the cars. Now part of their parade system was to keep the doors held open until the word of command and then to close them in unison. We just got in and slammed the things shut – nobody had told us. That went down like a fart in a sauna so we had to do it all again.

We arrived with a basic licence and after the first assessment in which I got ripped to shreds I realised I couldn't cheat on this one. We drove a variety of vehicles over a number of different roads and, once into the national speed limit areas, as fast as was safe. There were two sets of traffic signs that you got to know very well by their alternate names and the first one was the national speed limit sign or the diagonal black line on a white background. The national speed limit on ordinary roads was 70 mph but we came to know these as GLF signs. In other words, the 'go like fuck' sign!

Within normal speed limits you would observe the limit but once past the GLF sign there was no limit as far as we were concerned, provided what you were doing was safe. The other sign was the chevron sign at sharp bends (the black and white sign pointing in the direction of the bend). These came to be known as OFM signs or the 'oh fuck me' sign.

I'd actually been taught these phrases during my driving course on Camp Two during 14 Coy training. When I came out with these on the driving course the instructor didn't know what the initials stood for but after an explanation he had quite a laugh. The guy that taught me was a soft-spoken sergeant from Lancashire with a very dry sense of humour and I only had my hand slapped once when I ran an amber light at some road works. He was promoted to inspector after that course and sent to Skelmersdale. At the end of the day the policemen would mainly spend the evenings revising the Highway Code and the Roadcraft book (their Bible) as this was their career but after about half an hour, Mac and I would decide we'd had enough.

We got on well with the policemen and tried to get them out but none of them would except for an old Crime Squad guy who had had an accident and had to retake the course. His attitude was, 'If I don't get a class one pass so fucking what? I'm not traffic so what will they do, boot me off the fucking Crime Squad?'

He took us to a pub in Preston one night, near the prison, that was supposed to be really good.

'When we get there,' he said, 'just walk in with me and don't say anything.'

The reason for that was he just flashed his warrant card and we all walked in, with Mac and me trying to look casual, giving our Starsky and Hutch impressions. This place was one of the early theme pubs and the barmaids and barmen were all dressed in skimpy shorts and running shirts – great! After a while we noticed that the DJ was a raving poof and was giving everyone a bit of a hard time. If anyone tried to get lippy with him he just called one of the bouncers and these fucking gorillas would come over and have a chat with whoever it was. At one point I was standing there on my own because the other two had gone to get the beers in and I just caught the DJ saying, 'Ooh look at him over there on his own, isn't he a big boy.'

I was having a bit of a laugh because I thought someone else was getting the piss taken out of them but, after a while, I realised it was me he was talking about. I looked around for the other two for some moral support and saw them standing at the bar laughing like drains. When The DJ had decided to pick on someone else they came back and I asked, 'Why the fuck didn't you come back and give me some support?'

'You must be fucking joking,' Mac said. 'Did you think we'd want to be associated with you with him going on like that, dear?'

The DJ did play some good records though and the highlight was that every now and again when a particular record came on the bar staff would just jump on to the bar and start dancing. The women in their running kit were great and Mac and I just stood there, gobsmacked.

Just outside the HQ was a good pub with a cracking Indian restaurant next door so that's where we spent most of our evenings. The barmaids were gorgeous and so was some of the talent that used to get in there. Sometimes we weren't all that popular in the car the next day after ten pints of Guinness and a vindaloo! As usual, at the end of the course there were the usual exams and driving tests and I managed to get a class one pass, the same as the motorway police. Not bad from a load of shite on day one, eh! It actually pissed some of the policemen off that they had done all the courses, studied hard for four weeks and could only manage a class two while some of us, like me, would turn up having done nothing, spend four weeks on the piss and come away with a class one.

When I was on the course I was referred to at one point as King Farouk because I had long hair, a beard and because it was summer I had a cool pair of shades. I was behind the wheel of a Range Rover just outside Blackburn and was in a slow-moving line of traffic when we were overtaken by what turned out to be a rep.

The instructor just turned to me, pointed a finger and said, 'Catch him.'

Fucking great, I thought, here we go. It was two tones on, out of the line of traffic and the chase was on. It took him a little while to realise what was going on because the Range Rover behind him flashing its lights was all white with no police markings and there was a fucking hippie driving. He eventually stopped and the instructor got out, in uniform, and had a quiet word before letting him continue. I quite enjoyed that bit!

Although I was operational from when I had finished the German course I wasn't allowed to drive the Ops cars until I had completed the advanced driving course. Now, after a short time back in the navvie's (navigator's) seat I was able to get behind the wheel of some nice powerful cars. We had BMW 3 series, 5 series, an Opel Monza, a Mercedes, a Golf GTI and some other fairly powerful cars. We toured the whole of the British sector and to remember all the places we went to would be impossible, as I couldn't even do that at the end of the tour, never mind fifteen years later.

As usual with most squaddies, whatever background you come from, you work the system to the best of your advantage. At that time we were accommodated in hotels whenever we were deployed and when you are out the army give you money for hotels and living expenses called nightly rate of subsistence allowance (NRSA). Prior to that the Det used to move into woods and sleep in the cars for days on end. Not a very comfortable existence, so I was told.

The question asked was, 'Why do the Ruperts get more NRSA than the Toms [soldiers]?'

'Was it because their side of the car was more comfortable and they had *The Times* delivered while we only got *The Sun*?'

Anyway this could work out at up to DM200 or £50 per day and obviously there was some mileage to be gained out of this. We would find the seediest hotel and share maybe four or five to a room. As the charge was for the room we would split it and the rest was ours. A nice little earner while it lasted but all good things come to an end and the Army cottoned on to that one. Their counter was that they would pay for the hotel and we would get half NRSA. No problem, we thought. After that we booked into decent hotels with single rooms and after buying a cheap meal had enough for a couple of beers and could still make on the deal. It was a standing joke on both my tours in the Det that we could be in the middle of nowhere and I could still sniff out somewhere to eat as well as the cheapest restaurants in town.

Whenever we were deployed in a hotel we all carried bleepers to give us a warning of when a car had left the compound and might be starting a tour. This thing could go off any time of the day and night and depending on where you were depended on the time you had to get to your stake-out position. This could vary from anything from five minutes to one hour. We spent a couple of weeks deployed during one particularly hot summer and we were on a one-hour reaction time. The town we were in had an open-air swimming pool and we were not far from our stake-out locations. That meant we could be by the pool and had plenty of time to get dressed and make our stake-out when the bleeper went off – it was really good. When I was first deployed I used to lay awake half the night waiting for the fucking thing to go off; I spent nearly two years doing that. Since that time I have never been able to sleep properly and sometimes might only get a couple of hours a night before I am wide awake again. My doctor has actually told me that because of everything I have done in my life my sleep pattern is totally destroyed and it will probably never return to normal; having lived with this for thirty years I think I believe him. However, partly as a result of my first tour with 14 Coy, with me being away a lot with 28 and various other factors, my second wife and I split up in 1986 and subsequently divorced in 1988, fortunately without children. In fact, I drove her home to her mother's house and took Ben for his last run because he had been staying with her brother while we were in Germany. Although we had no children he was the nearest thing to a baby I had. It was this and the fact that I still loved my wife that I drove off and stopped the car somewhere quiet and just cried my eyes out. Big tough Special Forces soldier or what: bullshit. It broke my heart! Some things you just can't keep in.

Very often when we picked up a tour car first thing in the morning they would tour around for a couple of hours and then disappear for a while, usually in or near a forest. The normal practice was to stake the area out and then, hopefully, pick them up when they reappeared anything up to two hours later. It was not known what was happening in the wood because we did not go in after them.

One time I said to my partner, 'Why the fuck do we keep on sitting here waiting to see what happens when they could be in there doing anything? I'm going foxtrot to try to find out what's going on.'

I got my German parka on and went for a stroll in the woods keeping my eyes peeled for the car and anyone else out foxtrot. After a while I could hear that they still hadn't reappeared so kept walking. After about fifteen minutes I saw the car and they were all out standing around.

I was pretty sure that I hadn't been spotted and thought, Great, now we'll find out what you bastards are up to.

I skirted around them at a distance so that, even if spotted, I would either be walking away from or parallel with them until I could get to a position where I was out of sight. Once I was in dead ground I went to ground and cautiously made my way towards them then stopped short, in cover, so I could observe them without being seen. The biggest danger at this point was that if they were waiting for someone, that person might just walk up and see me lying there. There was no knowing what their reaction to that would be but with the Sov mentality I was likely to get the shit kicked out of me if I was found out. Mind you, at that stage I was running ten kilometres per day so they would have had to be fucking quick. I'd been watching them for about half an hour when they got back into the vehicle and drove off.

'Stand by, stand by. That's Pluto [all the Sov vehicles were given nicknames] now mobile south towards the main.'

I then continued to watch the area where they had been. Ideally, given the manpower, we would have mounted an OP to watch the area in case it had been a DLB (dead letter box). In other words, had they left something there for an agent to pick up or, indeed, had they picked up something an agent had left them? Because of lack of manpower and the fact that they were deemed priority the team went after them and I went over to where they had been to see what I could see. My partner in the car had by now driven down to the area and we had a look around and there it was.

After all this time we discovered why they went into forests early in the morning because we now had the evidence – eggshells and empty tuna cans; they had stopped for breakfast! We had a good search of the area anyway but found nothing and no marks that might have indicated that a DLB had been filled. We took photographs of the location and then got ourselves back into the chase.

Because it was a military mission they, and our people in their sector, were supposed to wear uniform. Quite often what used to happen is that they would drive up to Hamburg and go shopping in the tax-free shops. When they did this they would take off their uniform tunics and put leather jackets over their shirts so as not to attract attention to themselves. It is possible that there may have been something going on with the shopkeepers but that's doubtful. We all thought it was just a case of them getting Western products at good tax-free prices. Perks of the job! What we also did on one of these trips was to try the car to see if they had left it unlocked, which they hadn't. Whenever they were on tour the tour officer would always carry a briefcase and we wanted to see what was in it, especially if there was a weapon, as they weren't supposed to be armed. I also gave it a couple of good hard knocks with my shoulder to see if the alarm, if they had one, went off – it didn't. The person I don't think we positively identified was the political officer but we had a good idea who he was because he never went on the shopping trips.

One other incident demonstrates the German attitude to authority and that was when I'd lost my ID card and a couple more things I kept in a small wallet. I was stopped in the docks in Hamburg by the police and asked what I was doing there. I explained I was working and showed them the necessary paperwork and they went happily on their way. It was only about two hours later that I wanted something out of that wallet and I looked for it but couldn't find it; I went into panic mode. After a while I knew I'd lost it. Now the Germans have lost-property offices in the big towns and the people are told that if they find something they are to hand it in at the office. A couple of weeks later an envelope arrived at the Det from the lost property office in Hamburg, containing my wallet with everything intact. Some public-spirited citizen had found it and handed it in and the authorities had approached the British and it was traced back to me. Lucky or what?

As in the Det across the water when we weren't operational we would conduct Hare and Hounds. These would sometimes last just for the day but on other occasions we would deploy somewhere and stay in hotels and simulate taking a real target. We would all stay in the same hotel and in the morning we would stake the place out, pick the target up and place him/her under surveillance for the day before binning it and debriefing. One of the favourite places to go was Hamburg, for obvious reasons apart from working. Hamburg is served by a good motorway system so we would start from Herford and have a take-up to Hamburg with the target throwing in all sorts of funnies, especially around Fallingbostel, as the Sovs would if we had them under control. We also then had the option of working in a big city with all the fuck-up factors it had to offer. We would also cover the places where they went shopping so we knew the places to park and the best positions to cover from. Once the day's work was finished, Hamburg was also a great place to go out and socialise. Anyone who has never been to Hamburg should go at least once. There are some brilliant bars on the Reeperbahn and the atmosphere is great. After a night out in Hamburg it was nearly always the case that the surveillance the next morning was always on foot as hardly anyone would have been fit to drive.

There is also the other side of it with one place in particular called Davidstrasse. This is a street with a chicane at the start and finish, and it is where the whores sit in the windows and ply their trade. Some of them are gorgeous but some are real Chihuahuas. There was one particular place called the Eros centre and it was like an underground car park. The only difference was that it was well furnished and it was wall-to-wall fanny. There appeared to be hundreds of them in there and it was great to go in one end and do a run through, coming out of the other end with your eyes hanging out. This is the one thing I cannot understand about England. Everyone knows it goes on so why not put it all under one roof, control it, ensure the girls have regular medical check-ups and *tax* it all. It is, after all, the world's oldest profession so there is plenty of money to be made. They also say that soldiering is the world's second oldest profession. Perhaps there is a comparison to be drawn there somewhere! The girls are clean and safe and there is none of the stupid prudity that is endemic in England.

During my tour I was asked if I would like to go on what was called OP Sidecar back in England – or Southsea, to be more precise. This was a week where we were to act as a hostile surveillance team for the SIS (Secret Intelligence Service) or MI6, students undertaking their final exercise. It was supposed to be a good exercise although it involved a lot of work. There is a fort on the seafront near Southsea where the exercise was run from and we were booked into a hotel not too far away.

When we arrived we checked into the hotel and went to the fort for a briefing before the students arrived where we were told exactly what we were expected to produce in the way of reports. We then had time to recce some of the locations they would be using so that we would be familiar with the layout of certain shopping centres and other buildings. The students were aware that there would be surveillance on them at some stage but we were given selective targets, the time they would leave the fort, and imposed surveillance on an individual at different periods during the week.

As far as they were concerned they were to meet contacts in an environment, as they would do when posted abroad as intelligence officers. They would also have to fill and empty DLBs (dead letter boxes). A DLB is a safer form of communication for both the intelligence officer and the agent, there being no face-to-face contact. This means that the chance of the two being seen together by a third party is negligible. Certainly by this method it may be the case that the officer and agent might never meet but communication is maintained. The case officer controlling the agent would have briefed him on where the DLBs were and there would be a system of signs to say if there was anything in the drop waiting to be collected. Both the agent and officer would check these positions on certain days looking for such things as chalk marks to say there was something ready for collection. Another alternative would be to park your car in a car park with the window slightly open, and the agent would throw whatever he had into the car.

Another method of communication would be a 'brush contact' or 'brush' between the agent and handler. This works by the two passing at a prearranged point and handing over something surreptitiously. This method involves the agent and handler actually knowing each other. Usually for this method a quiet area such as an alleyway with an entrance at either end would be used. The two people would be in the same area and eye contact would be made, then they would walk down the alley from either end and pass whatever they had in the alleyway. This is difficult for a surveillance team to spot because to follow either one into the alley would give away the fact that they were under surveillance. Therefore, you would know one of the parties involved because you would have him under surveillance but unless you knew the other party you would not know a brush had taken place.

With all this in mind we were given timings of when the officer in question was leaving the fort and his car details and it was then up to us to impose surveillance on him. Most of the activity took place in and around Southsea centre and it soon became apparent that although they had done separate recces they were all looking for roughly the same place to service their DLBs. The first couple of people we took always seemed to disappear into a small alleyway to the rear of the main shopping centre and we were sure that there was something going on there. They would drive to the car park and park their car before going into the shopping centre. We would leave one car covering their car in case we lost them so that at least we would be able to pick them up again. The rest of the team would then take them wherever they went. We would build up a log of their movements and also take as much covert photography as possible.

We had a bit of an ace up our sleeves in the centre that none of them picked up on. One of the lads had been quite badly injured in a car crash a few years earlier but was still operating as an instructor. What we did was put him in the middle of the shopping centre in a wheelchair. It worked a treat because no one took any notice of the cripple in the wheelchair and he was able to get some good covert photography. Once they had been in the shopping centre for a while to try to identify if they were under surveillance they would move out the back to a small footpath. The first couple of times this caught us unawares but then we twigged that they must be using it for either a brush or a DLB. The next time one of them went into the centre we had people positioned outside, ready for it. This one poor sod must have thought he was doing everything OK but when he made his move there was half the team tripping over themselves to get in the alley with him and sure enough he was seen servicing a DLB. One of them did make the effort to vary things slightly and we took him to a wood on the outskirts of Portsmouth. He parked in the car park and went into the woods. The next thing he knew, there were at least three cars in with him and people out in walking gear and with binoculars doing the old bird-watching trick. He later said he didn't suspect a thing.

One particular occasion I saw a guy doing a recce of a small alleyway between some shops; by his behaviour I surmised that he was looking for a suitable location for a brush contact. I briefed the rest of the team and later that afternoon when he went back to the same area we staked the place out.

As I was covering one end of the alley I noticed someone else lurking around as well. He attracted my attention because he was dressed more or less the same as me. In other words, to me, he looked like a surveillance operator and I think he recognised me for what I was. It takes one to know one! I kept him in the back of my mind and though I didn't see him again it bothered me for a while after. It wasn't until we were debriefed at the end that I saw him again and he turned out to be one of their instructors.

At the end of the week we gave a presentation to the students. We were in there first and we had boards set up for each student showing a summary of what they had been up to during the week and the photography that had been taken. They were then shown in and introduced to us and although a couple said they had noticed one or two of us in various places they hadn't put two and two together at the time. If it had been done properly they probably wouldn't have seen a thing. It was because we only had a short time in which to observe them that we had to go in and hit hard. There was one incident that shows the effectiveness of a change of appearance. One of the blokes thought he'd had too much exposure to a particular target. He changed his jacket, plastered his hair back with some Brylcreem from Boots the chemist, put on a pair of thick-rimmed glasses and went and sat next to the target in McDonald's. The guy didn't notice a thing with all the other people around.

They were quite appreciative of our efforts and in the bar afterwards they picked our brains about how to try to spot surveillance. There was one guy in the bar who made a comment I will never forget which just goes to show the arrogance of some of these people. It was arrogance to the point of criminality not just to him but to any agent he might have been handling. His comment was, 'I've been doing this for twenty-five years and I can honestly say I have never been under surveillance.' Bollocks!

After my first tour in 28 I went back to 14 Coy in January 1987 for my second tour and was there until June 1988.

I arrived back in Germany in January 1991, not long after the Berlin Wall had come down, an occasion that was to alter drastically the way the Det operated. In fact to start with nobody knew what role we were to play in the new order of things and it was rumoured that we might even close. The CO at the time was fairly upbeat about things and assured us that a role would be found for us, if only temporary. Little did I know what we would be doing or actually be a part of in eighteen months' time. Obviously with the wall coming down the role of SOXMIS was finished, as was the role of the allied missions. They pulled out of Bünde and gutted the place.

Like the Det across the water we tended to socialise amongst ourselves, so there were always functions going on in the Sect and people had BBQs in the summer that everyone was invited to. We actually ended up with quite a good social life. Most of the functions had a theme to them and everyone entered into the swing of things. There was one when we had a 'Beach Night', which meant beachwear with various activities. At one point during the evening I ended up dancing on the coffee table with someone else and it wasn't very secure. When he jumped off I fell off and forgot about it but afterwards when we left I noticed that my foot was horribly swollen. I went and saw the medic the next day and he made the usual medic's diagnosis: 'Don't worry, it's only a sprain.'

He strapped it and gave me two painkillers called Brufen. So for the next week I was still walking around and driving at high speed but it wasn't getting any better. The day after the accident my wife was full of sympathy and even made me mow the lawn! In the end the Boss's wife, who was a nurse, insisted I go to the hospital for an X-ray, which I did. The doctor got the results, took a look at them and said, 'Hmm, that's quite a nasty break there; I think we'll have to put it in plaster.'

I was in plaster for six weeks and my faith in Army medics went rapidly downhill after that. The worst part about it was that I was confined to the office after that, manning the Ops room. I have never been one for being stuck in an office and that time, for me, was hell especially as the Sect got a really good job during this period. I was hearing reports of these targets going all over the place and felt jealous as fuck. I felt so bad that I even offered to do the report at the end of it.

Each Christmas we used to have a party for the kids in the Sect and that was always a good laugh because we would buy them presents and someone would be nominated as 'Santa'. There would also be spoof presents bought by members of the Section for the others. After the broken leg incident my present turned out to be a dinosaur with an overt video camera and one of its legs in plaster. Were they trying to tell me something or what? Mind you at that time, pushing forty, I could still run most of them into the ground.

On the day of the party, we would all arrive and while the kids were stuffing themselves with sandwiches and jelly, the parents and singlies were stuffing themselves with Herforder Pils and whatever else. The building we were housed in was a big civvy block outside the barracks. There were four flats on two floors converted into offices, and a bar, of course. Towards the present-giving time Santa would go upstairs and get into his costume and because we had a balcony on the first floor he was lowered by rope to the balcony below, accompanied by much screaming from the kids. He would call each kid's name in turn, have a little chat, and then give them their presents.

Now, because there were quite a lot of kids, Santa, who was a singly (single soldier), was kept supplied with liberal quantities of the hard stuff or 'coke' as far as the kids were concerned. After a while it was the turn of the wives to get their presents and Santa, half pissed by this time, took great pleasure in making the wives sit on his knee. At the end of the proceedings Santa would say his farewells and put his foot in the rope waiting to be hauled up and this is where the hard part came in. Three or four blokes upstairs were not enough to pull him up, as he was quite a big lad, and he was left dangling in mid air with the kids waving and cheering and Santa, half pissed, thinking, Get me the fuck out of here. The kids never worked out why that, shortly after their dads had disappeared, Santa suddenly went skywards at the speed of a space shuttle.

Germany, with its central location in Europe, was a good springboard for holidays and we had a few European holidays while we were there. I'll mention one because it ended up with quite an amusing tale.

I had had a back problem since my first tour in the Det but apart from a few twinges it didn't really bother me except when I was weight training in the Sect and it just clicked, leaving me collapsed on the floor.

We'd been for a holiday in Italy and on the way back we stopped off in one of the American Forces hotels.

That night my wife was putting the two little ones to bed when her back went. She was in agony all night and we managed to get to a doctor the next day before we drove back to Germany. When we arrived home she went straight to bed and I sorted the kids and car out and started to get the washing in the washing machine. On the first load I got quite a twinge in my back and thought, Hmm, haven't felt one that bad before, but thought no more of it.

When I took the first load out to put the next load in I bent down and suddenly I just felt as if someone had whacked me across the lower back with an iron bar; I collapsed in a heap on the floor of the cellar.

What could I do? I was flat out on the cellar floor and my wife was in bed two floors up, of no use to me. If it hadn't been so painful it would have been fucking hilarious as that sort of thing only happens in comedies. After about ten minutes I rolled over on to my hands and knees and crawled to the cellar steps and managed to get upright to crawl up the stairs. I told my wife what had happened and said I was sleeping on the floor downstairs to see if that would do any good. The next morning I got breakfast for the kids and it went again. I ended up trying to support myself between two chairs but also having to fling my strides (trousers) on without bending down. Not an easy thing to do in this situation! We called an ambulance and it took me up to the Medical Centre. I stood up in the back of the ambulance all the way because it was agony to try to lie down.

I saw the doctor who had a trainee with him; he said to the trainee, 'Look at this; you can actually see the muscles moving.'

Of course you could see the bloody things moving because they were spasming. Anyway, he gave me this tablet which was a class A drug and the next best thing to morphine – they take the pain away but send you gaga. I still have a load of them just in case but I haven't had to take one for a couple of years. Anyway, I ended up in hospital later that morning. When I was admitted there was a Billy Connolly video on the TV. Now I find Billy funny at the best of times, the only trouble was that this time whenever I laughed my back went into spasm. I was in fucking agony! Things got better at lunchtime when the Sister told me that my wife had been admitted as well and a friend was looking after the kids. I discharged myself after a week, which was probably a bit early but I wanted to get home. It happened once more when I was in a car working in London. Fortunately I wasn't driving. Since then, by good back management, I have found that I am still able to train but do exercises where my back is supported. Most people tend to dismiss back pain because you can't see any form of injury. I can honestly say it is absolute agony.

Most towns in Germany have a brewery and I think there are about 2,500 private breweries; Herford was no exception. We had one bloke there, whom I worked with again later in my career in London, who could and did organise a piss-up in a brewery. He did it on more than one occasion as well. On the first occasion we went down in a minibus and got dropped off where we were met by the tour guide. The tour was interesting to see just how the beer was made and stored.

The brewery was actually called the Felsenkeller, which in German means stone cellar. The beer is brewed and stored underground in the rock caves under the brewery. The normal Herforder Pils in the pubs is good but this stuff in the brewery was just out of this world. At one point in the tour we all decided that we wanted to become horses. They still have dray horses for certain events and these animals were magnificent but more importantly they were given eight litres of beer per day! The workers were allowed four litres and the office staff two litres.

After the tour it was into the bar for as much beer as you could drink in two hours. They also gave us some really big croissants filled with ham and cheese. We left that place very happy teddies indeed. About a year later we applied for another tour and were given a date to go so we all turned up again and we ended up with the same guide. He took one look at us and said, 'You have been here before, Ja?' To which we replied that we had.

'Ok, zen, ve vill not do ze tour but ve vill go straight to ze bar, Ja?' Outstanding: what a player.

We were finally given the role of an ATST or anti-terrorist survey team. Basically we would be given a town and we would have to adopt the role of terrorists to find and recce the camp, the married quarter (MQ) areas, and any British shopping facilities that we could find. We would be told there were barracks somewhere and that was it; we had to find everything from information to hand that everyone else could get hold of. There were a number of ways of doing this before we even left our own location. There are a number of publications that are for the

British Army but are freely available to anyone with half a mind to get hold of them. In these soldiers always advertise things and more often than not give a phone number in the publication. If not the other way is to look in the phone book for that area and pick out any English-sounding names and make a note.

Once you have these you at least have a starting point before you are even on the ground. Once we had identified these places and recce'd them we would identify the weaknesses and report on how easy or not it would be to mount an attack on the facilities or personnel from a terrorist point of view. Although we carried ID cards at all times, if we had been challenged and had to show them then we were considered to have been caught.

One of our first tasks was to conduct a survey on the British Army of the Rhine Headquarters at Rheindahlen, near Moenchen Gladbach. We did our background work before we deployed to the area, taking most of our assets with us including the OP van just in case, and also some pushbikes that proved invaluable. Although Rheindahlen is a military base, it has a German bus route running through it, which it made it easy to gain access. The bus was never stopped as it went in and there were bus stops inside. All we had to do was get on the bus outside and then get off inside and we were free to walk around and see what we wanted. There were also other entry points where you could either walk through or go in by bike. The latter made it easier as the whole complex is huge. After we had studied the base and found the areas of interest we decided to come up with an alternative. We knew the British General worked there and we had seen the place where he was likely to have worked but had to confirm it. We also found no trace of a house inside the base big enough for a General so we assumed (although assumption is generally regarded as the mother of all fuck-ups) he must live outside and that was the first priority. If he lived outside the base he would be more than likely to have an escort for protection. To try to confirm this we put someone into the base keeping an eye on the main gate, an OP watching the access road that led on to the main road and cars to cover left and right. At close of play that night the guy on the gate gave what he thought was a possible as there was a staff car with what appeared to be an escort car in front. The guy in the OP confirmed this and the car turned left at the main road but did not reach the car that was staking out that road further up. That meant he must have turned off somewhere along that stretch.

We then began searching both sides of the road, which had tracks running into the woods on both sides. An extensive search of the right-hand side proved a negative so we concentrated on the left-hand side. We found a large house with a fairly high wooden fence surrounding it with civilian guards on the gate so we thought this was a very good possibility. We lifted off that night and deployed early the next morning to see if we were correct. We positioned the blokes again and someone went past the house on a bike, there was also a car parked outside with its sidelights on. Shortly after, a staff car came out and tucked in behind the other car and they both set off now fairly obviously confirmed as a staff car with what appeared to be a Royal Military Police Close Protection vehicle leading. As they went through the main gate the guy on his bike tucked in behind them and the car went into another compound to what was known as the Big House where it stopped and a high-ranking officer stepped out. We were now convinced we had the house and workplace of the General. We managed to take covert photography of the entrance to the house and also some of the insides of the grounds with a video camera mounted in the roof of the van. The next task was how to find a place to simulate taking him out. We carried on this routine for the rest of the working week and there didn't seem to be any way we could get near him.

The weekend came and there was no activity except that he seemed to have a reception on Saturday night. On Sunday came the breakthrough when he left the house in his own car but with no escort. He drove into the camp but we lost him so it was everyone on bikes and foot to try to locate the car.

After a while we found the car in the car park of one of the churches in the camp. The car was watched and he came out of the church and got straight into the car and drove home. We now thought we had the weakness and decided that next Sunday we would carry out the attack. Normal practice in Germany at that time was to check under the vehicle for under vehicle booby traps

(UVBTs) – he didn't, obviously thinking that he was safe on the base. His movements were monitored the following week to make sure he didn't go anywhere and on the Sunday we were going to go for it. We had people in position to trigger him away from the house, see him into the camp and watch the car park. Once he was in the car park we took photographs of one of the team going up to the car and simulating placing a UVBT on it. We also had photographs of the General coming out and getting into the car without checking it – BANG, we had just 'killed' the British General and during all the time we were in the base no one had challenged us for identification. Can you imagine what a coup that would have been for PIRA if it were they that had taken him out in what he obviously considered to be his 'safe' base?

On another occasion we had information that the Sovs – or their agents – had targeted an American missile base with the intention of monitoring traffic that went in and out during exercise periods. We, along with the Americans, were given the task of trying to locate the beacons that had, supposedly, been dug in around the road that led to the entrance of the base.

We turned up, having been briefed and shown diagrams of what these things would look like, with metal detectors, trowels and shovels, hoping to find something. We spent days there and found nothing except an old scoop to a bulldozer that had been buried. Because we had Americans with us, lunchtimes were spent throwing a baseball. After three days I never did get the hang of catching the ball in one of those fucking great mitts. I couldn't understand it but they used to get a bit pear-shaped if we asked them if they were playing rounders again at lunchtime.

Because the Berlin Wall had now come down we were now able to go to the Berlin Security Section. They were only a small section but had the ability to carry out very limited surveillance so we would be called up for any surveillance jobs. However, before we were able to do that we would have to carry out recces of the city. This also gave us the chance to do quite a bit of sightseeing when we weren't actually working. Apart from the main tourist attractions such as the Blue Church, Europa centre and KaDeWe's, the biggest department store in Berlin, the things that struck me most were the remnants of the wall and looking from the west on to what used to be East Berlin, over the killing ground to the dreary buildings opposite. The former Gestapo headquarters in Prinz Albrecht Strasse and the mound in No Man's Land that was supposed to be all that was left of Hitler's bunker. The Brandenburg Gate had been cut off from the west and the former Reichstag, Hitler's old HQ. Just behind the Reichstag is a small memorial garden with crosses to remember those who tried to get over the wall and also to swim the river from the east to the west. If you walked down the Unter Den Linden you would see nicely kept Embassy buildings but once you moved off that street you were in areas that hadn't changed since the Second World War. Even some of the public and administration buildings were still pockmarked with bullet holes. The Sovs weren't going to waste money that they didn't have on the Germans. I took the S Bahn to a suburb called Pankow one time and had a look around. The buildings were falling apart and decaying; they had been doing so for fifty years. At first glance you also wondered why the main roads in East Berlin were so wide – this was so that the panzers could move freely in case of an uprising or any other trouble.

We went up a few times, once by train but more often than not by car. It was quite eerie driving through the corridor and past some of the old Sov barracks now falling to bits through lack of money. It was hard to believe that what you saw now was once the most feared enemy on the earth as far as the west was concerned. Rumour had it that money was in such short supply that when the sanitation systems broke down in some barracks they just ran the waste pipes straight down to the cellars and filled them.

In Berlin we would carry out hare runs in the city that took in mobile and foot surveillance using the U Bahn (Underground) and S Bahn (over ground elevated railways) systems. We only ever had two proper jobs in Berlin, for one of which we acted as the stake-out and surveillance team for a CIA operation. This particular guy in a block of flats was supposed to have very sophisticated computer and transmission kit and was supposed to be in contact with agents and then transmitting their information back to Bulgaria, I believe it was.

The plan was for us to stake the flat out and when he left, to place him under surveillance and as long as he was under control the two CIA guys would go in and look over the kit and get what information they could from it and then extract. We had an OP van in position and that stayed for the duration with the same team in.

Other agencies that I worked for later would find it acceptable to change the teams in the van even when it had the trigger on the target, a practice that I could never accept. Before the van went in, however, it had to be established if the guy was in the flat. This was established because the Berlin Section had had a pile of pizza delivery fliers printed and a good German speaker went around the flats knocking on doors and handing them over. He did a few blocks, just in case afterwards the target asked anyone else if they had had them delivered, before he went into the target's block. He identified him and confirmed that he was in and on his way out immobilised the lock to the outside door so that it wouldn't lock. In German flats there is usually an intercom at the front door so that when you press a bell you can be identified before you are let in. Once his presence had been established the OP van went in and the long wait began.

The van must have been in place for nearly twelve hours before the target moved. When he did, the trigger was given and the surveillance team imposed control. Once he was safely away from the target area the CIA team moved in and because the front door had been immobilised they were able to go straight to his flat and gain access. They did what they had to do in the flat and then withdrew, their part in the operation completed. They must have had some other input that we were not aware of because we were told that he was expected to move within twenty-four hours of returning to the flat. Some time later he returned and we staked the flat out.

As expected he moved again within the time frame and he was carrying a bag. We were told not to lose him as the bag was reported to contain some computer components that could be used as evidence if charges were brought against him. We kept him under control and he eventually made his way into the Turkish quarter of the city; so far we hadn't had any problems. It was thought he might be going somewhere to make a drop and in cases such as that his senses would be at hyper level and he would expect to be under surveillance and would obviously try to carry out drills to drop it. We saw him carry out some fairly basic drills but then he went into an area that had a lot of small alleyways. We'd been in this area before so we knew the hazards. To follow him down these straight away was not a good idea as it might be just us and him in the alley and he might get a bit suspicious. He went down one and was left to run and when he came out the other end he was negative bag – he must have either ditched it or made a drop. Some of the team stuck with him and a couple of others stayed at either end of the alley to see if anyone came out – they didn't! The area of the alley was combed later, particularly the skips, but nothing was found and it was assumed he had made the drop to someone waiting in the alley. I never did find out what became of him.

Apart from our role as an ATST we were still being promised this 'new work' that the CO kept hinting about, but all he would say was that it was taking time because it had to be cleared at the highest political levels. We did have one thing though and that if it was successful it would be referred to as Operation Predial. We kept on with the ATSTs until one day about eighteen months after we'd started them we'd heard that Predial had finally come through and that we'd be shortly starting that. The CO came to the Det to brief us fully on the background, what we'd be doing and whom we'd be ultimately working for. Basically there was an Irish threat in Germany as had been reported in the newspapers. People had been killed in Roermond just across the border, car bombs had been found in Germany and soldiers had been shot dead and wounded – all the work of the IRA. The Germans thought that this was mainly a British problem as we were the targets and their resources were stretched to the limit with the Wall coming down. They had a flood of migrants from the east into the west and also they now had responsibility for the former DDR (Deutches Democratic Republic). They were also having problems with the neo-Nazis who were firebombing refugee hostels and the resulting interracial problems that occurred. To the ordered German mentality it would be simpler if the British problem was taken care of by the British and thereby the Army's surveillance asset or 28 Sect.

In the SOXMIS days, this wouldn't have presented a problem because to all intents and purposes we were still the 'occupying power' as it were, although the significance of that had gone to ratshit years ago. Now the problem was a political one. We had a unified Germany free from the four powers agreement of the Second World War, so how were they to allow a foreign surveillance asset to operate, uninhibited, in Germany? The answer they came up with was to make us members of the BfV – the Office of the Protection of the State, or the German Security Service. This is why the political clearance took so long. We had photographs taken and all the documentation was produced which, when finished, made us accredited members of the BfV (*Bundesamt fur Verwassungschutz*, pronounced 'fervassungschutz'). It would have been politically unacceptable, I believe, to all concerned to have us running around with this caveat all the time so we were really part-time members.

When deployed on Predial operations we would draw and sign for our BfV paperwork so that if necessary we could flash it to the German *Polizei* if we were caught out. We carried out operations all over Germany but were not deployed in the former DDR because I don't think even the Irish were daft enough to go over there. I would put it down to the professionalism of the team during the time I was there that although we carried the BfV paperwork, at no time was anyone challenged and required to produce it. Prior to the first deployment on behalf of the BfV we all had to travel down to the Cologne area to be briefed on the background to the organisation. We were also very carefully briefed by their lawyer on their remit and what our parameters were, especially as to the use of their paperwork. After this initial briefing, when the Ops officer was away, I would quite often travel down to their headquarters outside Cologne to be briefed on forthcoming jobs and also to be debriefed on certain jobs we had carried out.

On one particular job that was slightly sensitive I took one of the BfV operators to the target area to brief him fully on the layout of where the target worked and the problems we might encounter in the area. I also showed him where the guy lived and the problems we had covering his address. His house was at the end of a quiet cul-de-sac, the place I would have chosen to live – impossible to cover by car. It would have been the ideal spot except that he was right next to a wood. This meant that someone could get in the wood during the hours of darkness for a standing (short-term) OP to cover the address. The reason for the sensitivity in this case was that usually we worked against Irish targets or people associated with the Irish. The difference in this case and the reason for the sensitivity was that the guy in question was a German national. He ran an import/export firm and was believed to be involved in some form of espionage. Exactly what, we would never find out except for what we saw when he was under surveillance. What we did find out was that he was dealing with some pretty undesirable characters outside Germany and had some offshore bank accounts. The whole operation was to build up a picture of his activities so that the BfV could get some sort of lever on him. We must have had had some sort of success because after we had been working on him for quite a while the BfV decided they were going to pay him a visit with the intention of turning him. We were covering him one day when it was planned to have two senior operatives from the BfV call at his house. I was in the OP at the time covering the house and the all clear was given to the guys who went into the house. They were in there for a while and afterwards we all got curious and asked them if he had decided to play ball. They apparently had so much on him at that time that they were able to give him an ultimatum – play ball or go away for a very long time. He agreed to play ball and sang like a canary. What the long-term result was of any future operations they mounted against other people he implicated, I do not know.

Because of our surveillance expertise we were invited to act as observers on exercises run by the German Customs service that took place in the former American Sector but now was open to us with reunification. It was the final exercise for people wanting to join the Customs undercover surveillance team. We were given where they were going to operate and all we had to do initially was to drive around looking for anything out of the ordinary in some of the car parks they were using. In one area the target moved to a marina because he was going to get on to a motor launch and go off for a meet. His route led him down this lane so I parked my car in the lane and pretended to be fiddling with the engine. I got some great photos of the team as they followed him because I had a video camera mounted in the boot. Normally if we were changing plates we would find somewhere quiet where there was no chance of the third party seeing. The Customs lads didn't seem too concerned about that and would quite openly change plates in car parks. Their mentality once again of having the authority had the potential to blow an operation that had been going on a long time and could maybe put lives at risk. We then moved to a café area outside the American PX (basically the same as their commissary but it holds all the luxury consumables) and waited for the targets (whom we knew) and the team to arrive. We saw the targets park their vehicle in the car park and meet someone outside before taking a table on the terrace and we waited for the team to show up. It didn't take long and it looked as if the place had been invaded; they were everywhere and not being too covert about it either. They were wandering up and down the road in front of the targets and loitering in bus stops and, instead of getting into a position out of sight of the target to observe them, were giving them the full frontal evil eye.

Because of evidential requirements, Customs were required to get photography of all meets and new faces so now with a new face appearing we knew they would be going for photographs. If it were the Sect doing it we would be using covert camera bags so that the opposition would not see a camera and not know they were being photographed. This is a quite simple process of obtaining a suitable bag and making a frame inside to hold the camera that could be either a stills camera or a video with the aperture maybe put into a luggage tag. Alternatively you would replace the tag with some dark coloured plastic that would let enough light in for the camera but would shield the lens from the third party. A camera wrapped in a plastic carrier bag was also effective.

We were looking at these people to see which one of them was going to come in to do the photography and then we spotted him. Here was a man with a mission! He was coming through the car park like a cruise missile – nothing was going to deflect him. He had his bag with him and his eyes were glued to the targets as though defying them to move. You could almost hear his thought process (in German): 'I've seen where I'm going to go, now don't you fucking well move.'

Now normally we would sit at another table and angle the bag casually towards the target. Not this guy, he sat at the same table as the targets – a bit of a no-no, but there weren't many spare tables – and put his bag on the table. OK, we thought, at least he's getting some form of covert photography. Wrong! The next thing is he opens the zip and starts fiddling around inside – OK, might just get away with that one but no, he hasn't finished yet. The next thing is the fucking camera comes out of the bag and he starts filming the targets! Well, you could have dropped me with a feather. We had a debrief later and pointed all these things out to them but they just said that photography was all-important and just getting that bit of footage might be enough to put someone away. Fine, but what if as you're pulling your camera out, he pulls his pistol out and wastes you? Not the way we'd have played it, but each to his own. They'd taken over a hotel to stay in and laid on a good BBQ afterwards with as much beer as you could drink, so who were we to complain!

It was during this period of operations that I was the Assistant Operations Officer in the Det. The Operations Officer (Ops Offr) and I would take it in turns to run the jobs and afterwards write the reports at the end. The reports were very detailed and went to both the German and British Security Services. Because we covered such large areas it was impractical and impossible to have a base location where all the radio traffic would be relayed. The shortage of manpower also made this impossible, as virtually everyone would be deployed on the ground. We therefore had a mobile Ops room – in other words, the SC's (Sierra Charlie – the commander) car. He would be part of the team but was responsible for co-ordinating the team and making detailed notes as the team was moving because some of the guys would be one up and couldn't make their own notes. During operations it would be the OC or me. It was quite a conjurer's trick at times when an operator was trying to take notes, watch the target, swap map books around and transmit on the radio. If it were night you'd also be holding a small torch to see the map, as you couldn't have the interior light on. In Ireland, in the cuds, you'd have the torch in your mouth, as your hands would be busy doing other things. You might be able to memorise the city and towns but not the whole of the cuds. At the end of the day, at the debrief, he would be able to give everybody detailed timings of when they were in control so they could write their own detailed reports. At the end of an operation that may have lasted for ten days the SC would then have to produce a detailed report on the operation and a surveillance log for the duration of the job. One particular job I can remember doing the surveillance log consisted of over forty pages of timings, minute by minute, of what the target had done when we had him under control.

In most of the major towns and cities you will always find at least one Irish pub selling traditional beer such as Guinness as well as the German beers. Guinness is popular because it is the only beer from abroad, apart from those on the Continent, which passes the German purity laws on brewing. All their beer is brewed from natural ingredients and does not have any chemicals. You will not find any British bitter in German bars. Needless to say, these pubs were very popular with the Sect, whenever we went away, even though some of them, such as the one in the Europa centre in Berlin, were out of bounds to soldiers. That's OK, we thought, because we didn't really look like soldiers anyway and they were the best places to go. They also featured sometimes as haunts for some of our targets.

One such target was reported to be the assistant manager of a Guinness promotions company and one of his jobs was to travel Germany promoting Guinness. Fantastic, we thought, we'd really get to go places with this target now. He had an office in Düsseldorf and that was the start point we were given.

The office wasn't that difficult to cover as it was in the one-way system and he was channelled out a certain way if he was moving by car. There were some four wheel drive vehicles associated with the office that were used for promotions and we thought that if he moved in one of these we'd be OK, as they were very distinctive. In all the time we watched him, however he didn't go outside Düsseldorf so once again the info was duff at this point. One of the reasons of interest in this firm was that because they ran promotions they were hired on a regular basis by British Army units holding summer fairs. Because it would be a promotion they would give some concessions and the Army, always on the lookout for a bargain, would hire them. What better and easier way would there be for someone to gain access to British bases? Even though the pubs were in Germany, all the bar staff were Irish.

When we started covering this guy it was soon apparent that he did not have ready access to transport and walked everywhere. It was also thought at first that he was quite switched on because he used to time his walks to and from the trams and the U Bahn stops so that he would get there as the train was there and jump straight on. After a while we discovered that he did this all the time and because the German transport system is so punctual he knew exactly when to leave work in the evening and where he lived in the morning. We eventually tracked him to where he lived – it was above the Irish bar in the Altstadt in Düsseldorf. This is a great place to work and also to socialise, as there are some great bars there and some really cheap places to eat. In other words, my sort of place. We were able to cover the bar from a café opposite and also from some benches down towards the river. If for some reason you had to leave your car around that area you had to be very careful where you left it because there were a lot of parking restrictions and the Germans don't mess about. One of the lads left his car in a parking area and went to cover the target but what he didn't realise that after a certain time that place became a taxi rank. When he went back to his car, it was gone! We had to go to the car pound with him and pay to get it back. The authorities do not mess about. On another occasion we were sitting in the car by the river in Düsseldorf and just watched as a fleet of trucks arrived and cleared the whole side of the street of cars that were illegally parked. After we had worked on him for quite a while we were pulled off and went on to something else, we never did get to know if we had found anything of interest.

When I was on my second tour with the Section the codes had been changed once again and this time some bright spark of a Rupert had come up with the idea of using numbers as a brevity code. I looked at this and thought, what a load of bollocks. I had been used to using clear speech, because we had secure comms. Everyone understood these codes with both 14 Coy and the Section on my first tour and now everything was fucked up as far as I was concerned. A few examples would be when you first saw the target or if he did something you were waiting for, the call would be, 'Stand by, stand by,' said with urgency. Now it was 'Seven Seven, Seven Seven.'

Apart from it not rolling off the tongue with the same urgency, you were now using twenty letters instead of fourteen, so where was the brevity in that? Mind you, it was at least a bit better than when I worked for the British Security Service and the target appeared out of his front door. All you would get then was, 'That's out now.' More often than not it was said in such a quiet voice that you wondered what the fuck was happening and had to ask for a repeat. Without going through all the codes I will mention one other because of an incident that happened when we had a target under surveillance.

The code I had always used for having control of the target was, 'I have.' Now it was, 'Five Five.' Once again now it was eight letters instead of five so it also failed the brevity test! Needless to say, these new codes and I did not see eye to eye. But the story!

We had this target under surveillance one day, going through a town in Germany. It was summer and he had his sunroof open at the time. We'd had him for quite a while and he didn't appear to be switched on at all. My partner and I had control at the time and I was acting as SC. Suddenly his fist came out of the sunroof and he opened his hand twice showing his five fingers. I turned to my partner and said, 'Fuck me, Five Five, I wonder who he's got control of. Tell him we're backing!'

Also during this tour, because of the work we were involved in, we visited some of the bigger towns and cities in Germany and they could be quite an eye-opener. Some of the airports we recce'd actually had sex cinemas in them – I suppose to take your mind off things if you were a bit nervous about flying. I found a few beers in the bar worked better but that was just a personal preference. The whole attitude towards sex in Germany is completely different to that in England and it was quite common in most towns to be able to find sex shops that sold hardcore pornography. Even the video rental shops used to rent them out. Perhaps the best places I found to go when we were deployed were the *Hauptbahnhofs* (main railway stations). Not only were there usually quite a few cheap places to eat but just to watch the cross section of people was fascinating. Since my days in the Group I have been a great people watcher and I found these places ideal to do this. Not only do you see normal people going about their business but in these places you also get the dregs of society. Apart from the numerous drunks all over the place there were also the drug addicts who seemed to go about their business without caring who saw them. I was on the escalator in one of these stations and saw a couple of junkies shooting up on the stairs, making no attempt to conceal what they were doing. I have also seen some people walking around the station with large plastic bottles filled with some sort of smoke and a tube taped into it, inhaling the contents.

I found this surprising compared to the attitude of the *Polizei* in other ways. Fare dodging is something they appear to crack down on heavily. On the U Bahn and S Bahn systems you bought a ticket from a machine and when you got on the train you would put it into another machine that would punch it and validate it. If you were caught without a ticket or one that was not validated it was an on-the-spot fine. Some people actually rode the odds and reckoned that it was cheaper to pay the fine for the few times they were caught than to buy a ticket every time. The transport police in Berlin didn't mess about though. They used to board the trains mob-handed dressed for the part and some of them would actually have Rottweilers that were muzzled. If they found you without a ticket and you couldn't pay the fine they would handcuff you to the railings until they had swept the train and then come back and deal with you. There was no fucking about with these Germans.

When you think you are under surveillance there are two ways of trying to confirm this. We already knew one method and were shown the other method and practised it in Berlin. The first method of detection is anti-surveillance; this is a series of drills you can do yourself to try to spot if you are under surveillance.

The idea is to be covert about it and not to let the surveillance team know that you are looking for them. There are many little things you can do to try to pick out a team just by going about your normal day-to-day business. If you think you are under surveillance then the team has to pick you up from somewhere and in most cases the easiest places are either from your home or from work. If you are at home there are certain things you can do in the morning. If you have a dog, take it for a walk because there is nothing more natural. Choose a route that takes in most of the streets surrounding your house because unless there is an OP in a house overlooking your house, the trigger will normally be in the street.

This could be a van or more likely an occupied car. Sometimes, though very rarely in England, it could be someone in the boot of a car looking through an aperture. This method is not favoured in this country but was quite common in NI and Germany. Although it can be uncomfortable I have known someone spend ten hours in a boot before he was lifted off.

For a trigger in a car, in England but never across the water, you would be looking for possibly two people and they would probably be reading or one would be sleeping. There would more than likely be a pile of junk on the back seat such as a couple of coats and bags or briefcases. If there were no Styrofoam cups on the dashboard then there would probably be the rings from where they had been. Also in the winter their bonnet would more than likely be frost-free, as they would have driven there and will more than likely run the engine to stop themselves getting cold. If it is raining their windscreen will probably be clear, as they will use their windscreen wipers to maintain a clear view of the target. If it were across the water you would call someone else to come in and take the trigger, as his windscreen would be clear as he arrived. You would never clear your windscreen sitting in a street watching a target; it only means one thing to a switched-on target – surveillance. If it is suspected that the OP might be in a house, then look for curtains that are always closed but don't always expect to see people going in and out as changeovers may be done through the back door and at night. Alternatively, a video camera with a radio relay might be used. If you are walking, try to pick a route that involves a couple of natural road crossings such as going to a shop or posting a letter. The letterbox gives you an ideal, innocent way of looking behind you as you put the letter in the box. Any of these will give you an ideal opportunity to look behind you without appearing suspicious. Newspaper shops on a corner are handy because as you turn the corner you can dive into one. As the team clear the corner you are nowhere to be seen so they will go into search mode and you might just get a rather flustered looking operator coming into the shop. Most people when they enter premises will make eye contact but a surveillance operator will studiously avoid eye contact. Shop windows are also very handy things to use to see if there is someone acting suspiciously behind you; they can be used as mirrors and give an excellent view of the street behind.

The other more difficult method for a team to spot is counter surveillance. Source handlers, who want to make sure that their tout is clear before they make their meet, favour this method. We used this method a couple of times in Germany to clear source meets. The handler would first of all brief the tout of the route he was to take to the meet and you would build in a couple of natural stops such as paper shops, cafés and a route that took in a quiet area after a busy area. The ideal situation is for the same people in the counter team to be at each stop, so that they would be able to see if the same people turned up, but sometimes this is not possible. In these cases we would keep in touch by radio and describe anyone suspicious. The idea would be that the tout walked through a certain point at a certain time and you would be in a position to observe him and anyone that might be tailing him. When he made his first stop for maybe a paper you would be looking for someone that might get into a position you would yourself use to trigger him away. When he moves off, watch who moves with him and see if it was the same person that stopped when he stopped.

The next stop might be a café but it would be chosen so that another café overlooked it. This would be because the counter team would be off the street and observing him but also anyone following him would also be looking for somewhere to get off the street and would probably choose your café if there was no other available. Also moving from a busy area to a quiet area would help isolate those people you might already have had under suspicion because they would have to go with him. By moving back to a busy area you would be able to confirm this if they were still with him. Thus by building in stops you are looking for the same people who turn up at every stop and react to the target's movements.

Towards the end of the route and prior to the meet you would have arranged a physical signal to the handler to say if he was clear or not. This has the advantage of a definite clear because sod's law states that just as you are about to give the signal over the radio the fucking thing breaks down or the battery runs out. It could be something so simple as 'If he's clear I'll blow my nose, if he's not I won't'.

7

WIND DOWN

When I was in 28 Section the opportunity arose to go to London on attachment to A4, the surveillance side of the security service or MI5. I jumped at the opportunity because until now all my surveillance had been done in either a hostile environment or in an environment where my language skills were not brilliant. I had always wanted to work in this country as I could speak the language and know everything that was going on. When the opportunity came up to other members of the section I took the Rupert to one side and told him not to dare to leave me out of this one.

I had to wait for a few months before my time came and then I made it to London to begin my time in A4 for the next two and a half years. My introduction was auspicious enough as I arrived in a big black overcoat only to be called 'Batman' with my suit and tie on. I had worn this only because it was my first day, otherwise I would have been in jeans. We completed the first day after which there were going to be initial interviews before the first week's training began. I heard via the back door that they were thinking of binning me at that stage because they thought I was too tall.

That afternoon when it was coffee time I collared the one of the instructors and said, 'Look, I've heard a rumour that I might be getting binned because I'm too tall. I can't see why because there are at least half a dozen people I've seen here today that are about as tall as me, so what's the score? If you're going to bin me then do it now because I'm not staying here for a week wasting my time to get binned at the end.'

He said, 'It wouldn't be my choice but these guys were hired when we were short of recruits and we had to relax the rules a bit.'

'That's fine,' I said, 'but if you look around London, not everyone is a short-arsed bastard under 5 ' 10 ". Apart from that I know you're still short of recruits and that is why you've got the Army attached to you. You've got us on the cheap because the Army is paying our wages.'

I spent the rest of the afternoon thinking that my time in that office was going to be very short and tomorrow I would be on the train back to Ashford. At the close of play that day I was called into the Chief Instructor's office and he assured me that I was there to stay and would not be binned at the end of the week. Fine by me, I thought, and that's where I stayed for two and a half years. If you actually look around London the height difference varies enormously. Their stipulation of 5 ' 10 " is way out of date. It is OK to say that the smaller you are the less likely you are to get noticed but that is a load of bollocks because in some places you need big guys in crowds to be able to look over what is going on and that is something these short bastards can't do. On one particular job in Regent's Park the only way we could keep control of the target was by looking over a hedge and guess who was the only one tall enough to do this?

Once the week's training period was over we were given our identification badges, which meant we were now accredited members of the Security Service. Not bad considering that just a couple of months earlier I had been working for the German Security Service.

Surveillance always comes down to how you act and react in a crowd and in a situation. After I had been in a surveillance unit in a hostile environment across the water there were places that I would go in London that some people felt uncomfortable with. I felt perfectly comfortable in these situations and it became known that if a particular target went into a certain pub, then I would be the one that went in after him, or I would be in there waiting for him to arrive. In this pub I actually got on nodding terms with the regulars. They'd probably be nodding to me with a smile on their faces but saying to each other, 'Look, the spy's in again.'

I was also told that in some of these Irish pubs some of the regulars would pat you down to see if you were carrying a weapon or wearing a covert radio. Some people when they went in pubs would actually take off their covert radios; that's if they ever wore them. It was very common to be in a car behind a target and when he got out to go foxtrot you would have these MI5 people scrabbling around trying to put a radio on without losing the target, which was a distinct possibility. Sometimes they would get out without a radio so that if they had control of the target they couldn't tell anyone what was going on. If your radio is on you're ready to go. I'm afraid in some cases it came down to professionalism, or the lack of. If, without their radio, they got in the shit, how were we to know when to help them? I suppose that when they came flying out of the pub window it was a good indication that they were in the shit! I never took my radio off and no one ever tried to pat me down, even in the heartland of Kilburn. You would go into these pubs and pay for the beer and claim the money back later, so I can actually say with no word of a lie that I have drunk for Britain and had it bought for me. The Guinness in Kilburn is as good as across the water.

Kilburn became a priority, because it is the heart of the Irish community in London and inevitably someone of interest turned up. We were briefed on a particular target and as all targets had code names I'll call this one Slimy Snail, or SS. Initially the brief was that SS was working on a building and was in fact renovating an old bank, so that was where we were deployed. All we had was an old photograph and a description so first of all we had to try to find out which of the blokes on the site was SS. After some time and with no sightings someone that could fit his description was seen on the first floor and when they all came down for a tea break it was confirmed that this was he.

In the Dets, in Ireland, the same people covered the same target until the job was completed, but here it was different. You might start work on one target but the next shift you turned up for work you might be on a totally different target and might not work the original one again for days or even weeks. This changes however if an operation requires all resources to the exclusion of all others, as I shall describe later on. When he'd finished work that evening he was taken back to Kilburn and he went into the pub he always used on Kilburn High Road, where he seemed to spend a lot of his time. It eventually turned out that he worked for quite a prosperous builder who had projects all over north London and employed casual labour, especially this guy. At the time it was rumoured that he was employed because he might have some hold on the builder from across the water but after a while this was discounted in favour of him being a grafter. He was so much of a grafter that after having worked all day on a building site he would go off and claim disability benefit.

We eventually found out where he lived and he was then triggered away from the house by a remote camera in a friendly house as occupied vehicles attracted too much attention and the police were called on a couple of occasions. He invariably walked towards Kilburn High Road, bought a paper and, depending where he was working, would stand at a particular bus stop to go either north or south. Whichever one he was at we would get someone on at the previous stop so that if the cars got held up at least we would have the place where he got off to start looking. In fact, depending on the target and the assets you had at your disposal, you could actually keep hold of a target for quite a while, even in central London. We had some excellent motorcyclists who would lurk at the back of the team just waiting for heavy traffic and then come forward and take the target before dropping back when the cars caught up. The London black cab is also a tremendous asset because they are incongruous and they can also use the bus lanes to beat the traffic. I remember having control of a particular target in Oxford Street while he was on a bus and I was foxtrot. The bus was moving so slowly that I was able to keep up. I only had to break into a trot as it got into clearer traffic at the end but by this time the cars were there.

Anyway, back to SS. Depending where he worked he got into a bit of a routine and trigger positions became few and far between. A very popular trigger among A4 operators is the bus stop but there are only a certain number of buses you can let go by before people start to notice. In fact, depending on the bus route, you might even see the same bus driver coming around again wondering why you are still standing there. Because of their fixation with bus stops, when I left A4 I actually presented them with one of London Transport's temporary bus stops that I had 'found lying around'. Now they need never be short of a trigger position.

No matter where SS worked there was one thing you could more or less depend on and that was that at the end of the day he would end up in his favourite pub until closing time. As I said, I had no problems going in there and didn't feel intimidated at all. Some weekends when he went in it was good to go in and watch the sport on TV and discuss what was going on with some of the old regulars you'd seen quite a lot of before.

One of the reasons why I wouldn't take my radio off is that he used to use the phone quite a lot and our base location, 0, wanted to know whenever he was on the phone, presumably for monitoring purposes. With me having long hair again, my earpiece couldn't be seen.

If you are in there with someone else talking then you can get away with transmitting what is happening because to all intents and purposes you are having a conversation. If you are on your own it is slightly different. OK if you're pissed and burbling to yourself but otherwise it comes down to clicks. In the Dets, as already mentioned, the method was two clicks for yes and zero clicks for no. The reason for this is if you just heard one click you would immediately get the response, 'That was just one click, is that a yes?'

The reason being is that sometimes you would get spurious clicks over the air so you had to confirm. The A4 method was two clicks for yes and one click for no. What if the guy meant yes but only one click came across? A recipe for disaster, but they wouldn't see sense.

The only concern I had was if I stayed there too long and SS got pissed and started a fight, as he had been known to do. He was about 5'10" but well built and looked like a hard bastard. Rumour had it that he once saw a bloke in a chippy that he was having a bit of a feud with. Anyway, he put his arm through the plate glass window and dragged this bloke out. He cut himself so badly and lost so much blood that he was apparently given the last rites but obviously made a full recovery. Whilst we were working in London we used to be accommodated in officer's maisonettes in Kingston upon Thames, which was a very nice area to live in. Richmond was a good place to go and there were some good pubs by the river in Kingston. Travel used to be handy as well because we were given an all zones transport pass, which meant that all public transport was free within the greater London area. We were also given extra money per day in order to feed ourselves. Unless I actually ate out, which I did maybe once, it was amazing how cheaply I could eat if I cooked for myself. I know accommodation is expensive in London but I found that because I don't eat an awful lot, I could actually feed myself for between one and two pounds per day depending on how extravagant I wanted to be. One pint of beer actually cost more than my food bill per day.

On another occasion we were covering a target in Tottenham, north London, and on this particular occasion we had to cover an address in a housing estate as the target was believed to be involved in some form of subversive activity. It was impossible to get a trigger on his flat as he lived in a block but we did have a trigger on the main door to the block and an indication of where the flat was so that, hopefully, any activity might be indicated by lights going off or coming on. It's only after I'd been in there for a while and noticed that we were getting some funny – and in some cases not so much funny but hostile – looks from the ethnic minorities that I asked what this estate was called.

'Oh it's the Broadwater Farm Estate, didn't you know?' replied my partner.

Fucking outstanding I thought, here I am at the scene of one of the bloodiest riots London has seen and nothing to defend myself with if it comes to it.

The next time I was on that estate, this time one up, I made sure the first thing I did was find all the escape routes just in case. I did also have a good look around out of interest and located the Tangmere block that had featured heavily in the riots. Some of the other estates in London were just as bad with tower blocks accessed by walkways so that you could walk all around them without actually coming to ground level. Sometimes you had to walk through them at night if you were in control of a target when perhaps, sensibly and on other occasions, you wouldn't go near the place.

On another job on another target I ended up in one of these places in control of the target and he went for the lift. I had two choices and the first was to get into the lift with him, which I didn't think was a good idea at the time. He was a member of the Armed Islamic Group (GIA), an Islamic fundamentalist group in Algeria, and I didn't want to get cornered with him and give him the chance to speak to me. If you do find yourself in the lift with the target make sure you are by the buttons – that way you dominate the lift and ask what floor he wants. Whatever one he says, you get out either on the floor above or below. My other alternative, which I took, was to go through the entrance door to the flats and I found myself in a long corridor with doors on either side. Now I'd committed myself I couldn't turn around and walk out in case he was still waiting there, so I walked the length of the corridor and out the door at the other end. I was having flashbacks of the Rossville flats in Londonderry except that this time I didn't have my friend Mr Browning with me. Another character who lived in the same flats was under some form of death threat from extremists he had informed on and, apparently, used to carry a hand grenade around in his pocket – lovely people!

Other targets included people from all different groups in London and sometimes you would work on them for a period of time, or else might do just one or two serials on them and not see them again for a long time. There was one particular group and one person in particular who was reported to be a member of the GIA. He was in fact an Imam, or spiritual leader, and once again this shows that in some cases violence goes hand in hand with religion. The GIA is a particularly ruthless group that operates mainly in Algeria where they have committed many atrocities in the name of religion. I feel I can say this with some authority because at the time of writing this I am working as a Security Advisor in Algeria and have seen reports of massacres of over 400 people including children, in one incident, from the same village, in circumstances that don't bear thinking about. Reports of children being dismembered in front of their parents were not uncommon. One of the worst times of the year for killings is the Muslim holy month of Ramadan. This is the most holy time of the year when they fast from dawn until dusk and they are not allowed to smoke or engage in sexual relations during the hours of daylight. Once dusk arrives they spend most of the night eating and drinking, with hardly any sleep. This will go on for four weeks and it can be quite a dangerous time for anyone working in a Muslim country – not so much for the violence but because after a couple of weeks they are so tired that they are walking around like zombies. Their driving becomes even more erratic and they will wander across the roads without looking and tempers become frayed. I came to a conclusion not long after I arrived here that Algerians don't drive: they put their foot to the floor, aim the car and hope everyone else gets out of the way. There is a saying here and that is '*Insh' Allah*', which means 'As Allah wills'. Their attitude toward everything is '*Insh' Allah*', be it crashing their car or whatever. They really don't care if they live or die because it all comes down to 'As Allah wills'. It's sometimes very difficult for expatriates to understand. Expats are encouraged to be more understanding during this difficult period. For some reason the GIA regards this as an auspicious time for killing and they go on the rampage. Although this sort of thing does not happen in Britain, interest was shown in these people because they are known to raise and supply money and also bomb-making equipment.

This guy lived in a relatively middle-class, mixed area of north London and was thought to be helping with funding for the GIA. We stayed with him for quite a while and helped build up a pattern of movement and also contacts. Unlike the Det where you would, more often than not, see an end result, it was unlikely in some of these cases as they would drag on for a long time and the desk officers were not prone to giving results or information. We took him to various addresses including mosques in different parts of London. Being an Imam it could be said that the reason for him being there was to conduct prayer meetings. On such an occasion, an outsider would have stuck out like the proverbial dog's bollocks; hence it was an ideal opportunity for him to meet other GIA members. One of his favourite haunts was the Regent's Park Mosque and he would drive his car in there effectively ending all form of surveillance until he came out again. It would then be a case of staking the area out until he came out again.

Another 'Imam' who came to light at this time was a veteran of Afghanistan with no legs, no arms and one eye. He must have been a very dedicated 'Imam' to get into situations where he would receive such injuries.

Anyway, back to my original Imam. There was one occasion where we had him under control and one of his favourite shopping haunts was a vegetable stall on Kilburn High Road about a mile or so from where SS used to go on the piss. The Imam would often make long phone calls from nearby public phone boxes before he bought his veggies. On one occasion another member of the team came up on the net and said they thought there was another team on him. He described two blokes who appeared to be acting in the same manner that we would be and also talking into their lapels – in other words into radio mikes. Some of the team stayed with the target and a couple of others thought of having a go at these two. They managed to get them on a bus but lost them soon afterwards. It was felt at the time, by the descriptions and gut feeling on the team, that they might have been Israelis. Did they have him under surveillance as well or did they have some other form of intention? We never did find out.

We actually spent a fair bit of time covering the GIA but I wasn't really aware of how much of a threat they were until I came to Algeria. They are very dangerous people and they have declared a Jihad (holy war) against the government and authorities in Algeria. They have stated that the war will not end until they have a pure Islamic state. The government and military will not allow that to happen so it really is deadlock. A lot of money flows into the GIA coffers from European countries, especially Britain, as well as electronic parts for bomb-making. A while back there was a report that a shipment of electrical and small computer parts from Britain had been intercepted hidden in tins of baby milk and talcum powder. These would be used for some of the more sophisticated bombs the GIA manufacture. To get hold of this stuff is not all that difficult because the organisation in Britain is very sophisticated and it doesn't cost them all that much money.

What they do is apply for a number of different credit cards under false names and then buy the kit by running the card to the limit. By the time the card company realises that the name and address is false, because the payments aren't being made, it is too late. If one man can apply for and get half a dozen credit/store cards, imagine what a whole organisation could do! It's also not uncommon for these people to be signing on at different DSS offices for dole, housing benefit and whatever else they can get. So the organisation in Britain is quite well funded, apart from what the local community and business people contribute willingly or otherwise. We spent an afternoon covering some guys going around the computer/electrical shops in Tottenham Court Road and another guy on another occasion going around a computer fair. With the relaxation of border controls on the continent it is little wonder there have been cases of Algerian terrorism in France and Belgium. Apart from some of the bombings in France in the late 90s attributed to Algerian extremists, there was an incident in 1999 where Belgian Special Forces raided a flat in Brussels where some more Algerian extremists were holed up.

Perhaps the most important operation I was involved in, along with most other people at the time, was the operation that culminated in the shooting in Hammersmith when the police stormed a hotel room. We were given information that a couple of blokes were on the scene and were thought to be part of an ASU planning a bombing campaign in London. We were given an address of where they were staying – just off the Hammersmith roundabout. As I have explained already I would not be fully aware of all the activity that went on with this ASU, because I may have been on another target from time to time and had leave. I can only describe it as I took part. Over the next few months we identified a further two English members of the ASU making four in all. They visited a number of addresses in London and although the other two members played their part the main players were thought to be the two Irishmen. As in previous operations they visited a number of storage facilities probably with the idea of storing kit there for their campaign. They themselves did not have a car but one of the ASU members did and also on one occasion hired a car when his was off the road.

They were eventually taken to an industrial estate and seen to enter a lock up premises. After they had left, the premises were searched that night and a large quantity of explosives was found. From that moment on they became the priority targets in London and A4 went to twenty-four-hour coverage of their every movement.

They tended to stick to the Hammersmith and Shepherd's Bush areas when they socialised and to frequent certain pubs including one just south of Hammersmith Bridge. We had a bit of trouble at first trying to pick them up from time to time but they were known to use the tube quite a lot. This problem was partially solved by using the cameras in London that can be seen on most junctions and covering tube entrances. I was on shift on the night when the raid went in but finished a couple of hours previously. There were three of them out drinking that night in the Hammersmith area and the young lad may have had a premonition that something was going to happen, because he looked a bit uneasy. They left the pub at closing time and we tracked all three of them back to the hotel. Obviously the powers that be must have had information that we were not aware of because a couple of hours later the police raided the flat and the young lad was shot dead. I believe at the time that the flat was bugged and this might have initiated the police response, although I cannot be certain. For everyone involved on the surveillance side it was a good job. It was also during this period that yet another attempt was made to bomb Hammersmith Bridge with a suitcase bomb and although the initiation device exploded the main charge didn't. It was put down to this ASU but there was never any proof as far as we knew.

There were jobs that, because of their sensitivity, we Army personnel were not involved in. Although I know of some of these jobs it is not my intention to put these into print because these could still be live operations and it is not my intention to compromise national security or individual personnel.

I remember another job though when we were deployed to try to gain access to a flat in London once the occupant had gone out. This took place in the area of Russell Square just south of Euston Station. The plan was for someone to enter through the front door and make their way to the emergency exit and let the rest of the team in. The couple doing the trigger were acting the part of a courting couple on a landing. They would give the occupants away and the entry team would gain access. My job was to drop off part of the team and then act as cover in Russell Square. I parked right next to the park in the square and I'd been there for about ten minutes when I noticed that it was actually very busy for that time of night. I then noticed that most of the activity was taking place amongst blokes. I'd only parked next to a fucking bender's paradise. You could see them walking around inside the park in groups and then darting off into the bushes. Other times a car would arrive and the driver would run in and then reappear a few minutes later and drive off. I'm not too sure of the outcome of the job but I came away a few hundred quid richer!

On one particular occasion we were covering a Russian diplomat in the Holland Park area of London and had taken him around quite a bit of London before housing him at his home address. Just about the end of the job now, I thought. I'd heard from the people at work about certain people in these relatively affluent areas being targeted by young blacks who would stalk and then mug them. The methodology was fairly simple but the results were nearly always the same. What they would do was hang around the shops and watch for anyone of interest who might be wearing expensive jewellery. Favourites were Asian women because, if they came from well-to-do families, they would wear heavy gold necklaces, bangles and watches, and they were also hardly likely to fight back. I'd been sitting in Holland Park for a while and I saw this young Asian woman turn the corner into what was a relatively quiet square. She was closely followed by two young black youths who were looking around a bit nervously. This did not look right so I switched on to it right away. Suddenly they made their move and grabbed her from behind. At this point I thought fuck the target; she could end up stabbed, raped or both. I started the car, put the headlights on full beam and went across the road, horn blaring, intending to ram the bastards if I could. I just missed one of them as he came out between two parked cars and the other one ran off down the street. I skidded to a halt and jumped out the car to try to get the one I missed but he wasn't having any of it and legged it down the street. My first thought now was for the woman; I made sure she was OK and, after telling her to stay where she was, followed them after informing the rest of the team and getting someone to phone the old bill. I searched the roads and back alleys but I couldn't find the little bastards. I went back to the woman and made sure she was OK and asked her what had been stolen and she said her Rolex that was worth about £15,000 and a necklace. The old bill turned up and I gave them details of what I'd seen and the action I'd taken. I had to declare whom I was working for because they wanted to know what I was doing sitting around there. By this time some of the woman's family had turned up and they took her away once the police had finished. After that bit of excitement the job was called off and I went back to Kingston.

I know everyone should have the right to walk the streets in peace but in London, but with all the muggings that go on, why walk around on your own at night with a £15,000 Rolex on your wrist? When I told my wife what had happened she went fucking apeshit and called me all the stupid buggers under the sun saying I had my own family and I could have been knifed. True, but someone has to stand up to these little toerags and I would hope that if the same thing happened to her someone else would have a go. Except it's not quite the same with a Timex! I was right anyway. It was the end of the job but not in the way I'd imagined!

One of the places I'd heard a lot about was Saughie Hall Street in Glasgow but I'd never been until one time we had a job come up there. We were tasked to cover a member of one of the Protestant paramilitaries who was coming over to watch the Rangers v Celtic Cup Final and also to take part in an Orange Order march. We were given a photo of the guy and told that he would be arriving at the airport on the Friday evening.

We drove up to Glasgow on the Thursday and checked into the Hilton Hotel (no crap for these guys). We would spend the next day carrying out orientation but that night had a few beers along the length of Saughie Hall Street and that was quite an experience.

On Friday evening we drove out to the airport and a few of us went inside in order to pick him up as he arrived. We were told that he would probably be picked up at the airport but there were no further details. In the airport we had to be careful, as we did not know who the third party was or how alert he/she would be. We went up to the bar and had a coffee because if anyone was waiting there was a good chance they might be in there as well. In the bar we had a look around and spotted someone who might have fitted the bill. The airport wasn't very crowded and this guy kept looking at his watch and checking the arrivals board. Come the time when the plane was due to arrive the guy paid his bill and went downstairs. We had someone on the airside of the airport because the police in Ireland had phoned through his description and the clothes that he was wearing. He was identified at the baggage reclaim and descriptions of him and his luggage were given and we waited for him to come into arrivals. Him and the guy from upstairs met up and walked out of the terminal. The priority now was to get the VRN (vehicle registration number) of the car. Two of us made our way out into the car park, watched them get into a car and then when they went mobile passed the VRN over the net. The vehicle was picked up and housed at an address just outside Glasgow, which gave us a start point the next day.

The following day we deployed to the area where the vehicle was housed and waited for him to emerge to pick him up. We knew where he would be going later that day and there were numerous volunteers to go complete in the stadium to watch him – and the match. But the Special Branch knew what seat he would be sitting in so they would control him by surveillance camera once he was inside – bloody spoilsports!

He was picked up coming out of the address and went into a pub for a pre-match warm-up. When he came out some time later to board a coach he was, to a layman's point of view, half pissed. On board the coach he sat at the back, which was ideal for a surveillance team. Some of the time I had the coach under control and he was definitely well on the way. We got the VRN of the coach and took it into the area of the stadium and got people out on foot to take him to the stadium. Once at the stadium they lifted off and it was left to the police in the ground to control him. At the end of the match he was triggered away and picked up as he approached the coach. The coach then drove back to the original pub where he went for a warm-down. After a couple of hours we lifted off, as the state he was in it was hardly likely that he was going anywhere except back to his pit. The next day we deployed to the same area as he was supposed to be taking a leading part in an Orange Order march at around lunchtime that day.

Earlier that morning I'd gone for a walk just up from the Hilton and watched the marchers forming up in a square before setting off for Glasgow City Centre, with fifes and drums playing. I'd worked for a number of years in Ireland by this time but this was the first time I had ever seen, at close hand, such solidarity with the Loyalist movement on the mainland. I had great admiration for David Trimble and how he persevered with the peace process despite intense opposition. There will, however, always be some faction that will not want peace. In many countries there is organised crime and I believe it is, and has been, rife in the province for many years. There is too much money to be made to have everything stopped completely. Call it the Irish Mafia if you like but I believe it exists and therefore I do not believe that all their weapons will be handed over either. I think there is still deep suspicion in both communities that if one faction decommissions completely they will be left undefended if it all breaks down and starts again. OK, so they will hand over some weapons and some explosives, but I believe that some stuff will remain hidden. There will always be weapons there ready for the day to come! It is also bred into the people from a very early age, as my experience in the Turf Lodge many years ago bore out.

Anyway, we went back to the area and watched him play quite a prominent part in the march before he went for a few pints. We thought it unlikely that he would get tanked up as he was supposed to be flying out that evening.

He came out not much later and went back to the address he was using. We had located the car he used on the Friday night and now waited for that to make a move back towards the airport. Early in the evening the car appeared with him as a passenger, drove to the airport and he went through and on to the plane. Once he was through we were lifted off and it was back to the hotel and out for a few beers before we drove back to London the next day.

Towards the end of my time in A4 I was asked if I might be interested in joining the Security Service once I'd left the Army. Now I can say that the majority of the people were great and I'd have no hesitation in working with them in the mainland environment. About ninety-five per cent of them wouldn't last five minutes across the water, but that comes down to environment and training. There are a lot of ex-service people in the organisation; one or two I had worked with before, and were good but the Service was getting their expertise on the cheap. I honestly don't know how they manage to live in London on the salary they are on because I couldn't.

Anyway, my answer to their question was yes with certain conditions: that they give me a safe house to live in and top whack salary for the grade I'd be starting on. I couldn't understand why they said no! When I spoke to my brother about this, he told me that they had tried exactly the same ploy with him in 1990 because of his expertise in counter-terrorist search ops. He had turned them down on money grounds as well – mercenaries or what!

As I have said, there are some very good people in the Service but like every organisation they have their share of wankers. The way the shift pattern worked was that you would work a late shift and start at 1430 hours and finish at about 2000 hours providing you weren't involved in a take with the target. After the shift had ended there were always people who lived in approximately the same areas so you would be teamed up with someone to get a lift home and be picked up in the morning to start an early shift. At this time we had a bloke from the Regiment who had worked with 14 Coy and now was attached to the Service. On this particular late shift this guy, who was brought up in Toxteth in Liverpool and was actually a bit of a hard bastard, was partnered with one of two brothers. At the end of the shift this bloke wouldn't give the Regiment guy a lift home because he said he had to take his dog to the vet in the morning. I think at the time the guy was too stunned to say anything and ended up having to get the train home that night and into work in the morning. He wasn't too impressed. He went into work the next morning and got this guy in a quiet corner and basically told him that if he ever pulled a stunt like that again he would beat the living shit out of him. These two were part of the same ten-man team so working together after that might have caused a bit of friction! The Service guy asked to be taken off surveillance duties because of the stress caused by that incident and he was put into the photographer's office. He wouldn't do surveillance again until the Regiment guy had left.

During one of our trips to Anglesey to cover the ferries from Ireland I was given a message from the team leader to phone Ashford the next day. There was no further message – just to phone first thing in the morning, as it was urgent. Shit, I thought, wondering what this could be, so I phoned my wife to make sure everything was OK, which it was and pondered the rest of the night as to what could possibly be wrong. First thing the next morning I phoned Repton Manor and got through to the secretary.

'Good morning, this is Sgt Major Alexander. I've had a message to phone the Boss first thing this morning, what's it all about?'

'I'm sorry, I can't tell you but I'll put you through straight away.'

By now I was panicking like fuck, wondering what had gone wrong or what I had done.

I was eventually put through and my first words were, 'Morning Boss, I was told to phone you first thing, what's the matter?'

'Nothing,' he said, 'I just wanted to be the first to congratulate you. You've just been awarded the MBE.'

You could have knocked me down with the proverbial feather. I mumbled something about thanks and put the phone down. I spent the rest of the day in something of a daze. Things like that don't happen to people like me for just, in effect, doing your job. Well, I phoned my wife that night and told her the good news and got a drink in for the rest of the team.

A few months later when I was at home, the invitations, car passes and everything came through for the investiture. The only trouble was I only had three invitations (which was standard) but I had four people to go – a wife and three kids. I phoned the

Palace and explained the situation to them but they explained that nobody got more than three tickets so I had to leave someone behind, which I thought was bloody unfair when you saw other people there with no guests. We went and stayed the night before the investiture in the flat in Kingston where I lived and then drove into London the next day.

We stopped in Hyde Park so I could put my uniform jacket on, took a couple of happy snappies, and then drove to the palace. I actually got quite a kick driving through the crowds, through the gates of the palace. After we'd had the car searched and invitations checked, we continued into the inner courtyard. I was then separated from the family who were seated and we were taken elsewhere and briefed on what to do and what to expect. As you do some of us got talking and with one bloke I was talking to, the chat got round to 14 Coy. I asked him what he did and he said he was an ATO (Ammunition Technical Officer) or bomb disposal expert and had done some work for the Group. I asked him what award he was getting and he said the George Medal, which is only the bloody highest peacetime award for gallantry. I considered what I had done in my life and some of the risks I had taken against the risks he would have taken and I suddenly felt quite humble in company such as that. Another person who was invested that day was Sir Cliff Richard. My wife was sitting almost next to him and she was really thrilled. We had our pictures taken afterwards (not with Cliff though) and I think my little lads were chuffed to bits. I have the video of me receiving my medal from Her Majesty and a photo of the family outside with the two boys holding the box, showing off the medal. It was yet another unforgettable experience. I will also say that when I was seven years old in Singapore (in 1961), Cliff was my idol and I used to comb my hair just like him and his record, *Bachelor Boy*, was the first pop record I ever bought.

It was just before this that I left A4 and was presented with an inscribed hip flask but what I appreciated most was a Security Service plaque they gave me. These were, apparently, very hard to come by and the team leader at the time had to call in a few favours to get me one. That, with some of my other memorabilia, occupies a prominent place in my house. As I mentioned earlier I also presented them with their portable trigger position!

While I was attached to A4 I knew the promotions board was coming around and I went to Ashford to see the guy who did the postings plot to find out about my promotion, which was due, and where I would be going next. His answer floored me when he said there was no way I was going to get any more promotion and as for posting he had me pencilled in for A4 for the foreseeable future as that was one less post for him to worry about. Apparently, although I had been getting excellent reports with all the recommendations for promotion, what everyone had failed to tell me that unless you made Warrant Officer (WO) Class One (I was a WO2 now) by the time you were forty-one you wouldn't get it, as you were considered too old. I was about six months short of forty-one at this stage and was told that even if I was picked up on the next promotions board I would be 41 before I would have got it so I would be ineligible. I asked to see the Brigadier Int Corps to see if it was worth applying for a commission.

Although he sympathised (he was an old friend of my brother) he really didn't see any way round it. What he did say was that as he sat on the board he would give me a heads-up after the board had sat to see if it was worth reapplying in the future if I failed this time. I didn't make it that time and I was told not to hold my breath. Too specialised, I was told. As far as I was concerned, in the game I had been involved in you needed people who were specialised and had the operating experience. If you look at some of the people who are still operating with A4 there are some who are no longer spring chickens but are perfectly capable of doing the job in London. I had two choices at this stage: the first to stay in as a WO2 for the next five years, the second to get out now while I was still young enough to be employable.

8

AFTER SHOCK

They say fate takes a hand in everything and it did with me on this occasion. I went to see the lady who held details on jobs that might be on offer on the outside and her office was in the medical centre. Passing through the med centre I saw a bloke from the Regiment whom I'd known on and off for a few years and he was doing a bit of medic work. I asked him what he was up to and he said he was on his resettlement course as he was getting out of the Army. I asked him what he was doing and he said he was going to work for a company called Rapport Research and Analysis, based in London but with contracts in Africa. I asked him what the money was like and what he told me was more than I was getting at the time. He also gave me the phone number and told me to get in touch. I did that and called into the London office. What I heard sounded OK, so I asked if there were any jobs going and mentioned that I would have to give twelve months' notice in to the army. The answer was fairly positive so I went back to Ashford and handed my notice in. I left the Army on 12 September 1997 and started a new job as a security advisor to a seismic survey crew in Algeria in October of that year. I have been in Algeria now for nearly five years working four weeks on and four weeks off for a firm that has been taken over so many times the guys put the company logo on their coveralls with Velcro.

I spent two years in the office in a place called Hassi Messaoud, went out to the desert for eighteen months and I'm now back in Hassi. The guys themselves are sound and I would say it's the nearest thing you could get that could be compared to camaraderie in the Army.

The first company, Rapport, actually turned out to be a nightmare. They were a relatively small company but with offices in Mayfair and one of the directors was a guy called Charlie

Pettifer who went on to marry Tiggy Legge-Bourke, Prince Harry and Prince Wills' nanny. Charlie was a nice enough guy but the guys here in Algeria got the feeling that this was a bit of a hobby for him.

The situation was that we would work for four weeks out here and then not be paid while we were at home. That wasn't a problem on paper because you could budget for that and the money over the year was good. What fucked everyone about was they assured us that we would get our money three weeks after we had gone home. This happened once or twice but more often than not the money would not go into the bank until after you were back in Algeria. One guy actually went three months before he was paid. Towards the end of 1999 they lost the contract to DSL (Defence Systems Limited), a much bigger firm. Because we had been with Western for a while and had done a good job for them they wanted to keep us on so we transferred across to DSL. Because of takeovers I have worked with other security firm firms. I finished my last stint for Rapport in December 1999 and it was towards the end of March that I finally got the last of my money from them. In the end, I resorted to threats of physical violence if we weren't paid and there were definitely a few of us prepared to go down and carry the threats out.

As to the seismic side, for those who have never seen a seismic crew (as I hadn't before I came out here) they are like a band of wandering gypsies: 'seismic scum' as they are known in the trade, or more commonly known as Doodlebuggers. This does not have the sexual connotations as people may think but more after one of the types of vehicle they use known as a Doodlebuggy. Unlike a drilling platform – that is, static and comfortable – these guys are mobile and must be able to move locations, and even countries, as and when required. Therefore everything is contained in trailers on wheels and so it is a case of hitching it up to a truck and off you go. The problem when you move is that some of the trucks or buggies cannot go that fast so the normal travelling speed is down to around 25 kph.

Doing this for eight hours per day over six days (which my last camp move was) gets a bit tedious. It's all very civilised though because at the end of the day the camp forms up in a suitable location and everything is connected so you have hot food, hot showers and a bed to sleep in. These guys, because they have done it for so long, have got it down to a fine art and in the mornings it only takes about an hour to pack it all up again and get back on the road. I suppose one of the perks of a camp move is that there are usually a couple of crates of beer available when you stop each night. Just to break the monotony, you understand!

Some of these guys have spent years in the industry and this is the next best thing they have to family. Their break schedule is six on and three off so the trailer where they live is really their home. The actual facilities they have are quite comfortable considering the harsh working conditions. The trailers are air-conditioned in the summer and heated in the winter. We have hot showers and flushing toilets and more than an adequate supply of drinking water. There is, surprisingly, a hell of a lot of water in the desert; you just can't see it. You may have to drill down a couple of hundred metres to get it but it's there. We also have a well-equipped kitchen and the cooks produce some really good food. Perhaps the biggest gripe amongst the lads is that they have to share a cabin in bunk beds. Some of these guys aren't spring chickens or sylph-like anymore, so to have to climb on to the top bunk is a pain in the arse for some of them. In one trailer there are four cabins and each one is about 10' x 8' so space is at a premium.

Many people may not realise but there are extremes of temperature in the desert – it isn't always hot. In the middle of the summer I have known temperatures of 55 degrees Celsius (over 130 degrees Fahrenheit) during the day and that may only fall to 30 Celsius at night so it is a case of having the air conditioning on twenty-four hours a day. During the winter it is definitely a case of wearing a fleece in the evenings and in the mornings until the sun comes up and then it may get down to a chilly 20–22 Celsius. Anything below 30 and the Algerians are wrapping themselves up in jumpers and coats whereas we Westerners are still walking around in shorts and T-shirts. Also in the winter we have had snow, ice, frost, magnetic storms and absolute deluges of rain. I try telling my kids that we have had snow and ice in the Sahara desert and they look at me as though my name has suddenly changed to Grimm. At the time of writing this, Remembrance Day 2000, the temperature is a cool 27 degrees Celsius.

We have worked in the tallest sand dunes in the world and they are about 300 m high. It is like looking at a range of hills except that these are sand and moving. To try to drive through these and navigate can be quite an experience. We are equipped with a handheld Global Positioning System, or (GPS), and that makes the whole thing quite simple, giving your position to within 100 m. It amazes me the way some of the Algerians don't even need one of these things; it all seems to be in their head.

If you were to say to one, 'OK Abdullah, I need to go to so-and-so,' he would think for a couple of seconds and say, 'OK Mr Sam, let's go,' and off you'd go and actually get there.

For people who have seen any news on Algeria they may think the whole country is dangerous with massacres taking place everywhere every couple of days. This is not the case in the main areas of the oil industry. Oil and gas comprise more than ninety-five per cent of the Algerian economy so it is in their interests to keep those areas well protected. Most of the trouble is in the mountainous areas in the north and on the coast. The main threat in the southern areas is the threat of banditry and smugglers. With this threat the main problem is theft, especially of Toyota 4 x 4s. These are the workhorses of the industry here and in the big sand you wouldn't get anywhere without one. To this end each drill crew or seismic crew that is operating out here, provided there are expats on crew, will have a detachment of military or gendarmes as their protection force. These guys are here to guard the base camp and to provide armed escorts to expats who need to go off into the desert to work. Some of them can be good but some are indifferent. There is still National Service in Algeria and although some of the more senior ranks may be professionals the majority are just kids doing their time. As long as they have their satellite TV, a football, a bed to sleep in, good food and the occasional packet of fags, they are OK. Every now and again the commander will get bored and come up with a new set of demands and that is why all the security advisors out here are ex-military. Having been there before you can understand where they are coming from and can either reason with them or put them off for a while or just say no. They know the score and as long as you are firm but fair with them they will play ball with you. They might say that they are not going to do this and that, but you can point out to them that they are here to protect the expats and that if they try to rock the boat you will report them to his Commandant. The threat of replacement is usually enough to make them toe the line. While they are here in the south they are happily away from the fighting in the north of the country and some of them have no wish to go up there.

Although Algeria is a third-world country, the people are glad to be in work (there is about thirty-five percent unemployment and more below the poverty line), especially for any firm to do with the oil and gas industry. Desert crews can have anywhere between 120 and 300 local workers and I do not see how the local labourers manage to work in such conditions.

The way seismic works basically is that a front crew lays out a line of geophones on the ground, and the vibrators go along and shake the ground. The signals are then passed back to a machine called a recorder where the data is 'recorded' and then more labourers known as the back crew pick up the geophones that have been used. These guys, in the summer when the temperature is in excess of 50 degrees Celsius, are walking along laying these geophones out and in some conditions they have to walk up and down these massive sand dunes for twelve hours a day.

They work eight weeks on and two weeks off and the working day is 0600–1800 with no day off. It must be especially bad for them during Ramadan where from dawn until dusk they are not allowed to eat or drink. Although I haven't seen it when Ramadan occurs in the summer they apparently drop like flies and I can't blame them. The expats on the crew work the same hours for their six weeks on and three weeks off and once again there are no days off, so it is a pretty harsh regime for all concerned.

I do not want to get into mentioning all the characters by name or description because there are too many, but I will mention two. In one of the *Blackadder* series he describes the Welsh as 'huge gangs of tough, sinewy men who roam the valleys terrifying people with their close harmony singing'. Well, there was someone similar to that on the crew except that he wandered around the dunes.

He's grey now but the rest of the description fits him to a tee, especially after a few beers when he starts singing and doing his Tom Jones impression. Good luck, Bach!

When I first came to Algeria I didn't know what to expect or whom I would meet so I asked, at the Rapport offices, if there was anyone else going over whom I could perhaps make myself known to. Yes there was, I was told, I'd probably (definitely) find him in the bar. Just look for the world's oldest man with a droopy moustache, long sideburns and earrings. Well I got to the bar in the Moat House hotel at Gatwick and there he was; you couldn't miss the wizened old bugger. I introduced myself and have known him ever since. All the best, you twat.

Being a security advisor in Algeria, certainly on a seismic crew, involves having a certain amount of time to yourself and it is difficult to find some form of leisure pursuit to fill your time. After a while going for a walk in the dunes loses its appeal and so I turned to learning French again, because it is one of the main languages spoken over here. However, Arabic and English are slowly replacing French. A lot of the people employed here are ex-Foreign Legion for the obvious language ability, but I'm afraid it doesn't come easily to me. I quite often find that I think in German as that comes easier. Certainly when I went back to college to brush up on my French, before I came over here, I was thinking in German and then translating it into French. Perhaps one of my biggest leisure pursuits on the crew was reading. I used to read a lot but let it fall by the wayside. I have now started again in a big way. I have read most of the Andy McNab and Chris Ryan books and I think anyone from the background I was involved in will naturally gravitate towards that type of book. Spy stories and most thriller novels are the sorts of things that I will go for.

I was given a book to read a while back and I must admit, when I was first told the title, I thought it was all about sport parachuting and nearly didn't bother until I read the front and back covers. Once I got my teeth into it I couldn't put it down. The book was called *Freefall* by Tom Read. Without giving too much away it was about a former member of the Regiment who suffered a psychotic breakdown and went through years of therapy. He then killed himself by jumping from a plane without a parachute; his burden was that big. Read later in the book and you might pick up on some of the conflict people feel. It was one of the most fascinating books I had read in years. Some people might say, 'OK, it's easy to pick up on something you've just read and try to make something out of it.' That's true, but I have only mentioned it because there are certain passages in the book I can relate to and if I hadn't read the book I wouldn't have mentioned them here. As far as I was concerned, this stage in my life was finished, until I read Tom's book, for the reasons I will describe later.

The reason for my interest is that some of the things he described in his book were some of the things I have been going through over the last few years, certainly since leaving the Army, and talking to other people who have left, especially, Special Forces. This does not stop there, because there are people from other Elite units – namely the Royal Marines and the Parachute Regiment – who feel the same way. Unless, however, someone points these things out to you, you don't realise they are bloody well happening. You can be in total naive oblivion. As he pointed out, for anyone in the Army, your life was pretty well ordered and you didn't have an awful lot to worry about. The troubles begin when you come out and suddenly find you are in the big bad world all on your own.

The first hurdle comes when you have decided to leave the security of the Army and have to find a job that is going to keep you in the fairly decent lifestyle that you have become used to. For someone with this sort of background, and not that many qualifications, that sort of job is hard to find in the UK and unless you are lucky enough to get one, other jobs don't pay enough. You are therefore drawn naturally to working abroad in this line of work and although you are away from home the money is there for the family.

I found that this was where the pressure – more often than not self-induced pressure – started. Although I slagged Rapport off for what happened towards the end of the contract, I will always be grateful to them for the start they gave me. I started work, on good money when I got it, one month after I left the Army. I have known blokes to spend in excess of one year out of work and they have had to accept that whatever job they get will pay a lot less than the Army.

While I was working in London we bought a house that was to be the family home and suited us apart from the elderly neighbours, who proved to be a pain in the arse towards the kids. I suppose it didn't help when I was doing some DIY and was trying to open up a chimney and went through to their living room; my last DIY project. I think it was around this time that things started to go wrong in my personal life. A lot of it was of my own making but not exclusively, as you will read later. Things, apart from that, were quite settled, and after a while I started working abroad. We then moved to a larger house because of school boundaries and other circumstances. Having been part of a team doing some very good jobs and in a lot of cases some very important ones I found that I wasn't getting that buzz any more and started to resent it. Some of it might have been due to the circumstances in which I found it necessary to leave the Army because I thought they had fucked me over. When I talked about the sequence of orders during the CTR phase I referred over and over again to 'what if?'

Well now it was my turn for the 'what ifs?' and they were things like, 'What if I lose my job and can't pay the mortgage? What if this happens and what if that happens? What will happen to the kids (because I will feel as though I've let them down and they'll think I'm a failure)? What if, because I haven't got the qualifications I can't go for anything else?'

I started to suffer from mood swings. When things were going well everything was OK, but when the pressure started to build up I would go into black moods and unfortunately, the most important people to me, my family, would suffer. At this time just little things would start me shouting, even at the kids, for no apparent reason. It might have been something as stupid as something I had mislaid. That was it. No matter what I was doing, it went on hold. It was obsessive behaviour and it didn't matter whether it took me five minutes or one hour – I had to find it. Once that had happened, the atmosphere in the family had gone until my mood had changed.

Sometimes that atmosphere would last from the day before up until the morning I was going away again. I would always get a kiss and a cuddle from my two youngest but quite often my wife and I would just walk past each other, say 'bye' and she would walk out the door and go off to work. I would then just walk around the house feeling fucking miserable and looking at things that seemed important to me in the knowledge that I wouldn't see them again for another four weeks. I would then spend sleepless nights thinking about how, and more importantly why, I'd fucked up and made the break a misery for all concerned – but it didn't stop it from happening again.

I think the hardest part about coming home was the fact that everyone seemed to be getting on fine without me. I don't know what I expected when I arrived home but my wife would say, 'Well, what did you expect? Did you think we'd fall apart just because you weren't here?'

The kids seemed fine, the house was OK and everything was ticking over. I suppose I should have felt good because it showed a strong family unit that didn't cave in. After a while, however, I got to question where I fitted in to all this because I felt they obviously didn't seem to need me except for the money that was coming in each month. I got more and more withdrawn and at that time, although I felt resentful, I couldn't understand why or how it had started.

I found that my appetite went and, although I'd already been on a diet for years, I just wouldn't eat because I was paranoid about trying to keep my weight down to what it was when I was as fit as fuck twenty years ago. I found that I was drinking too much because there wasn't anything to do and that was a Catch-22 situation. I was drinking because I felt worthless and because I was drinking too much it used to cause arguments with my wife and consequently I would think, fuck it, what's the point? and drink more, causing more arguments. I felt I was on a downhill spiral and couldn't stop. I felt as if I had pressed the self-destruct button. I became paranoid and felt that if something went wrong it was a conspiracy and that people were out to get me and trip me up.

Even during the first few days I was home I felt I couldn't relax because I felt as if there was always someone watching and waiting for me to fuck up. I'd always been so confident in my own ability and now I wasn't, except when I was at work. When I was at home I liked to go and pick the kids up from school but when I used to walk into the playground I would always stand on my own. There used to be some of my wife's friends there but I'm not the sort of person who will go and force myself into other people's company. So, if there was a group of them talking, I would just stand on my own – no problem to me. Also on some of my days at home, especially on the first one or two, I would maybe go into town and, because I just wanted somewhere quiet and be able to relax, I would go for a pint in one of the pubs in town. After that, I might not even bother for the rest of the break and I certainly didn't go out in the evenings. This was always on my own because apart from my wife's friends I didn't have friends of my own where we lived; that's the nature of the business unfortunately. I would do it just to feel that I was back home where I belonged and also to do some people watching again. While I was there if I had the car I would never have more than one pint and if I was on the bus I would have two, max. Now, you can have one pint or you can have five pints, it doesn't matter because the alcohol will remain on your breath for quite a while.

My wife came in one day and asked me if I had been drinking at lunchtime. I replied yes, I'd had one pint in town while I was there and enquired why she was asking. It turned out I'd picked the kids up from school and was talking to one of her friends and she'd bubbled me because she could smell alcohol on my breath. So fucking what! At that time I was a grown man in my mid-forties who worked away from home for four weeks at a time and if I couldn't have a beer without someone putting his or her nose in then what the fuck was the point? I then went through a stage of thinking I couldn't even have a beer at lunchtime because someone would bubble me to my wife and I'd be in the shit again. I nearly reached the stage of telling the kids to walk home on their own but in the end I thought fuck them (the other adults) they're not going to do it to me.

I was finding that my sleep pattern was becoming increasingly disrupted and I was going to bed late and getting up in the early hours of the morning. It might have been just a noise outside that woke me up but once awake my mind would immediately start racing and I couldn't get back to sleep. Rather than wake my wife up with my tossing and turning I would get up and retreat to my reclining chair in the living room with a duvet and watch videos for the rest of the night. The time when I'd get up could range from anything from 1 a.m. to 4.30 a.m. If I managed to get three hours' sleep a night I considered myself lucky. Sometimes I would be downstairs dreading the rest of the family getting up because that would disturb my lethargy. I got to feel that all I came home for was to cook and look after the house and apart from that I was of no use to anyone. While I was at work I was fine, apart from feeling like shit because I had fucked up yet another break. At work, I was doing something and I felt as though I had something to contribute and people actually seemed to appreciate what I was doing.

I found that everything was getting on top of me and I just couldn't see any way out of it. In particular it came to a head in the few months leading up to and over Christmas 1999. The company I was working for in Algeria was restructuring and it looked for a while as if I would lose my job and I didn't know how to handle it. Up to then I had always been in control and as far as I was concerned nothing touched me. Suddenly the prospect loomed of no job and I was panicking at not being in control any more. After that things, to me, seemed to feel as if they couldn't get any worse. I really felt as if I was losing it. I went to a football match with my cousin Mac and we had a few beers on the way. I don't know whether it was the beer or the state of mind I was in at the time but we went for a kebab before the match. I asked him to spare me a few minutes while I tried to explain. We sat down and I told him that I had never felt so low in my entire life and then explained a bit about how I felt but then I decided that he didn't want to hear all my troubles and stopped. It was shortly after that I found out what was happening to me. In Algeria we used to get a company health magazine each month and there were some quite good tips in there sometimes. I was reading this small article on stress one day and I just looked at it and thought, those symptoms they are describing are exactly what

I'm suffering from. I have, actually, sought advice about this from the medical profession and found that it has worked because I have an understanding doctor.

The symptoms were weight loss, excessive drinking, temporary loss of memory, lack of concentration and loss of interest in life in general. The excessive drinking would only occur at home though because alcohol at work was strictly controlled. I now discovered that I was suffering from depression and looking back now if things had kept on the way they were, I would have headed for a breakdown.

I suddenly felt as if a great weight had been lifted from my shoulders because now I knew what it was I could do something about it. I decided that, fuck it, you only live once so get a grip and be grateful for what you've got.

In the past my wife had tried to persuade me to go to Relate when our marriage had hit rocky patches because of my moods (because of events later that I now believe were manipulative) but I had always refused to let any outsider in on what was, to me, my business. As they say in the Forces, what happens in the Mess stays in the Mess. I always felt that we should be able to sort it out ourselves and I felt the same way now because I knew that once I had identified the problem I could find my own way of dealing with it. I wasn't going to start taking drugs to combat it because I think that once you are on them it is very difficult to get off.

My prescription was to kick myself up the arse and to adopt a more positive mental attitude, and I have found that that has worked. Since then (although now separated) I have become very careful about my moods. If I could see them coming I tried to back off before they got out of hand but sometimes it wasn't easy and sometimes I couldn't help it. For example, if something had gone missing before everyone, including the kids, would probably have felt like shit and disappeared to their bedrooms until Dad had found whatever it was he was looking for. Then I thought so what, if I find it I find it. It will be there somewhere. It just wasn't worth making the whole house feel afraid of you because of some stupid piece of kit. I still had my bad days but they got fewer and farther between. My sleep pattern was, and is, still bad, mainly through stress. Years later, I still got the feeling sometimes that I didn't want to go to sleep because the time I used to have at home with the family was so precious that I didn't want to waste it on sleep. I'd rather catnap in the chair so I was making the most of it.

Part of the problem was being afraid of not waking up again and what I'd miss. It didn't matter if they were asleep; so long as I was awake I knew they were there and that they'd be OK; I miss that now. I also found another small article in another edition of the same company publication that I cut out and used to carry in my wallet until I put it through the washing machine along with my bloody mobile phone. It was by M. Scott Peck, MD, whom I presume is or was an American and it's about being valuable.

'The feeling of being valuable is the cornerstone of self-discipline, because when one considers oneself valuable, one will take care of oneself in all ways that are necessary. Self-discipline is self-caring.' When I wasn't feeling valuable (I might have been but I just didn't feel it) I was lethargic, I wasn't taking care of myself and I thought, fuck it, I just don't care any more. I wasn't eating and walked around in total lethargy but I also felt very angry and very aggressive, just waiting for someone outside the house to say something and I honestly think at that time I was waiting to punch somebody's fucking lights out. I would actually walk through town staring at people and waiting for a reaction.

What Scott Peak could have added to that passage is the importance of other people making you feel valuable. I was as guilty as anyone over that and used to take my kids for granted but not any more. As I said at the start my kids are my life but you can never take anything for granted with them, because when they're grown up you'll suddenly find that maybe they don't want to bother with you any more, if you haven't made the effort with them earlier.

I didn't know Tom Read but I have worked alongside some of the people he mentioned in his book (if they are the same ones I am thinking of) at Ponty. Although he was in 'B' Squadron he may well have known my mate whom I refer to as Ken because he was Boat Troop 'A' Squadron and they would have been in the Regiment at around the same time. My family will be surprised to read this because I don't even think they know how bad things got. They would all ask if I was OK and I would say I was fine knowing full well I wasn't and that there was this Mr Depressed But Fucking Angry just under the surface dying to get out. I was very fortunate not to go through the same experiences Tom Read did, and I am not trying to draw any form of comparison, but I would really like to have thanked him for telling his story. At the start of this passage I said I would give the reasons for writing this later. The main reason is that for someone who has gone through some of the experiences I have been through it is very difficult actually to admit to something like this because the feeling is that this sort of thing only happens to someone else and you don't want to admit to any form of weakness. It certainly wouldn't dare to affect someone like me – WRONG, because these things will affect you, no matter how hard or brave you are! So if I hadn't read his book I would never have had the guts to explain, and I would not have explained in this book, what I went through with my depression.

They say that a book never ends and that if you do not succeed at the first attempt to go back and try again. When I left the Service, because of the books that had been written, I was obliged to sign a non-disclosure document. At that time I was happy to do that and I still, to this day, would not give anything away that I thought would harm the interests of my country or, perhaps more importantly, the people I worked with or those people who are still risking their lives because most of the politicians don't give a shit.

What a lot of people fail to realise is that these people work in extremely difficult circumstances with no thought of themselves because that is what they joined for, but look how stretched we were in, say, September 2006. The Forces have suffered years of defence cuts but are expected to do more and more. The politicians need to wake up and realise that these people give their all, in some circumstances, but they are still human beings and have families. If Britain wants to be on a par with the Americans then let's spend a proportional amount of money to support our troops and enable them to do the job that the politicians want them to do. What a lot of people may not realise is that the troops have to go out and buy suitable equipment for themselves because the Army does not provide it – why? Perhaps the politicians these days (the vast majority of which have had no military experiences) need to go and have fruitful discussions with the troops. I don't mean talking to the Ruperts but talk to the guys on the ground one-to-one with no repercussions and no Ruperts present. My own son has recently joined the Army, of which I am so proud, but I took him into town to buy a lot of kit for him.

However, back to the non-disclosure document. It was my privilege to work with a lot of these people but I would like to mention why a lot of books about these organisations are written. For what you are expected to do in the armed forces as a whole and especially some specialised branches, the financial reward received for the risks taken does not balance. Please do not get me wrong because the people who do these jobs do not do it for the financial reward, they do it because they love doing it. It is just that when you leave and receive your pension you can see the inequality in what you have done compared to others in Civvy Street.

When I left I had the option, as does everyone else, of taking a reduced lump sum payout but receiving a slightly larger pension or a larger lump sum but reduced pension. My pension after over twenty-two years' service amounted to approximately £6,000 per year before tax. I chose to take the larger lump sum so that went down to just under £5,000 before tax. This is not likely to keep you financially secure so therefore you have to embark on a second career. Don't forget you have given over twenty-two years of your life to the service of your country with all the risks you would have taken. I read an article a while back, concerning the problems with pensions in industry. They quoted a steel worker who, after twenty years with the same company, would have walked away with a lump sum comparable to mine but with a yearly pension of £15,000. Could someone please explain to me the, as I see it, disproportionate levels of pensions? This is why you have people from the Forces writing these sorts of books because if their country won't look after them then they have to look after themselves. The Forces pension is non-contributory but I am sure, in today's financial climate, the opportunity to top this up with voluntary contributions towards a larger retirement pension would not be ignored by a lot of financially astute people. That doesn't just mean Ruperts either.

In the film *Bravo Two Zero* Andy McNab said that when they got back from the Gulf they were descended on by a load of psychiatrists looking for signs of post-traumatic stress disorder and that the psychiatrists were more stressed out than them. That's probably true because it is easier to come to terms with stress when you have your friends and guys you have worked with and shared experiences with around you. Remove that 'comfort zone' and things start to get harder. I think it would be very interesting to interview people a few years after they have left Special Forces and find out, if they would be truthful, how many are finding it difficult. Rub away the tough, macho exterior and you might find that you have some – and I'm not saying all, but some – who might be putting on a brave face to disguise what they are really feeling and going through. For anyone who had not seen the film I would recommend you to give Bravo Two Zero a viewing because it epitomises Special Forces life. It is an absolute insight in the way people are loyal to each other and the camaraderie of forces life in general.

With what I have said so far, things have a remarkable way of turning themselves around and this was just another chapter in my life so far. I was obliged to change jobs again in January 2003 – yet another fuck-about in my life. I walked into my new location not knowing what to expect but I was very fortunate to meet someone who has become a very good friend and someone who I could, and do, depend on sometimes to keep me sane with all the shit I have had to put up with over the last couple of years.

As I said, I walked in not knowing what to expect and was introduced to the two pilots. I took one look at this guy and he didn't look like what you would expect from a pilot. I introduced myself, as you do, and said, 'Hi, I'm Sam, the new security guy.'

His words were, 'Yes I know, I can tell.'

I just knew there was something different about this guy and after a while I found out what it was. He had spent quite a while with Belgian Special Forces and we were both on the same wavelength. I'd only been there a couple of days and some of the expats had a BBQ. At these occasions we were either invited or, after a while, there would be a coalition between the Belgian, the Malaysian (the other pilot) and me, the Brit, whereby we would gatecrash. There was never a problem as we were always good company. Even the bosses used to say that it was good to see the security guy joining in and having a couple of beers. This is one thing I have always done as the security man and that is to socialise. There are too many instances of the security keeping themselves aloof and not mixing. This leads to suspicion amongst the rest of the crew because they think that you are always looking for ways to trip them up. Not so in my case because I had looked at all the possibilities and the only way to get accepted was to socialise. If you do I have found that people respect you more because you can have a couple of beers but the next day you are still the professional and will tell these guys what they can and can't do. They do respect you for that.

Anyway, we were at this BBQ and me and Johann (he'll hate me for this) got talking about various things, and he just turned around and said, 'You can't let it go, can you?'

I looked him in the eyes, thought and said, 'No I can't.'

We talked for a while and he explained that when he came out he went through months of counselling to get him back into thinking straight. He then said that any time I wanted to talk to him about things just to knock on his door. After a while of thinking about things I did. Prior to this I went and saw a doctor and explained my problem and asked if he could put me in touch with a counsellor with whom I could talk my problem through.

Looking back at this now I feel as though my wife was pressuring me into this. She, by now, was in a job where part of it was to manipulate people. I was in a situation where nothing I did was right and it seemed to me that affection was handed out as and when she thought fit. If I tried to talk to her about my situation it was always the case of, 'I'm too tired,' 'I'm too busy,' or 'I've got things to do'.

Then again, it was also a case of with me being away and working abroad, that she didn't want to know. It was a major part of my life but she just did not want to know because she was at home all the time, had her own little clique of friends and I was just an intrusion. In the end I was being manipulated into what she thought I should be and eventually I saw through it and, once again, as in the rest of my life, started to rebel. It caused many arguments about the fact that I was not going to be dictated to and have my life ruled by someone else because I had my own life and nobody was going to dictate to me. Why should I be turned into someone that another person wants me to be, even if it is my wife?

I said earlier that my kids will be able to follow their own destiny without any constraints from me, so why can't I? I am no angel and there are things I have done that I regret to this day. Can you imagine, however, when you are on the phone from Algeria thinking everything is OK and all of a sudden you are told, 'I have made it my mission in life to destroy you emotionally.'

This continued to the day we split and it was a case of, 'You be a good boy and let's see how we get on.'

Bollocks, I'm made of stronger stuff than that. I will go so far to accommodate people but unless they start to accommodate me, especially when I can see through them, they can think again. Also with what was said about destroying me emotionally I can look back now and see there was a very subtle but gradual progression over the years to achieve this and it very nearly worked.

Can you imagine what it is like to be in a situation where you are away from home for four or more weeks at a time and in certain circumstances putting up with a load of shit? You go home and try to relax but you can't because someone is on your back giving you a hard time. I would arrive home on Thursday and always used to say, 'Give me the weekend to relax until Monday and then I'm yours.' That wasn't good enough, however, and invariably by Saturday night she would blow a fuse and that would set the scene for the rest of the break. Was this manipulation or was I, perhaps, being too sensitive? I don't think it was the latter. You try to explain what it is like but she doesn't know or will never understand what it is like because she has never been there. To try to explain to someone who has never been involved in things in my past and what I am doing now is extremely difficult when firstly they can never understand because they have never been there and done it and secondly when they are not interested.

It's not just not being involved in this; it also comes down to the fact that you cannot even have an in-depth conversation about life in general. I think it also relates to a line in the film, *A Few Good Men*, starring Jack Nicholson. When he is being questioned in court about an order called 'Code Red', he rejoinders with, 'You can't handle the truth.' Some people in their sheltered little lives either do not want to know, or are happy to ignore, the truth. As I tell people from time to time, 'The reason why people like you can sleep safe in your beds at night is because people like me are out there doing the shit that you either don't want to get involved in or are not interested in. Why get involved in other people's problems when you have your own cushy life to lead?'

When I am working away I come into contact with some very intelligent people and people who keep an eye on what's going on in the world. We can have some really good conversations on all sorts of subjects and people appreciate your point of view and I theirs. I have had conversations with senior British and Foreign politicians and very senior British military personnel. When trying to get into an in-depth conversation at home it would go to a certain point where my wife either knew nothing about the subject or had a go hinting that I didn't know what I was talking about.

I must have been doing something right in the jobs I am managing to hold down and the fact that other companies are prepared to make me offers. I have always been able to fit into any environment and that might be part of the problem at home; I think it comes down to jealousy again as I will mention once more later. When trying to have an in-depth conversation at home the same thing used to happen when it started to get too deep or intellectual; it became a case of, 'Oh don't be so bloody stupid, you don't know what you are talking about.'

Sometimes it would degenerate to her face six inches from mine ranting and raving because that was the only way she could handle it and then give me a right hook to the jaw, which made me laugh the first time it happened. She had given it her best shot and I just stood there laughing and quoted a Billy Connolly line: 'Is that the best you can do?' It didn't hurt but can you imagine the shit I could have got into if I had retaliated. The hook end of a coat hanger coming at your face was not quite so funny but it was just a question of restraint.

Anyway, most of the time I do know what I am talking about because if I don't I will listen to other people and debate the subject with them. I then got round to that way of feeling, why should I fucking bother because she's not interested in my life?

It was then a case of, 'You never talk to me.'

What the fuck could I talk about if I couldn't explain how I felt without her getting bored because, as far as I was concerned, there was no interest and the attention span was minimal!

Anyway, back to Johann. I talked to him about all of this and found that he was the one person with whom I could talk to; he could understand me and I him. The main thing is that he was normally at the end of a phone or on the email so I could talk things through. I thought about a counsellor but how could they relate to me if they hadn't been through the same things I have? How can you describe to a stranger the feeling of what it is like and the rush you get? To have that elation of getting back from a job without being killed or worse, as would have been in my and my colleagues' cases, being captured and brutally tortured before being killed. On a lighter note, I would come back sometimes and say, and I still repeat it to this day, 'I'm still here, ya bastards.' This is why I could talk to Johann, because we had something in common. At home, my two brothers-in-law are golfing fanatics. When we were at a get-together and you tried talking, the chat invariably got around to golf. I tried to be interested but in the end it was just the two of them talking about fucking golf. There was polite conversation about what I was doing but invariably the obvious happened and it got turned around to, for example, 'Did you see who the Captain (or lady Captain) was sitting with last Sunday?'

Who fucking cares?

The same happened if I went out with my wife's friends because the talk was always about their work and each other. Where did I fit in? If I tried to steer the talk around to what I was doing it was once again a case of, 'Yeah, OK.'

It was then back to them. The only time I got to have a conversation in that company was with another husband or boyfriend who didn't work with them, because they got dragged along and were just as bored to fuck with what's happening at their wife or girlfriend's work. In fact, thinking about it, you very rarely got another husband there because like me they'd probably learnt their lesson.

In fact it got to the stage where I became fed up of all my wife's family preaching to, and trying to alter, me that I eventually turned around to her and said that as far as I was concerned the whole lot could go and fuck themselves and I haven't seen them since. Drastic or what!

So, once again, I think why should I fucking bother? As I mentioned earlier, Johann said that when he came out of the Special Forces he had to go through months of counselling to talk through it and get back to normal. I kept saying to my wife, 'You will never understand.'

To which I was told, 'Oh be quiet will you, you're just a wannabe.'

Well, I'm sorry, but after having read this book I'm sure you'll agree that I'm not a wannabe because I've actually done it. I sometimes got the impression of jealousy because I've actually done a lot with my life and I have the awards and respect, from my peers, to show for it. I am now coming to terms that it was not just me, but I was the one that underwent a determined constant effort to grind me down and a deliberate effort to undermine my confidence and make me feel inferior. What have I got to feel inferior about? I have done some of the hardest courses in the world.

I have honours other people could only dream about and the respect of the people I work and have worked with. That is good enough for me. If it is not good enough for other people then fuck them! For example, the Mention in Despatches is only a small bronze Oak Leaf attached to another medal but it is, in fact, the oldest form of recognition of Gallantry in the United Kingdom armed forces: think about that!

My wife and I, in 2005, finally separated after all those years; the end to yet possibly one of the final chapters in my life. We are still friends but after all the years of problems we just can't live together. I now have a new three-bed apartment only ten minutes' drive from the family home and my kids are regular visitors as I have made the apartment as I want it and they have their own bedrooms. It makes a good stopover for them as most of their friends are in the area where I now live. It is also on the seafront overlooking the Welsh hills which gives me the space and freedom I enjoy instead of being in, what I felt became, a depressing and claustrophobic row of detached four-bed houses. Within two minutes of leaving my front door I am on the seafront with the opportunity to walk out to an island that boasts a seal colony – bloody marvellous! I do not want to pontificate on the subject but sometimes a sacrifice on one's own part is often better for the communal good. Certainly I feel now that my kids are getting stronger emotionally because they can see their dad as he used to be years ago instead of the shell that he became.

However, I would like to include a poem by one of our finest writers who, being born in India during the British Raj had a somewhat clearer vision of the mentality of the British soldier (and sometimes it takes some understanding for those who can't and won't understand) in some of the other poems he wrote; it is something my mother gave me years ago and I still have it.

If – by Rudyard Kipling

If you can keep your head when all about you
Are losing theirs and blaming it on you;
If you can trust yourself when all men doubt you,
But make allowance for their doubting too;
If you can wait and not be tired by waiting,
Or, being lied about, don't deal in lies,
Or, being hated, don't give way to hating,
And yet don't look too good, nor talk too wise;
If you can dream – and not make dreams your master;
If you can think – and not make thoughts your aim;
If you can meet with triumph and disaster
And treat those two imposters just the same;
If you can bear to hear the truth you've spoken
Twisted by knaves to make a trap for fools,
Or watch the things you gave your life to broken,

And stoop and build 'em up with worn out tools;
If you can make one heap of all your winnings
And risk it on one turn of pitch-and-toss,
And lose, and start again at your beginnings
And never breathe a word about your loss;
If you can force your heart and nerve and sinew
To serve your turn long after they are gone,
And so hold on when there is nothing in you
Except the Will which says to them: 'Hold on!'
If you can talk with crowds and keep your virtue,
Or walk with kings – nor lose the common touch;
If neither foes nor loving friends can hurt you;
If all men count with you, but none too much;
If you can fill the unforgiving minute
With sixty seconds' worth of distance run –
Yours is the Earth and everything that's in it,
And – which is more – you'll be a Man my son!

'Or, being lied about, don't deal in lies,' reminds you to be very
careful because some people who deal in lies do it because they
see you as a threat and it is the only way they can undermine you.
In my business, disinformation was a major factor because if you
throw enough shit about, some of it will stick. However, it works
both ways. If you spread disinformation to certain people, and see
where that information goes and how it comes back to you, then
you know whom the tout is and whom to avoid. However, to a
lot of people without this sort of background, they don't even
know it is happening because they are so wound up in their own
little world of intrigue and deception; it works both ways but is
more effective in the hands of those trained to use it. My father
used to say, 'My time will come.' Give people enough rope to
hang themselves and eventually they will do it without even
realising it. Spending days and hours in an OP or in a car attunes
the mind whereby you have that unique ability to see beyond the
day-to-day banality of life so that you possess that gift of being
able to see the futility of what other people are sometimes doing.
Being laid back and giving people the impression of being
easygoing has the effect of lulling people into a false sense of
security because deep down you have a fuller picture than they.

POSTSCRIPT

As I mentioned in the Foreword of this book it has not been my intention to reveal any secrets or to give a glorified account of everyday occurrences as other books have done, but what to me was just part of the job. My aim has been to give an insight into what, for me, was an interesting and at times fascinating career. I think that in eighteen years in the Intelligence Corps I spent around fifteen months in Army uniform so I wonder sometimes, what my uniform really was. This included fifteen years in covert organisations including six years in the Special Forces. Although I would not change anything I have done, and chose to do, I hope my kids come away with more qualifications than I did and end up with something better; this is the mission I have made in my life. If anyone who has managed to fight their way to the end of this book can put it down with perhaps a hint of a smile, and maybe go away with a thought of how the other half lived then to me, it will all have been worthwhile.

As a finale I would like to pay tribute to the British soldier; the finest ambassador this country has. Why are they ambassadors? Because most of them are married with children, they have compassion and won't tolerate brutality. There are bad eggs in any organisation but the decency of the rest will seek them out and they will be punished through the legal process if not from their own section or troop. Some people might consider them to be warmongers but it is not them who choose this, it is the politicians; we do as we are told. In the Malayan, Borneo and other campaigns the Regiment, in particular, and all other British Regiments made a point of carrying out what was called 'Hearts and Minds'. It was a case of going out into the indigenous population, speaking to them and treating their sick in the case of the Regiment's medics. This got the people on the side of the soldiers against the terrorists and is something the American Forces got to grips with after the British example. The mind of the average British soldier is sometimes difficult to understand. It is one of the few Forces in the world whereby decisions are sometimes put on to the least ranking soldier in the Forces and they are encouraged to think for themselves. If there is no officer or ranking person present what happens – does the battle stop? I don't think so.

The best, and most recent, example in recent times took place in 2005 where Private Bahari took a decision, saved the lives of his comrades and, although wounded, extricated himself and his comrades. He then went back for a second go and was wounded again! He was awarded the Victoria Cross. It is no wonder then that if there is any conflict in the world (if not hijacked by the Americans) most countries want the British soldier to step in. I salute you and always will.

Printed in the United Kingdom by
Lightning Source UK Ltd., Milton Keynes
137755UK00001B/8/P